D1600023

Date Due

Information and Elections

Michigan Studies in Political Analysis

Michigan Studies in Political Analysis promotes the development and dissemination of innovative scholarship in the field of methodology in political science and the social sciences in general. Methodology is defined to include statistical methods, mathematical modeling, measurement, research design, and other topics related to the conduct and development of analytical work. The series includes works that develop a new model or method applicable to social sciences, as well as those that, through innovative combination and presentation of current analytical tools, substantially extend the use of these tools by other researchers.

GENERAL EDITORS: John E. Jackson and Christopher H. Achen

Keith Krehbiel
Information and Legislative Organization

Donald R. Kinder and Thomas R. Palfrey, Editors
Experimental Foundations of Political Science

John Brehm
The Phantom Respondents: Opinion Surveys and Political Representation

William T. Bianco
Trust: Representatives and Constituents

Melvin J. Hinich and Michael C. Munger
Ideology and the Theory of Political Choice

John Brehm and Scott Gates
Working, Shirking, and Sabotage: Bureaucratic Response to a Democratic Public

R. Michael Alvarez
Information and Elections

Information and Elections

R. Michael Alvarez

Ann Arbor

THE UNIVERSITY OF MICHIGAN PRESS

Copyright © by the University of Michigan 1997
All rights reserved
Published in the United States of America by
The University of Michigan Press
Manufactured in the United States of America
♾ Printed on acid-free paper

2000   1999   1998   1997   4   3   2   1

A CIP catalogue record for this book is available from the British Library.

Library of Congress Cataloging-in-Publication Data

Alvarez, R. Michael, 1964–
    Information and elections / R. Michael Alvarez.
       p.   cm. — (Michigan studies in political analysis)
    Includes bibliographical references and index.
    ISBN 0-472-10779-8 (cloth)
       1. Presidents—United States—Elections. 2. Voting—United
States. 3. Electioneering—United States. 4. Communication in
politics—United States. I. Title. II. Series.
JK576.A43 1997
324.973092—dc21   96-49175
                                                            CIP

In America the people appoint both those who make the laws and those who execute them; the people form the jury which punishes breaches of the law. The institutions are democratic not only in principle but also in all their developments; thus the people directly *nominate their representatives and generally choose them annually so as to hold them more completely dependent. So direction really comes from the people, and though the form of government is representative, it is clear that the opinions, prejudices, interests, and even passions of the people can find no lasting obstacles preventing them from being manifest in the daily conduct of society.*

—Alexis de Tocqueville, *Democracy in America*

Contents

Acknowledgments

This book has evolved in two stages. The first stage of this project began with the development of my dissertation at Duke University. John Aldrich, my dissertation adviser, got me rolling on this project, and helped me bring it to successful completion. Peter Lange, while not my dissertation adviser, deserves credit for his contributions to my research and to my professional development. The remaining members of my dissertation committee, by sharing their unique professional and intellectual insights, greatly improved this research; I thank Robert Bates, John Brehm, and David Canon.

While on the political science job market, I presented components of this research in a number of seminars. I thank seminar participants at Duke University, the Massachusetts Institute of Technology, Princeton University, Rice University, the University of Rochester, and Yale University. During this period, the insights of many people were helpful: Larry Bartels, William Bianco, Janet Box-Steffensmeier, Peter Feaver, Charles Franklin, Elizabeth Gerber, Paul Gronke, William Keech, Dean Lacy, Brian Loynd, Jonathan Nagler, Philip Paolino, Samuel Popkin, Wendy Rahn, Matthew Schousen, Patrick Sellers, Kenneth Shepsle, and John Zaller. The empirical work in chapters 6 and 10 were presented at successive American Political Science Association Annual Meetings (1992 and 1993). I thank Charles Franklin, Walter Mebane, and B. Dan Wood for their comments.

The second stage of this project came after my arrival at the California Institute of Technology. Here I have found a perfect working environment, fantastic colleagues, and smart students. Discussions with Mark Fey, Jonathan Katz, and Tom Palfrey were important in my early revisions, and Rod Kiewiet had the patience to wade through the entire manuscript and provide written commentary. Kim Border's advice on finishing a book helped me to get the second stage of this project done, and Scott Page helped insure that I maintained some balance personally, professionally, and on the basketball court. Scott read the manuscript, and from him I got the economist's seal of approval. A set of diligent students at Caltech served as test cases for this book; I thank

Tara Butterfield, Garrett Glasgow, James Honaker, Heidi King, Tony Kwasnica, Reginald Roberts, and Julie Scott for reading, discussing, and critiquing this manuscript. Throughout this process, Abby Delman, Eloisa Imel and Gail Nash provided indispensable secretarial assistance.

Also, some of the material in chapter 4 was presented at seminars at the University of California, San Diego, the University of California, Riverside, and at the Hoover Institution of Stanford University. The comments and critiques in these three forums were enormously useful, and I thank Neal Beck, Shaun Bowler, John Ferejohn, Jonathan Katz, Skip Lupia, Mat McCubbins, Jonathan Nagler, Sam Popkin, Doug Rivers, Barbara Sinclair and Barry Weingast, for their hospitality and talks about this material.

In the past two years, my collaboration with Charles Franklin on a related project has helped sharpen my theories and analysis. With his hard work and help, the direct survey–based measures of uncertainty have been included in a number of surveys, and we have analyzed their properties in joint work. Charles also read an early version of the manuscript, and provided helpful comments and advice.

Malcolm DeBevoise of Princeton University Press, Larry Bartels, and an anonymous reviewer all worked hard to get this manuscript into shape and to convince me to let Princeton publish this book. I thank them for their efforts and advice. Ultimately Colin Day won the fight, and he has proved to be the perfect editor who knows the right combination of tactics to help a young scholar publish his first book. Malcolm Litchfield and then Charles Myers both provided their editorial assistance at the University of Michigan Press. I thank John Jackson and Chris Achen, editors of the series in which this book appears, for their advice and support throughout this process.

On more practical matters, the survey data I utilize in this dissertation for the 1980–88 presidential elections was originally collected by the National Election Studies and was made available to me through the Inter-university Consortium for Political and Social Research. Thomas Patterson collected the panel data from the 1976 presidential election which I use extensively below, and this data was made available through the ICPSR. I am grateful to Thomas Patterson for lending me the sole remaining computer tape containing the data from his 1976 content analysis of the presidential election media coverage and for his help in using this unique data. I thank Stacy Kerkela for her hard work during the summer of 1993 undertaking the analysis of the 1980 campaign and the content analysis of the *Los Angeles Times* presented in chapter 10; Stacy's work was supported by the Summer Undergraduate Research Fellowship program at Caltech. Warren Miller, of the Federal Election Commission, provided useful information about the requirements of federal campaign finance laws.

I typeset this manuscript using the LaTeX document processing system. However, I would not have been able to produce this book without the assistance of John Brehm; John produced many of the macros necessary to format this document, and he kindly answered all of my questions, no matter how silly or minor. Also, Jonathan Katz and Eloisa Imel helped me to wander through the complexities of LaTeX and postscript.

Special thanks go to the John M. Olin Foundation, who gave me a Faculty Fellowship during the 1994–95 academic year to concentrate on completing this project. In addition, John Ledyard saw fit to enhance this fellowship with additional research support from Caltech and elimination of my teaching responsibilities during that academic year.

In the end, having a supportive and understanding family is of the most help in getting a book finished. My parents, Ramon and Mary Alvarez, and my sister, Kelly Mace, got me started on this path, and with their unwavering support I have made it this far. The person who was there day in and day out, always there to support me was my wife Sarah Hamm-Alvarez. She helped to get me on course, and she has been the source of great friendship during the past eight years. This book is dedicated to her.

CHAPTER 1

Introduction

Those who wrote the Constitution might be baffled by modern presidential elections. The system they envisioned certainly had no role for political parties, the mass media, primaries and caucuses, party conventions, or the hundreds of millions of dollars which are spent by the presidential candidates running for office. Rather, they desired that a small number of prominent political figures in each state would gather together in the Electoral College every four years to choose the next president and vice president. That the founders of the American republic preferred indirect election of national executives over direct and popular elections seems puzzling today.[1]

Why did the Founders desire such an elitist system for choosing a president? Hamilton wrote in *Federalist 68:*

It was equally desirable that the immediate election should be made by men most capable of analyzing the qualities adapted to the station and acting under circumstances favorable to deliberation, and to a judicious combination of all the reasons and inducements which were proper to govern their choice. A small number of persons, selected by their fellow-citizens from the general mass, will be most likely to possess the information and discernment requisite to so complicated an investigation.

Thus, in Hamilton's view, electoral choice should be methodical and deliberate, made only by those presumed to possess enough information to make a proper choice. The Founders believed that this could be insured only through indirect elections.

Yet the presidential election system we have today differs dramatically from that foreseen by the Founders. This system has evolved considerably over the past two hundred years, with the expansion of suffrage to greater numbers of citizens, the change from party-list voting to the Australian ballot, and the shift to virtually direct selection of presidential candidates in both the primary and general elections by the mass electorate.

---

1. This point is developed fully in Ceaser 1979.

These changes inevitably raise two questions. Like Hamilton, most academics would not question the importance of selecting a president. After all, this is one of the most powerful jobs in the world, since the American president bears direct responsibility for the lives and livelihoods of over two hundred fifty million Americans. But is the mass electorate equipped for this important task? Do those who participate in the selection of a new president every four years, in Hamilton's words, "possess the information and discernment requisite to so complicated an investigation?" Secondly, do presidential election campaigns as they are conducted today provide "circumstances favorable to deliberation"? That is, do campaigns produce a level of debate which allows voters to make an informed decision? These are the central questions examined in this book.

To paraphrase E. E. Schattschneider, political scientists have long assumed that the mass electorate should be composed of two hundred fifty million Aristotles—two hundred fifty million people who are interested and informed to meet the task of choosing a president. One early example concluded:

> The democratic citizen is expected to be well-informed about political affairs. He is supposed to know what the issues are, what their history is, what the relevant facts are, what alternatives are proposed, what the party stands for, what the likely consequences are. By such standards the voter falls short. (Berelson, Lazarsfeld, McPhee 1954, 308)

By beginning with these suppositions about American voters, it is not surprising that researchers over the past forty years have been exceptionally pessimistic about the ability of the mass electorate to make well-informed choices.

What might be found by starting with a different view of the democratic voter? Instead of assuming that voters are perfectly informed about political affairs, in this book I assume that voters have imperfect information. Specifically, I focus on what voters know about the policy positions of presidential candidates. While the focus on imperfect information about issues is restrictive, the general approach taken in this book can easily be generalized to other types of political information, since voters are imperfectly informed about all aspects of political affairs.

Chapter 2 contains an extensive discussion of past research into three questions: how well informed the electorate is on policy-relevant matters in presidential elections, whether the electorate is able to obtain any relevant information during the course of a presidential election, and how the electorate is influenced by this information.

In chapter 3 I turn to the theory which motivates my analysis. First, I define the term "uncertainty" as the imperfections which exist in a voter's information about a candidate's policy positions. Though I discuss uncertainty at length in the chapters that follow, the intuition behind my use of this term is that it expresses the relative clarity of the individual's perceptions of the candidate's policy stands. With this definition of uncertainty, I use spatial modeling to show how imperfect information or uncertainty influences voting under different conditions. I demonstrate that in some cases this uncertainty directly influences the voter's decision making process. Also, I show how the acquisition of information can influence this uncertainty and likewise the voter's perceptions and preferences.

Chapters 4 and 5 turn to methodological questions. In the fourth chapter, I discuss past attempts to measure this conception of uncertainty. Basically, these attempts involve indirect measurement of uncertainty, for example, inferring a voter's uncertainty from some combination of demographic characteristics. I argue that we should develop direct indicators of uncertainty, either by including measures of uncertainty in attitudinal surveys or by directly measuring uncertainty from existing survey data. I advocate a new operationalization of uncertainty using existing survey data, based on the variation in the voter's perception of the candidate's position relative to the actual position of the candidate on a number of policy issues. In the second part of the fourth chapter, I examine empirically the direct and indirect measures of uncertainty, using some new survey questions from the 1993 National Election Study Pilot Survey. These results demonstrate the superiority of direct measures of uncertainty, one of which I use for the remainder of the empirical analyses in the book.

Chapter 5 discusses the statistical models I employ to examine the variation of uncertainty across the electorate and to test the hypotheses generated by the spatial model in chapter 3. A number of complicated empirical issues surface in this chapter, concerning the nature of the measure of uncertainty and voter evaluations of candidates I utilize, as well as the strong theoretical likelihood of a simultaneous relationship between uncertainty and candidate preferences. First I discuss the relative merits of the statistical models I use. Then I discuss briefly a further difficulty encountered in my empirical analysis—how interactive effects should be modeled.

In the remainder of the book I turn to a presentation of data from the 1976–92 series of presidential elections. These five presidential elections were chosen as cases for several reasons. First, prior to the 1976 election, the "rules of the game" of the presidential election system were substantially different. Many changes occurred during the 1960s and early 1970s in the presidential election system, ranging from dramatic changes in the selection of party nominees and in campaign finance to changes in the relative roles of parties and the mass media in the process. All of these changes have influenced how presidential elections are fought and reported by the media, and hence they have influenced voter decision making and the campaign strategies of candidates as they seek to influence voter choice. Since it would be difficult to control for these intervening changes, it would be difficult to compare empirical results from those earlier elections to those after 1976.

These five presidential elections also include a number of interesting contextual differences. There is election without a sitting incumbent president (1988), one with a nonelected incumbent (1976), and three with incumbents (1980, 1984, and 1992). Also, one involves a relatively obscure challenger (1976). Moreover in 1984 and 1992 the candidates were relatively polarized on most issues, a sharp contrast with the other elections involving less polarization (1980, 1988) and even relative similarity on most issues (1976). Last, two of these presidential elections (1980 and 1992) involve significant challenges to the two-party system by independent candidates. Identifying whether these different electoral contexts influence the dynamics of particular campaigns or how voters make decisions will be difficult, since there are more explanatory factors than can be precisely explored in only five elections.[2] Nonetheless, by studying multiple presidential elections, it is possible to determine how these contextual differences might influence voter decision making. This, in turn, provides insight into the ways in which presidential campaigns might be said to "matter." And last, the available survey data for these elections is consistent (containing relatively similar questions) and is amenable to the complicated measurement and statistical analysis necessary to accurately test the hypotheses derived from the formal models. The survey data employed is discussed in chapter 5.

Chapter 6 contains the first set of results from the statistical models. Here I present models of voter uncertainty of the policy positions of the candidates in each election. The fundamental question posed in this chapter concerns the determinants of voter uncertainty—which individuals are *systematically* more uncertain of a candidate's position than others?

Chapter 7 considers how uncertainty of the candidate's positions influences voters' decisions. The empirical models of voter evaluations show that uncertainty reduces voter support for presidential candidates. And, even in the presence of uncertainty, I also show that policy issues have strong influences in each of the elections I examine.

---

2. With more independent variables than objects to explain, this is a classic case of under-identification (Przeworski and Teune 1982).

In chapter 8, I examine the influence of uncertainty on voters' decision making. This chapter tests two hypotheses: that uncertainty of the candidate's positions reduces the ability of voters to employ their issue preferences in their decisions; and that under uncertainty, voters will turn to information other than the candidate's policy positions in their decision making. I find strong support for the first hypothesis, but surprisingly mixed evidence for the second.

The last two chapters focus on the campaign's effect on voter uncertainty. I compare the aggregate distributions of uncertainty about each candidate's positions across the elections under analysis in chapter 9. I then unravel the patterns apparent in the distributions of uncertainty both across the four elections and across the four candidates, and show that the patterns are quite understandable.

Finally, chapter 10 contains a detailed examination of the dynamics of the 1976 and 1980 presidential campaigns. I use content analyses of newspaper coverage of these two presidential elections and relate the dynamics of information made available about the candidates during each election year to changes apparent in voter uncertainty across the campaign. This chapter provides strong support for the model of voter learning that I advance, and for the argument that presidential election campaigns matter.

CHAPTER 2

Elections, Information, and Campaigns

Theories of how voters behave acquire importance not because of their effects on voters, who may proceed blithely unaware of them. They gain significance because of their effects, both potentially and in reality, on candidates and other political leaders.

—V. O. Key Jr., *The Responsible Electorate*

In the past half-century, political scientists have amassed a great deal of data about presidential elections. However, it is difficult to argue that we are any closer, after this half century of data collection and analysis, to answering some of the critical questions about the role of elections in a democratic society. Do elections constitute a link between constituents and representatives? Can candidates learn about the preferences of the electorate and consequently translate that into public policy? Can the electorate determine what these same candidates would do if elected, and can they then vote appropriately?

The literature on presidential elections has traditionally been pessimistic about these questions. Led by the conclusions garnered by pioneering works in the field, the conventional wisdom has long been that policy issues have little, if any, effect in presidential elections (and virtually no effect in other types of national elections). This conclusion has long been buttressed by a complementary conclusion, that the campaigns conducted by the candidates provide little, if any, information to the electorate—and that whatever information is disseminated by the campaigns is distorted by the mass media and even ignored by voters.

Since these conclusions shape how we view the development of public policy and the operation of political institutions, they also have broader implications. To the extent we are pessimistic about the role of policy issues in

7

national elections, we will consistently see policymakers having broad freedom in their ability to shape and implement public policy. Governmental institutions, then, should be designed in accordance with this model of an issue-ignorant electorate and basically unconstrained policymakers.[1] But if we find that the opposite is the case, that policy issues and political campaigns play an important role in our political system, we are led to a different set of normative conclusions—the actions of elected officials are constrained by their policy positions articulated to the electorate. Understanding the influence of campaigns on voter perceptions, and how these perceptions influence voting, are therefore critical for understanding whether our political institutions are responsive to public preferences.

In this chapter the past research on these two questions is discussed. First, I focus on the role of policy issues in presidential voting. I then discuss the research on the effects of presidential election campaigns. Each section closes with a summary of these two literatures, which provides the backdrop for remainder of this research.

The Pessimistic Election Studies

The point of departure for discussing the relative role of issues in presidential elections is the work of Campbell, Converse, Miller, and Stokes in *The American Voter*. In their studies of the 1952 and 1956 elections, they searched extensively for evidence of issue-knowledge in their survey samples. They argued that the necessary conditions for issue voting included:

• the voter must be aware of the issue and have an opinion concerning it,
• the issue must arouse a minimal intensity of feeling for the voter,
• the issue must be accompanied by a perception that one party or candidate represents the person's own position better than the other party or candidate.

When searching through their survey data for voters who fulfilled these criteria, they found in these elections that two-thirds of their sample *could* state a position on a particular issue and *could* describe what the government was doing regarding that issue. Of those who passed this "familiarity" level, they found that between 40 and 60 percent on any particular issue were able to perceive party differences and could locate one of the two parties as closer to their own position on the issue.

However, Campbell et al. interpreted their results pessimistically. They

---

1. This is the conclusion reached by Campbell, Converse, Miller, and Stokes in the last pages of *The American Voter*, unabridged edition, 1980, 543–44.

argued that these "low" percentages demonstrated that the electorate does not meet the necessary conditions for issue-based voting:

> We have, then, the portrait of an electorate almost wholly without detailed information about decision making in government . . . it knows little about what government has done on these issues or what the parties propose to do. It is almost completely unable to judge the rationality of government actions; knowing little of particular policies and what has led to them, the mass electorate is not able to appraise either its goals or the appropriateness of the means chosen to serve these goals. (Campbell et al. 1980, 543)

This interpretation of the data was used to support a number of other conclusions by the authors of *The American Voter*. One major conclusion concerned party identification, which in the absence of issue-based knowledge of the candidates and political parties was argued to be a useful decision-making cue. Party identification was seen as devoid of issue-content, as a socially determined construct. The absence of issue-based knowledge, and any apparent structure to this knowledge, meant that voters did not have a consistent issue or ideological means of understanding the political world.[2] Thus, these conclusions about these conditions for issue voting provided the crux for many of the early conclusions advanced in this literature.

But were these data correctly interpreted? Many did not think so, and in the forefront of the attack against these arguments was V. O. Key Jr., in his posthumously published *The Responsible Electorate*. In this book are scattered components of a number of critiques of Campbell et al., which subsequent research has expanded upon. But the most important point raised by Key was that "the electorate behaves about as rationally and responsibly as we should expect, given the clarity of the alternatives presented to it and the character of the information available to it" (1966, 7). Basically, voters are able to be informed about issues, and to use those issues in their voting decisions, only up to the limits established by the current political context. If that context does not facilitate issue-based voting, that will be reflected in the information voters appear to possess and in how they decide between presidential candidates. But if that context does facilitate the transmission of issue-based information, then we should see issue-based behavior by the electorate.

---

2. The initial development of this argument was in *The American Voter*. However, it was subsequently elaborated by Converse (1964).

A number of scholars in the decades following the publication of Key's book added to this debate. Pomper (1972) showed that two changes had occurred between 1956 and 1968, both of which called into question the Campbell et al. conclusions. First, Pomper showed that across six issues, the electorate increasingly perceived differences between the parties, and that the correlation between party identification and the voter's preferences on the particular issues had also increased. Pomper accounted for these changes by placing great weight on the Goldwater candidacy in 1964. But he argued more generally "the events and campaigns of the 1960s, I suggest, made politics more relevant and more dramatic to the mass electorate" (Pomper 1972, 421). Thus, the political context changed, the two parties diverged, and the electorate was able to perceive the distinctions between the parties with more clarity.

Subsequent research seemed to support this conclusion. Nie, Verba, and Petrocik (1976) presented data that showed that the effects of issues on presidential voting appeared to be correlated with the clarity of the alternatives presented to the electorate. In the 1956 election, they found that only 1 percent of the variation in presidential voting could be accounted for by the independent effect of policy issues. This rose to 9 percent in 1964 and 11 percent in 1972, when the electorate was offered clearer choices between parties and candidates, but fell to 2 percent in 1976 with more moderate and equivocal candidates (Nie, Verba, and Petrocik 1976, 375).

But the Nie, Verba, and Petrocik work was called into question on methodological grounds, the most damaging of which was the recognition that substantial evolution in the survey instruments across this period might have produced the observed changes in the level of issue voting. The early (pre-1964) National Election Studies issue format was a simple agree-or-disagree question for each policy issue. In 1964 the question format was changed to a choice between two opposing policy choices, in which respondents were asked to choose between policy choices and then to state which party would be more likely to undertake one of the policy options (1964–68). And in 1968 and 1972 the most dramatic change occurred, when the NES changed the format to the now dominant seven-point policy scales. Some critics have pointed out that the apparent changes in the amount of information possessed by the electorate might simply be artifacts of these changes in question wording (Bishop et al. 1978; Kessel 1972; Sullivan et al. 1978).[3]

Yet Page and Brody (1972) took advantage of the new question formats in the 1968 NES survey data to determine why the Vietnam War, a highly salient issue in 1968, did not appear to influence Nixon-Humphrey voting. They pro-

---

3. However, the direction of these potential biases is unclear. That is, did the previous format substantially *underestimate* the extent of issue voting? Or does the current format *overestimate* issue voting?

vided data which demonstrated that both Humphrey and Nixon avoided discussions of the war in their campaign pronouncements. When the Vietnam War was mentioned by either candidate during the campaign, both were deliberately vague in their rhetoric. This ambiguity was apparent in the electorate's perceptions of the candidate's position on Vietnam policies, since the mean perceptions of both Nixon's and Humphrey's positions were virtually identical and exceptionally moderate. This provided strong evidence that, just as Key argued, the ability of the electorate to bring policy issues into their decision-making process hinged on the nature of the campaign context.

Another early, but distinct source of criticism of the work of Campbell et al. came from RePass (1971). RePass utilized one of the new question formats adopted by the NES after the 1960 study, which are commonly known as the "most important problems" questions. Here survey respondents are asked, in an open-ended survey format, what they consider to be the most important problem, or problems, facing the country. RePass, building upon Converse's notion of "issue publics," argued that the responses to these questions could be taken as indicators of the salience, or weight, that voters attach to different issues. And RePass argued that, armed with the knowledge of a voter's concerns and which party is perceived to be best equipped to deal with these concerns, a considerable amount of leverage might be gained in accounting for vote choice (RePass 1971, 399).

The most serious problem with RePass's approach is how to include measures of salience in models of voting. In their examination of experimental salience items in the 1979 NES Pilot and 1980 NES general election studies, Niemi and Bartels (1985) found that weighting issues by the respondent's reported salience did not enhance their ability to predict voter choices (Niemi and Bartels 1985, 1218).[4] Other approaches have been suggested for this perplexing problem, but these attempts have involved unique data sets or complex estimation routines (Rabinowitz, Prothro, and Jacoby 1982; Rivers 1988).

While the level of issue voting might be influenced by the information made available during the campaign, and by the importance of issues to the electorate, it might also be influenced by the nature of the issues themselves. There are many possible differences in types of issues. One way of distinguishing issues was offered by Carmines and Stimson (1980), who differenti-

---

4. This finding might be the artifact of a problem in the experimental salience formats. My examination of the reported levels of salience in the 1979 Pilot revealed little variation in salience across respondents. For example, in the first wave of the survey, salience was measured on a 0 to 100 scale, with 100 being high salience. However, the average salience weights across the issues using this format were very high, ranging from approximately 60 to 75, with standard deviations of 20 to 25. The effect, then, in the work of Niemi and Bartels is that of multiplying the respondent's perceived distance to the candidates on each issue by a constant. It is not surprising that little difference was found in their salience-weighted and -unweighted models.

ated issues into "hard" or "easy" categories. They suggested that easy issues would be characterized by:

- Easy issues are symbolic rather than technical.
- Easy issues are more likely to involve policy ends rather than means.
- Easy issues are those that have long been in public discussion.

Their argument is simple. The body of research which I just discussed focused predominantly on hard issues. Carmines and Stimson suggest, then, that this focus on hard issues had underestimated dramatically the actual extent of issue voting. By including both forms of issue voting in our models, we would find a much greater incidence of issue voting in presidential elections.

The problem, though, becomes one of deciding which issues are hard and which are easy. Carmines and Stimson focus on the 1972 election and argue that the issue over withdrawal from Vietnam should be considered hard and that of racial desegregation easy. But the crux of their argument revolves around the empirical assignment of issues into hard and easy categories:

> How can we tell empirically whether a particular issue is easy or hard? Our theory suggests simply enough that the relationship between *hard* issues and vote should be *conditional* on level of political information possessed by voters. Issue position should exert a considerably stronger causal influence on the votes of the well-informed because they, more than the ill-informed, accurately map party and candidate issue stands.

So the assignment of issues into hard and easy categories is contingent on their relative effect on the vote choice, across levels of political information. And regarding the issue of withdrawal from Vietnam, they show that highly informed voters were more polarized in their positions on this issue than poorly informed voters, while on the desegregation issue, no information-based differences were apparent.

The work of Carmines and Stimson is a valuable contribution to the literature, since it highlights heterogeneity across voters (in terms of political information and salience) and issues (in terms of the hard/easy classification) in presidential elections. But the murky distinction between hard and easy issues, and the difficulty even Carmines and Stimson have in their attempt to operationalize this concept empirically, is a major problem.[5]

The source of the problem is the conflation of many possible factors making an issue hard or easy. For example, in 1972 there simply could have

---

5. See Sartori 1970 on the difficulties in operationalizing vague concepts.

been heterogeneity in the salience of these two issues across the information levels—highly informed voters might have been more concerned about ending the Vietnam than segregation. Or, the media might have focused more attention on the issue of ending the war, making voters who are more exposed to the media better informed about the issue and more polarized in their opinions. And in 1972, unlike 1968, the two candidates running for office did present different plans for ending the war, which may not have been the case for racial desegregation. Therefore, it might have been the nature of these two issues which made one hard and the other easy; but it might also have been any number of factors *specific to the 1972 election* which polarized high information voters on the Vietnam withdrawal issue and not the desegregation issue.[6]

Writing about the heterogeneity across issues in a similar fashion, Fiorina (1981) draws heavily on the distinction made by both Key (1966) and Downs (1957) between "prospective issues" (the sort discussed by Campbell et al.) and "retrospective issues." Key summarized the rationale behind retrospective voting: "Voters may reject what they have known; or they may approve what they have known. They are not likely to be attracted in great numbers by promises of the novel or unknown" (1966, 61). In the earlier work of Downs, the logic is more explicit, yet fundamentally the same. Downs begins with what is basically a prospective voting model, where voters choose the candidate who will bring them the greatest returns when in office, whether material or policy-related. But since this involves making predictions about future events and candidate responses, the voter's decision becomes quite complicated. So in Downs's argument, instead of embarking on a complicated forecasting procedure, the voter simply relies on readily available information in making their choice—what has the candidate's party done for me lately?[7]

Thus the importance of the work on retrospective issue voting, for the discussion at hand, is again the heterogeneity across issues. In the retrospective

---

6. Interestingly, this implies that there might be heterogeneity across both voters and issues in terms of how hard or easy they are. On some issues, variations in voter information, salience, or exposure to information might make one issue easy for some to conceptualize, while other issues might be more difficult to understand. But other voters might find the first issue difficult and the others easy.

7. Fiorina goes to great lengths to make a critical distinction between Key and Downs on this point. He argues that Key's "reward–punishment" notion of retrospective voting is outcome oriented; whereas in Downs, Fiorina asserts that the use of retrospective information is for a prospective inference about future policy actions. It is not clear that such a distinction can be supported, since Key's work is unfortunately vague on this very point. However, it should be remembered that Key does argue that the retrospective vote is based on the actions taken by the incumbent party, where the electorate judges "past events, past performance, and past actions" (Key 1966, 61). It is difficult to imagine that Key did not mean by "actions" policies undertaken by the incumbent, and thus, it is difficult to see that a retrospective vote is not policy oriented in Key's perspective.

voting literature, the heterogeneity is between retrospective issues and prospective issues. The implication is not that prospective issue voting does not occur, or that it is not important; rather by excluding retrospective issues the early work on presidential voting seriously underestimates the extent of issue voting.

Other than the distinction between retrospective and prospective issue voting, the work of Downs and Black (1958) has led to the development of the spatial model of voting. Here, an issue is depicted as a one-dimensional space, with both the voter and the candidate having positions along the dimension. Under certain conditions, voters prefer candidates with positions closer to their own on the issue. This spatial model of voting has been generalized to multiple issues, with the issues being independent or correlated (Davis and Hinich 1966; Davis, Hinich, and Ordeshook 1970; Enelow and Hinich 1984).

An early critic of the spatial issue voting model was Stokes (1963), who noted a number of potential problems with the assumptions of the spatial model. One of the more prominent criticisms was his distinction between positional and valence issues, where the latter are issues "that merely involve the linking of the parties with some condition that is positively or negatively valued by the electorate" (Stokes 1963, 373). Recently, Rabinowitz and Macdonald (1989) and Macdonald, Listaug, and Rabinowitz (1991) have built upon Stokes's criticisms of the spatial issue voting model. Instead of a focus on spatial distances between the voter and the candidate, their model asserts that the impact of a particular issue on an individual's decision is the product of "the directional compatability of the individual and the candidate (or party) and the intensity levels of the individual and the candidate" (Rabinowitz and Macdonald 1989, 96).

Their innovations in the "directional" issue voting model are twofold. First, the impetus for their model rests on the assertion that most issues have symbolic responses—and hence are like Stokes's valence issues—and that most voters are so poorly informed that they might understand directions on an issue, but not actual positions. Second, they have directly incorporated issue salience (as intensity) into their model in a very intuitive manner.

While innovative, this approach has a number of flaws in its present form. First, they have gone to great lengths in their work to compare the directional model to the standard spatial model, but the survey data do not support the empirical superiority of the directional model.[8] Also, the model has a number

8. In both articles, the empirical superiority of the directional model is asserted to rest on differences in variance explained and in differences in standardized regression coefficients. In table 1 of the 1989 article, the R^2 values are only different between the two models by 0.02, which is not likely to be statistically significant. The other elections they present data for in table 2 show similarly small differences in model fit. Also, examining differences in the standardized

of theoretical puzzles associated with it. One of these puzzles is the treatment of extreme candidates or parties. In their second article they add a term which effectively penalizes candidates or parties that are "too" extreme. This is not taken into account in their other work and appears to be simply ad hoc. Therefore, while intriguing, their directional theory of issue voting is clearly in theoretical development and will continue to be controversial until more definitive evidence is presented.

After covering this extensive literature, the general state of this area of research can be summarized in four general themes. First, most agree that the conclusions of the pioneering *The American Voter* were overstated. Whether on methodological or theoretical grounds, it is clear that most scholars are satisfied that policy issues play a significant role in presidential election voting. The major question, then, becomes where one is willing to draw the line— exactly how important are policy issues in presidential elections?

Second, the work which followed Campbell et al. emphasizes that a great deal of heterogeneity characterizes issue voting. Whether the heterogeneity is across voters, as in the different salience weights they might attach to different issues, or across issues, as in the hard/easy or retrospective/prospective categorizations, there seem to be many different forms that issue voting can take. Once these broader definitions of issues are taken into consideration, the role of issues in presidential elections increases, not surprisingly.

Third, certain attributes of individuals seem to influence their ability to understand policy issues and to use them in their voting decisions. Much of the post–*American Voter* work discusses the role that political information plays in issue voting in one of two ways. Some, like Carmines and Stimson, assert that political influences which voters employ which types of policy issues in their decision making. Others, from Key to Rabinowitz and Macdonald, advance a stronger argument—that the quality of available information about policy issues is so poor that voters may be unable to take them into consideration when voting. Ultimately this is an empirical question, and the literature is beginning to resolve which of these two effects of information might be operative.

Finally, most agree that the context of the election plays some role in issue voting. This notion can be traced to the writings of Key, but convincing evidence of the effect of the political context came first from Page and Brody. While Page and Brody focused directly on the spatial differentiation of the candidates on policy dimensions, other aspects of the political context of any particular election are related to the conduct of the campaign and the informa-

---

regression coefficients is a poor test since any differences observed could simply be differences introduced by the variations of the independent variables in the sample. Since the R^2 values are virtually identical between models, it is unlikely that even what appear to be large differences in the standardized coefficients are statistically discernible differences.

tion that might be dissiminated. It is to this literature, the effects of presidential campaigns, that I now turn.

The Pessimism about Presidential Campaigns

Just as there was an early pioneering work which set the stage for the issue voting literature, so there was work that laid down the research agenda for the work on presidential election campaigns. This is the work associated with the "Columbia School," in the companion volumes *The People's Choice,* by Lazarsfeld, Berelson, and Gaudet (1944), and *Voting,* by Berelson, Lazarsfeld, and McPhee (1954). These works set the agenda both methodologically and substantively for this literature, and I discuss each contribution in turn.

The Columbia researchers were concerned with measuring the effect of the campaign on the electorate, and to do this, they were the first to use the panel survey to study presidential elections. The first study analyzed in *The People's Choice* was conducted in Erie County, Ohio, between May and November 1940. Of an original sample of 3,000, interviewed in May, they took 4 samples of 600 individuals. One of these samples was reinterviewed each month until the election; the other three were each reinterviewed once. Concurrently, another group of researchers gathered monthly samplings of the events in the campaign, the candidate's statements, and the coverage in the media of the campaign.[9] The idea was to measure the changes in preferences which the Columbia researchers thought would occur during the electoral season and then match those changes in preferences with campaign events and information (Natchez 1985).

But instead of documenting any changes in preferences, the Columbia team found an amazing stability of preferences in the 1940 election. "What the political campaign did, so to speak, was not to form new opinions but to raise old opinions over the thresholds of awareness and decision. Political campaigns are important primarily because they *activate* latent predispositions" (Lazarsfeld, Berelson, and Gaudet 1944, 74). In terms of voting decisions, they found that the presidential campaign changed few minds, and for most voters, the campaign only reinforced their predispositions to vote for one candidate or the other. Thus they reached what should have been a startling conclusion: "In sum, then, this is what the campaign does: reinforcement (potential) 53 percent; activation 14 percent; reconversion 3 percent; partial conversion 6 percent; conversion 8 percent; no effect 16 percent" (Lazarsfeld, Berelson, and

---

9. The 1948 study which culminated in the publication of *Voting* also was quite innovative. The study focused on one community, Elmira, New York, and the panel consisted of interviews of respondents in June, August, October, and November. Data on the campaign were collected as well.

Gaudet 1944, 103). This is a remarkable finding, since only 14 percent of their sample *changed their voting decision* during the course of a presidential election campaign. Thus began what many working in this literature have come to call the "minimal effects" hypothesis—that campaigns and the mass media only influence mass preferences at the margin (Iyengar and Kinder 1987).

The second important substantive finding to come out of the Erie County study involved the informational context of the campaign. From a data set covering a number of major radio addresses by the candidates, radio news-casts, magazine editorials and articles, and front-page newspaper coverage, the Columbia team also set out to discover what information had been passed to the electorate during this campaign.[10] They found that an overwhelming proportion of campaign information concerned the campaign itself, campaign tactics, and the relative standings of the candidates in the race (over one third); with lesser coverage of Roosevelt's record (one quarter); and the remainder devoted to discussions of the candidates' personal characteristics and policy proposals.

These conclusions were buttressed by their analysis of the major radio addresses of the candidates in 1948. Again, they asserted that campaign information was not policy oriented—Truman's speeches covered general aspects of the campaign (35 percent), while Dewey concentrated on the symbolic issue of the 1948 race, the "unity of the American people" (26 percent). Additionally, in the 1948 data they found that "there was little meeting of the minds or joining of the issues between Dewey and Truman on some major topics" (Berelson, Lazarsfeld, and McPhee 1954, 236). Therefore, the major conclusions that came out of their early analysis of the informational content of the campaign was that little "substance" was discussed during the campaign, and that the candidates did little to force direct confrontation on issues in their campaign rhetoric. Yet the Columbia team did not relate either of these two findings to their conclusion that campaigns do not induce voters to alter their preferences.[11]

The last important finding in this work was articulated most clearly in *Voting*. Here they found that voters practiced selective exposure to informa-

---

10. It is not clear from the discussion in *The People's Choice* exactly what the criteria for inclusion of a news source, and consequently a particular campaign story, into this analysis were. Nor is the coding or classification scheme given. Their sketchy discussion is in footnote 2, page 168. They are also vague about their campaign data in *Voting*. The problems involved in gathering this type of data are discussed later in this chapter.

11. This is odd, since in the 1948 election they relate the shift toward Truman late in the campaign to the fact that the standards by which many voters evaluated Truman changed from his personal characteristics to his stands on labor and class issues (Berelson, Lazarsfeld, and McPhee 1954: 269). What makes it so odd is that their own data in the previous chapter shows that Truman stressed labor issues relatively heavily in his speeches (p. 236).

tion in different ways. First, some voters were systematically more exposed to political information, especially the mass media, than others. Second, voters were more likely to pay attention to information which was favorable to their preferred candidate. And lastly, they showed that voters tended to see their preferred candidate's stands on issues as similar to their own, and the opponent's as much different than theirs.

But even though selective exposure seemed pervasive, a number of interesting campaign effects can be observed in their data. Truman's policy positions, which were clearer and more confrontational than Dewey's, were much less subject to projection and misperception. Also, as the campaign progressed, perceptual accuracy about the issue positions of the candidates among voters increased. And last, those who were more exposed to campaign information were more accurate in their perceptions of the candidates' stands as well. Thus, even though the campaign may not have had an immediate impact on the preferences of most voters, it seemed to have an impact on the information obtained by the voters, and on their propensity to misperceive the positions of the candidates on policy issues.

The importance of the Columbia research cannot be underemphasized. First, this research was methodologically innovative, especially regarding the development of the panel study. Second, it established the subsequent research agenda with their conclusion that political campaigns had only marginal conversion (or persuasion) effects. Third, and typically understated in this literature, they found substantial evidence that political campaigns lead to significant changes in how voters perceive or misperceive candidates.

Interestingly, it has been the second finding of the Columbia research which has received the most attention in the political science literature. Writing specifically about the effects of the news media on the political perceptions of citizens, Patterson and McClure argued that "most network newscasts are neither very educational nor very powerful communications" (1976, 90). Their detailed analysis went even further than the Columbia results and led Patterson and McClure to conclude that television news had almost no political ramifications at all. And in a follow-up study, patterned closely on the Columbia studies (panel surveys during the 1976 campaign combined with extensive content analysis of the campaign coverage in the media), Patterson reached virtually the same conclusion:

> Election news carries scenes of action, not observations on the values represented by these scenes. Election news emphasizes what is different about events of the previous 24 hours rather than everyday political topics. Election news concentrates on competition and controversy instead of basic policy and leadership questions . . . the news is not an adequate

guide to political choice. The candidates' agendas are not readily evident in press coverage of the campaign. (1976, 174)

In most of the major studies which have followed up on the conclusions of the Columbia school, finding evidence that campaigns and mass media sources have little *persuasion* effects has not been very difficult (Finkel 1993).

This is not to say that campaigns and the mass media have no political effects. Perhaps looking for campaign or media persuasion is incorrect; instead of examining changes in voter preferences, research should look for the broader (and more important) impact of campaigns and the mass media in forming and changing the attitudes and perceptions of the electorate. Perhaps the Columbia school was correct—the information the campaign provides shapes voter attitudes and perceptions, not just preferences for candidates. Some recent studies from diverse methodological perspectives demonstrate this very point.[12]

One puzzling aspect of the "minimal effects" literature is that it is difficult to imagine that the mass media could have no political effects, given the exceptional amount of information which is present in the media in an election year. Graber (1988) conducted an intensive study of twenty-one voters during the 1976 election season, combined with a content analysis of the media outlets they were exposed to in Evansville, Illinois. In her breakdown of only politically relevant media coverage in the 1976 election, Graber found a total of 30,662 news topics covered in the local newspapers, and 38,510 news topics covered by the local and national television newscasts. In light of these numbers the question really is how individuals cope with such an enormous amount of political information.

Graber, working within a cognitive information processing framework, finds that the individuals in her analysis have very efficient methods of dealing with the flood of information. In the first stage, people simply ignore old and redundant information. Then, Graber argues, the stories they deem interesting or novel are processed schematically, allowing the individual to integrate the information into their existing knowledge structures. And since news is often repetitive, substantial learning does occur. Therefore, even with the seemingly haphazard approach taken by the individuals in her study, there is such a massive amount of information available during a presidential election that

---

12. I want to draw a distinction between preferences and perceptions in this book. By preferences I mean the narrow economic notion; if I present a voter with two candidates, and ask this voter how they compare, she will tell me that one candidate is better than the other. This is a preference for one candidate relative to another—which I will later assume is reflected when an individual votes for one candidate instead of another. Perceptions about candidates are more general attitudes about the candidates—their issue positions, their traits, or their leadership skills.

"Americans are capable of extracting enough meaningful political information from the flood of news to which they are exposed to perform the modest number of citizenship functions that American society expects of them" (Graber 1988, 252).

Additionally, Iyengar and Kinder (1987), combining survey data with a large number of experimental studies, offer convincing evidence against the "minimal effects" hypotheses. First, their analysis of the 1980 election shows that the media was capable during that election of inducing substantial changes in individual preferences. However, a number of special circumstances need to be present for substantial persuasion to occur during a political campaign— many voters must remain uncommitted until the last days of the race, late political events must be covered extensively by the media and be politically relevant, and these political events must favor one candidate.

Instead of persuasion, though, Iyengar and Kinder find substantial support for the notion that the television media has a great deal of political influence. And here their work ties directly into the findings by the Columbia school, in that the major effects of the campaign and television news "appears to rest not on persuasion but on commanding the public's attention (agenda-setting) and defining criteria underlying the public's judgments (priming)" (Iyengar and Kinder 1987, 116).

Yet more recently, there have been many important works supporting the notion that political campaigns and the mass media have a significant influence on the mass electorate—both on their preferences and the criteria underlying those preferences. In the 1976 presidential election, Conover and Feldman (1976) observed that misperceptions of the candidates' stands virtually disappeared as the general election campaign progressed. Working with data on presidential primaries, Bartels (1988) and Popkin (1991) have both shown that campaign events and changes in available information about candidates lead to substantial changes in the criteria voters use to judge candidates and hence to changes in their relative evaluations of primary candidates. With data from Senate elections, Franklin (1991) has shown that the information made available by the candidates competing for office influences voter perceptions. Working across these national elections, Zaller summarized his results (and the literature): "Campaigns bring about attitude change, as I have sought to show, not by producing a sudden conversion experience, but by producing incremental changes in the balance of considerations that underlie people's summary attitudes" (1989, 231).

Two immediate conclusions should be taken from this literature. Clearly, campaigns and the mass media matter. That is the most important point raised by the flurry of recent research on this topic. In fact, it strains the imagination to think that campaigns and the mass media do not have important electoral ramifications. So many events happen in a campaign, many of which are substantively important, and there is such a flood of campaign and political media coverage during the electoral season, that both must have some effect. If not, then why would candidates bother to campaign?

More importantly, this literature argues that the effects of campaigns and the mass media may not be expressed directly in changes in voter preferences— in Iyengar and Kinder's terms, in persuasion. Clearly it is difficult to change the minds of voters, and neither political campaigns nor the mass media are well suited for that task. However, perceptions are less malleable and are more subject to change. Perhaps even more subject to change are misperceptions, or the degree to which the perceptions of voters are inaccurate. Most of these works, from the Columbia research to the most recent work summarized above, argue that political campaigns and the mass media can and do influence voter perception and misperception and therefore, indirectly influence preferences as well. To study the impact of the political campaign and the media on the electorate, a better focus might be on the perceptions and misperceptions of voters.

While the evidence is slowly accumulating against the "minimal effects" hypothesis, there remain disturbing methodological problems in this literature. While the survey methodologies employed by these works are generally accepted, often the generation of the data for the study of the campaign or media effects is troubling. There are three approaches taken by these scholars, each with their own attendant problems. First, there is the media content analysis approach, employed by many different authors. Here, there are problems with the sampling procedures employed and with the coding of the data. As noted by Graber, there really is a flood of media coverage of presidential campaigns, and, without substantial resources, analyzing that flood of information can be overwhelming. Thus, a variety of sampling strategies are employed—sampling the media coverage from only a limited geographic area (Graber 1988), sampling randomly from national news sources (Patterson 1980), or sampling from selected sources (Graber 1980). Each sampling strategy has obvious implications for the results which might be obtained from the data.

Also, there are methodological questions about the content analysis of the media information. Here, the major problems are the categorization of stories and the ultimately subjective nature of the content analysis process. Regarding categorization of stories, the problem is that the literature cannot agree on a set of story "types" or "topics" (Graber 1983). This makes comparisions across works very difficult, if not impossible. The latter problem, subjectivity in the coding process, is of great concern to all of these researchers. Typically, however, single individuals code most of the media stories, with spot checks for reliability (Graber 1988; Patterson 1980). And works vary greatly in the level to which they document their coding processes.

The second approach is experimental analysis, undertaken by Iyengar and Kinder. They discuss in great detail the trade-offs associated with undertaking experimental analyses—maximizing experimental control of independent variables versus maximizing the generalizability of the findings. But they achieve a compromise in their analysis, since they combine their experimental results with results taken from accepted national surveys. This multimethod approach helps alleviate concerns about the generalizability of their findings.

The last approach taken in this literature is the most agnostic, since it simply avoids measuring media and campaign effects entirely. Many of the survey-based studies which have recently been published are of this variety. For example, both Bartels (1988) and Popkin (1991) observe that the basis of voter evaluations of Gary Hart early in the 1984 primary season changed dramatically after the Super Tuesday primaries, with deleterious consequences for his standings in the polls. Bartels argues these changes occurred due to the accumulation of information about the primary candidates, while Popkin points to campaign events, although neither provides more than verbal justification for these relationships. Basically, their argument *infers* certain campaign or media effects.

These different methodological approaches, especially content analysis and experimental studies, have led to serious disputes among the scholars working in this literature. And many point to data generation problems as the source of the poor development of the literature (Graber 1983). It is also quite likely that measurement problems have contributed to the persistence of the "minimal effects" hypothesis, since without precise measures of the information made available by the media and the campaign, demonstrating the correlation between this information and changes in voter perceptions is extremely difficult.

Conclusion

This chapter has set forth the background materials for the arguments developed in the remainder of this book. My research takes a different approach to the unresolved questions of issue voting and campaign effects. It is clear that the literature on issue voting has reached some consensus that information provided to the voters is critical in determining the extent of issue voting. Yet with few exceptions both the theoretical and empirical models assume that voters are perfectly informed about the positions of the candidates on policy issues.

It is also clear that the literature on the effects of campaigns and the mass media has begun drifting away from the minimal effects hypothesis. This movement has occurred mainly because there is a massive amount of information made available about the candidates during the campaign season. Additionally, the slow rejection of minimal effects has occurred due to the realization that the campaign and media influence perceptions and not just preferences.

My work in the following chapters takes an important new step by focusing directly upon imperfect information. I both theoretically and empirically incorporate imperfect information—conceptualized as uncertainty—into models of voter preferences and learning. The focus on uncertainty allows for a clearer understanding of how information influences voter behavior and how campaigns and the mass media influence voter perceptions.

In the next chapter, I move to a detailed theoretical discussion of the role that uncertainty plays in voter decision making. Then the analysis turns to how uncertainty changes in response to information; in other words, how information made available by political campaigns and the mass media influences voter perceptions. Both these arguments involve the development of formal models, which are presented in the next chapter.

CHAPTER 3

The Theory of Uncertainty and Elections

Even the most discriminating popular judgment can reflect only ambiguity, uncertainty, or even foolishness if those are the qualities of the input into the echo chamber . . . If the people can choose only from among rascals, they are certain to choose a rascal.

—V. O. Key Jr., *The Responsible Electorate*

As discussed in the previous chapter, voters often appear to be poorly informed about political affairs. In early studies, the findings regarding voter knowledge of political affairs were consistently negative—voters were believed to know little about vital issues of public policy, about where the two parties stood on these issues, and about the status of current federal policy on these issues (Campbell et al. 1960). The amount of information voters possessed about public affairs seemed bleak indeed.

Yet an important determinant of voter information levels is the context of the campaign—more specifically, how the available choices are framed by the candidates and the media during any particular campaign (Key 1966). In other words, what voters know or don't know of the candidates and the policy issues in any election is largely determined by the information, and the clarity of that information, presented to them during the presidential campaign.

Thus, instead of assuming that voters *should be perfectly informed* during a presidential election season, it is more appropriate to assume that they *are imperfectly informed* about candidates and policy issues. That Campbell et al. found the electorate was poorly informed about policy issues in the presidential elections of the 1950s should not have been surprising. The lack of information can be attributed to the lack of clear and emphasized differences between the presidential candidates on policy issues (Key 1966, 78). Page summarized this understanding:

To be sure, voters do not receive or retain every scrap of available information about politics: it would be costly and irrational to do so. But often the information is simply not available. The extreme ambiguity of candidates' policy stands—the low emphasis with which they are taken, and the lack of specificity in even the least ambiguous statements—add greatly to the costs of obtaining such information and sometimes make it altogether unobtainable. Candidate ambiguity is an important cause of misperception and nonperception by voters. (Page 1978, 281)

This insight led to fundamental reconsiderations of both candidate and voter behavior, revolving around the notions of ambiguity and uncertainty (Enelow and Hinich 1984; Page 1976, 1978; Page and Brody 1972; Shepsle 1972).

In these reconsiderations, the theoretical work has reached agreement on one point—candidates in many circumstances have strong incentives to present ambiguous policy stands to the electorate. However, the theoretical literature has not agreed about the underlying motivations for these incentives. Shepsle (1972) provided one of the early elaborations of these incentives based on the Downsian spatial model. The primary innovation in Shepsle's paper, however, lay in his supposition that candidates might prefer to take a "lottery" or probabilistic position on an issue dimension instead of taking a single-point stance. Shepsle's results hinged on three conditions: that all voters are nonstrategic decision makers, that a majority of voters are risk-takers or are risk-takers across a large portion of their utility function, and that there are issue dimensions upon which voters have intense and polarized preferences. The key result in Sheplse's paper was that he showed that if a majority of voters is risk-acceptant (or they possess intense preferences about the issue), then candidates and parties will have strong incentives to be equivocal in their issue stands (Shepsle 1972, 567).

Thus, under these conditions, Shepsle demonstrates that candidates might prefer an ambiguous (or probabilistic) position over a nonambiguous (or point) position. Shepsle's work is exceptionally important—it places uncertainty squarely in a model of electoral campaigns. Furthermore, the conceptualization of uncertainty in Shepsle's model, that a candidate's policy positions can be represented not only as points in an issue space, *but as probability distributions over points in that issue space*, provides a means to incorporate uncertainty in models of voter decision making.

Yet Page (1976, 1978) raises some serious critiques of Shepsle's model. In place of Shepsle's probabilistic model Page developed an "emphasis allocation theory" to account for candidate ambiguity. Here, beginning with the assumptions that political information is imperfect and that there are strong constraints on the ability of candidates to communicate their messages to voters, Page argued that candidates must allocate their resources either toward publicizing their policy stands or to other campaign strategies. But, Page stated:

> Specific policy proposals turn out to be relatively ineffective in winning votes. Candidates therefore devote most of their efforts to projecting a favorable personal image and making other productive appeals: policy stands are left ambiguous, with very low emphasis (Page 1976, 748).

Thus, candidate ambiguity in Page's model contains two aspects of uncertainty: candidate vagueness as well as a lack of campaign emphasis on policy issues.[1]

Page's work is important in two respects. First, since candidates must allocate scarce resources between policy-based campaigning and other, potentially more effective, types of personal or symbolic campaigning, we should not be surprised to find that voters are often poorly informed about policy issues. Second, and of equal importance, Page provides an opening into how voters might cope with this uncertainty about candidates—they use more reliable and inexpensive information, like retrospective assessments and evaluations of candidate personality and style, as cues in their decision making.

Yet, both of these models agree that candidates have strong incentives to present uncertain policy stands to the electorate. While both models have implications for voter decision making, these implications have not been systematically explored. Thus this chapter elaborates two related theoretical models depicting how voters react to uncertainty about candidate issue stands under certain assumptions. I first discuss my definition of voter uncertainty. Then I present a simple spatial model to demonstrate how uncertainty influences voter choices. The third section of this chapter turns to a dynamic model of voting, utilizing the insights of Bayes's Theorem, and discusses how the acquisition of information in a political campaign influences voter perceptions and hence their decision-making processes. Throughout this discussion, I present specific hypotheses which are tested in the subsequent chapters of this book.

What Is Uncertainty?

In this section, I discuss theoretical issues regarding voter uncertainty about candidate policy positions.[2] First, uncertainty is defined. In the next section

---

1. It is of interest to note that "emphasis allocation theory" implies that candidates will be ambiguous in both their *positions* on policy issues and the *importance or salience* they attach to different issues.

2. Why uncertainty about only candidate policy positions? Of course voters may be uncertain about other attributes of a candidate—their personal traits, abilities, or their future behavior.

I use this definition of uncertainty to show two ways in which the uncertainty voters have about candidate policy positions influences their voting behavior. One of the effects of uncertainty is on the general evaluations, or utility, of voters for presidential candidate. The other effect of uncertainty is on the ability of voters to use their policy preferences when they decide which candidate to support.

In this book, I adopt the usual decision-theoretic distinction between certain and uncertain information (Kreps 1990; Rasmussen 1989). Decision making under certainty is characterized by situations in which choices (C_i) lead to known outcomes (O_k). Thus, when faced with certainty, a particular course of action, some C_i, leads deterministically to a certain O_k. For example, certain information implies that I know that if I choose candidate 1 in an election, I will obtain policy outcome O_1, but if I choose candidate two, I will obtain policy outcome O_2. This is illustrated in equation 3.1:

$$C_1 \longrightarrow O_1 \tag{3.1}$$
$$C_2 \longrightarrow O_2$$

Certainty here means a direct mapping of candidate choice into policy outcome.

On the other hand, decision making under uncertainty occurs when actions C_i lead to outcomes O_k with some probability P_{ik}. In this situation, when an individual picks a particular C_i, there is a set of possible outcomes, each with an associated likelihood of occurrence. Thus, under uncertainty, the mapping of candidate choices into policy outcomes is not deterministic. For example, if I choose candidate 1, I know I can get policy outcome 1 with only probability .8, and policy outcome 2 with probability .2.

$$C_1 \longrightarrow O_1 \quad P = .8 \tag{3.2}$$
$$C_1 \longrightarrow O_2 \quad P = .2$$
$$C_2 \longrightarrow O_1 \quad P = .3$$
$$C_2 \longrightarrow O_2 \quad P = .7$$

And, as depicted in equation 3.2, I can achieve policy outcome 1 with probability of .3 by choosing candidate 2, and policy outcome 2 with probability of

---

Here I focus only on policy uncertainty, since that has been the area of most concern in the theoretical literature. The theoretical work in this chapter, and the empirical analysis of subsequent chapters, should be expanded in future research to encompass these other types of voter uncertainty. Just as candidates have incentives to present ambiguous policy positions, so might they be motivated to be ambiguous about their traits, credibility, and past record.

.7 by picking candidate 2.

However, how do individuals determine P_{ik}, the probability that an event would occur given a particular action? In the literature on decision making under uncertainty, a distinction is made between probabilities that are given exogenously to the decision maker (choice under risk) and probabilities that are determined endogenously by the decision maker (choice under uncertainty). This distinction is often a source of confusion in this literature, so it is necessary to grapple with the difference between the models in some depth, considering whether one better approximates the political world than the other.

To clarify this distinction, I return to Shepsle's model of candidate ambiguity. Here, Shepsle uses the choice-under-risk model of uncertainty, where the probabilities of candidate location in the issue space are given exogenously. Shepsle states, though, that "the three-part distinction (between certainty, risk, and uncertainty) is, for our purposes, somewhat artificial, and that we may conceive all contingencies as falling under the rubric of risk—a known probability distribution over outcomes" (Shepsle 1972, 559).

But when we think of candidates competing in national elections, we may want to reconsider this assumption. The representation used by Shepsle has the probability distribution of the candidate's position in the issue space being set by the candidate and known by the voter. Neither of these assumptions is appropriate. First, while candidates may *try* to define their positions in an issue space, they often are not very successful. Both the media and the candidate's opponents often intervene to influence where the electorate sees the candidate's position on policy issues. Second, it is not clear that voters know the probability distributions of the candidate's position in the issue space, since there is likely to be heterogeneity in the voter reception of candidate messages. Since these assumptions are inappropriate, a model that assumes the probability distributions of candidate positions to be known by voters is questionable.

Enelow and Hinich (1984, chap. 7) distinguish between these two types of uncertainty in a different fashion. First, they develop what they term *candidate-induced uncertainty*, which they define as uncertainty induced in the minds of voters when candidates announce changes in their position on a policy issue and voters believe this announcement only to a limited extent. In Enelow and Hinich's model, a candidate who has a past position later announces a new position, and the difference between the two announced positions leads voters to attach probabilities to these two locations. This yields a model very similar to choice under risk (Enelow and Hinich 1984, 119).

Second, they discuss *perceptual uncertainty*, which they define:

In any single election period, there are many reasons why voters may be unsure about precisely where a candidate is located on the predictive dimension. Political communication is a noisy process, and voters typically lack incentives to resolve uncertainties they may have about the candidates. (Enelow and Hinich 1984, 115–16)

Here the uncertainty of voters about the candidates is largely endogenous, in that they are unsure about the placement of candidates on issues due to imperfect and costly information (e.g., Downs 1957). This yields a model which is similar to the choice under uncertainty approach, where the uncertainty voters have about candidate policy stands is endogenous.

Yet while this distinction between choice under risk and uncertainty (exogenous versus endogenous uncertainty) is important to discuss, in practice it is difficult to distinguish between risk and uncertainty, since perceptual uncertainty encompasses both uncertainty from the candidates and the information transmission and acquisition process on the part of voters. Indeed, Enelow and Hinich encountered this very difficulty in their discussion of Carter in 1976: "*the voter's lack of familiarity with Carter, compounded by the personal focus of his campaign,* made it extremely difficult for them to decide where he was located on the predictive dimensions of the campaign" (Enelow and Hinich 1984, 122–23, emphasis added). Thus, perceptual uncertainty about a candidate's policy positions can be rooted both in the voters' own disincentives to gather and process costly information about candidates as well as the candidates' incentives to disseminate ambiguous information.

In this book, when I refer to uncertainty I am discussing the broader notion of perceptual uncertainty. While some of the uncertainty voters possess about the policy positions of candidates in an election clearly is the result of candidate ambiguity and equivocation, some of the uncertainty is also due to the voter's ability to gather and process costly political information. Thus, due to the presence of endogenously driven uncertainty in the minds of voters, I adopt the notion of perceptual uncertainty advanced by Enelow and Hinich, as well as the broader model of choice under uncertainty implied by this conception.

Uncertainty and Voter Decisions

Effects on Candidate Evaluations

I use the spatial model of voting to understand the impact of perceptual uncertainty on voter evaluations (or theoretically, utility) of candidates. Here, while I follow the path developed by Enelow and Hinich (1984) and Bartels (1986), the models presented below provide a foundation for understanding how imperfect information matters for voter decision making. Assume that there are two candidates under evaluation, J and G, and that there is only one policy dimension associated with this election. Due to the uncertain information that voter i has about the position of each candidate, the voter's perception of each candidate's position is represented as a random variable, P_{iJ} and P_{iG}, with a corresponding central tendency or actual position (focusing only on candidate J), p_J, and a variance in perception, v_{iJ}. Then, P_{iJ} is expressed as the sum of the actual position of the candidate and the perceptual uncertainty of the voter:

$$P_{iJ} = p_J + v_{iJ} \tag{3.3}$$

The spatial interpretation of equation 3.3 is that each voter's perception of the position of a candidate on a policy issue is composed of a central point and a distribution of points around that mean.[3] The smaller the distribution around that mean, the less uncertainty the voter has about that candidate on that issue.

Recall that uncertainty about a candidate's policy stance can be represented as a variance around some specific position.[4] A useful heuristic representation is the one-dimensional policy space, as depicted in figure 3.1. In the figure the set of potential candidate positions is given on the x-axis as falling on a continuum ranging from -4 to 4. The y-axis gives the possible distributions of the candidate's position. The three curves in the figure depict three levels of voter uncertainty about the candidate's position on this issue. In figure 3.1 the central tendency of the candidate's position is the same—centered around zero—yet the variances of the distributions are very different, showing differences in the voter's uncertainty. Under conditions of low uncertainty, as shown in figure 3.1, the variance in the voter's perceptions is quite small, and the distribution clusters around the central tendency. Under conditions of high uncertainty, however, the variance is quite large, and the distribution is very flat. Thus, with high uncertainty the voter has a difficult time discerning where in the issue space the candidate's position may be.

Now, using this conception of uncertainty, equation 3.3 is built into a spatial voting model under the assumptions that voters use quadratic utility functions and that preferences can be expressed with a Euclidean distance metric. For simplicity, assume that the voter's utility for candidate J (which can

---

3. Note that this generalizes to a set of policies, where the issue space is multidimensional (Bartels 1986).

4. Any number of functional forms might be used to represent a voter's perception of a candidate's policy stands. For example, Shepsle (1972) utilized a uniform distribution to make his work more tractable. Additionally, nonsymmetric distributions might be considered, since it is possible that due to certain characteristics of the campaign, candidate, or issue, the distribution of a voter's perceptions of the candidate's position might be skewed in one direction. An example would be the position of extremist candidates—like Barry Goldwater or Jesse Helms.

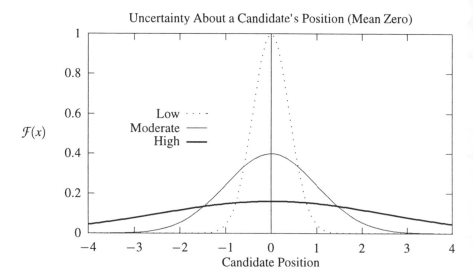

Fig. 3.1.   **Voter uncertainty of a candidate's position.**

also be termed the voter's evaluation of J), is composed of nonpolicy dimensions of candidate evaluation, c_{iJ}, and that the voter's issue preferences can be measured by the squared distance between the positions of the voter and the candidate on the issue, x_i, and P_{iJ}.

$$U_{iJ} = c_{iJ} - (P_{iJ} - x_i)^2 \tag{3.4}$$

But P_{iJ} is a probabilistic term, and decision making occurs in an uncertain world, so equation 3.4 is recast in terms of expected utilities:

$$E[U_{iJ}] = E[c_{iJ} - (P_{iJ} - x_i)^2] \tag{3.5}$$

Next, expand equation 3.5:

$$E[U_{iJ}] = E[c_{iJ} - (P_{iJ}^2 - 2P_{iJ}x_i + x_i^2)] \tag{3.6}$$

Then move the expectations operator through the right-hand side of the equation, and note that $E[c_{iJ}] = c_{iJ}; E[x_i] = x_i; E[P_{iJ}^2] = p_J^2 + v_{iJ}^2; E[v_{iJ}x_i] = 0; E[v_{iJ}^2] =$

σ_{iJ}^2; and that $E[P_{iJ}] = p_J$.[5] This yields:

$$E[U_{iJ}] = c_{iJ} - p_J^2 - \sigma_{iJ}^2 + 2p_J x_i - x_i^2 \tag{3.7}$$

Last, by collecting terms on the right-hand side:

$$E[U_{iJ}] = c_{iJ} - (p_J - x_i)^2 - \sigma_{iJ}^2 \tag{3.8}$$

This simple addition of perceptual uncertainty into the standard spatial model demonstrates one way in which voter uncertainty about candidate policy positions is important. Under the assumption that voters are risk-averse (implied by the assumption that voter utility functions are single-peaked and concave), perceptual uncertainty *depresses* the voter's utility for a candidate. This is an important theoretical prediction—the more uncertain a voter is about a candidate's policy stands, the lower their utility for that candidate.[6] Thus, this is the first way in which uncertainty influences voter decision making, since I expect that greater voter uncertainty about a candidate adversely influences his or her evaluation of that candidate and hence his or her preference for that candidate.

The utility the voter expects to obtain from the other candidate (G) can be expressed in a similar form:

$$E[U_{iG}] = c_{iG} - (p_G - x_i)^2 - \sigma_{iG}^2 \tag{3.9}$$

If the election involves these two candidates, then the decision rule for the

---

5. That $E[P_{iJ}^2] = p_J^2 + v_{iJ}^2$ may not be intuitive. However, define x to be a set of k observations of a variable, μ to be the mean of x across k, and σ^2 to be the expected squared deviation of x from μ. Then, $E(x - \mu)^2 = \sigma^2$. Simple rearrangement of the terms gives $\sigma^2 = E(x^2) - \mu^2$ and $E(x^2) = \mu^2 - \sigma^2$. The latter is equivalent to the expression given above.

6. Kenneth Shepsle has pointed out, however, that this prediction is not applicable to two classes of voters: those with globally convex utility functions, and those whose utility functions might have convex regions. The first type of voters we would call risk takers—they would always prefer an ambiguous candidate to a nonambiguous one. The latter class, though, might be visualized by thinking of a voter with a normally distributed utility function. Here, there would be convexity in the extremes, or the tails, of the utility function. Thus, if a voter encountered a candidate whose ambiguous position fell in the convex portion of their utility function, they might respond positively to that candidate's ambiguity. Therefore, there might be heterogeneity in voter responses to uncertainty and ambiguity, based both on the shape of voter utility functions and on the location of the candidate relative to the voter. It is also quite possible that voters might be risk neutral. In any case, the risk proclivities of voters are really empirical questions. In later chapters, I show strong support for the prediction of equation 3.8—which implies that the electorate is risk averse.

voter is simple: vote for candidate J if $E[U_{iJ}] \geq E[U_{iG}]$. Or:

$$c_{iJ} - (p_J - x_i)^2 - \sigma_{iJ}^2 \geq c_{iG} - (p_G - x_i)^2 - \sigma_{iG}^2 \tag{3.10}$$

This presentation in the context of a two-candidate race only serves to reinforce my conclusion drawn from equation 3.8. Here in equation 3.10, it is clear that if $c_{iJ} = c_{iG}$ and $(p_J - x_i)^2 = (p_G - x_i)^2$, then the voter's decision hinges on the relative magnitudes of σ_{iJ}^2 and σ_{iG}^2. Thus if the voter evaluates the two candidates identically on nonpolicy dimensions, *and* the voter is the same distance from *both* candidates on the issue, then they will support candidate J only if $\sigma_{iJ}^2 \leq \sigma_{iG}^2$ which is true only when they are more (or equally) certain of J's position on the issue.

How great, however, is this influence of voter uncertainty on candidate evaluations? To ascertain the potential magnitude of this influence, I translate the utility calculus equation 3.10 into a probabilistic model.[7] To depict the effect of uncertainty on voter evaluations of the candidate, I make two assumptions. First, I assume, for the sake of simplicity, that the expected utility of the voter for candidate G is zero, which simplifies these calculations. Second, I assume that the nonissue components of the voter's evaluation of candidate J are distributed normally and are independent of the voter's issue-based evaluation of the candidate. Note that these assumptions are only required to demonstrate this theoretical model probabilistically and are not relevant in subsequent empirical evaluation of the model. These assumptions allow me to take the expression in equation 3.10 and transform it into a probabilistic model. First, rearrange the terms:

$$- (p_J - x_i)^2 - \sigma_{iJ}^2 + c_{iJ} \geq 0 \tag{3.11}$$

$$- I_{iJ} + u_{iJ} \geq 0, \tag{3.12}$$

where $I_{iJ} = -(p_J - x_i)^2 - \sigma_{iJ}^2$ and $u_{iJ} = c_{iJ}$. Then, under the assumption that u_{iJ} is distributed normally and independently of I_{iJ}, the expression in equation 3.12 is written probabilistically,

$$P[-I_{iJ} + u_{iJ} \geq 0] = \int_{-\infty}^{I} \frac{1}{\sqrt{2\pi}} \exp^{\frac{-u^2}{2}} du \tag{3.13}$$

By inserting hypothetical values into the expression in equation 3.13, I can

---

7. Erikson and Romero (1990) present a similar set of simulations to explicate their model. However, their presentation concerns salience, not uncertainty.

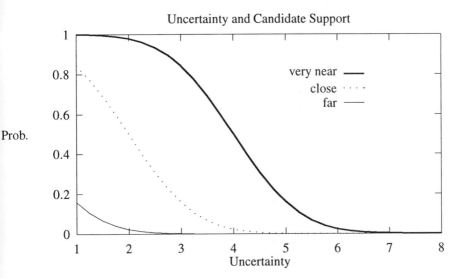

Fig. 3.2. Simulated effects of uncertainty on candidate support probabilities.

show graphically the relationship between the uncertainty the voter has about the candidate's policy positions and the probability that the voter would support the candidate. I present such a simulation in figure 3.2, where I show probabilities of candidate support, across a hypothetical range of candidate uncertainty, for a candidate at varying distances from the voter on the policy issue.[8]

In figure 3.2, the y-axis gives the probabilities that voter i would support candidate J, while the x-axis gives hypothetical values for the level of uncertainty the voter has about J's position on the issue. The dark line gives the effect of i's uncertainty on the probability of supporting J when the voter is very near the candidate on the issue, the dotted line when i is not as close to J, and the light line when the voter is distant from the candidate on the issue.

---

8. Estimating simulated probabilities of candidate support at various combinations of uncertainty and distance between the candidate and the voter is simple. Hypothetical values for each variable are combined as given by the theoretical model, and after adding an intercept term to produce reasonable z-scores, the area under the cumulative normal distribution was calculated for each hypothetical example. This last calculation produces the predicted probabilities shown in this figure. For a similar application, see Erickson and Romero 1990.

The influence of voter uncertainty on candidate policy positions is striking when the candidate is very close to the voter on the issue. For example, assume a hypothetical voter who is very close to the candidate on the issue, under the following situations. From figure 3.2, a voter who was relatively certain of the candidate's position (uncertainty = 1) would vote for the candidate with high probability, but one who was even only moderately uncertain (uncertainty = 4), would now be about 50 percent less likely to vote for the candidate, all things held constant. Even when the candidate is far from the voter on the issue, uncertainty acts to reduce the support of the voter for the candidate. Of course, the effect of uncertainty is greatly diminished due to the fact that the voter is not very likely, even when certain of the candidate's position on the issue, to vote for that candidate since she is not close to the candidate on the issue. This result leads to the first hypothesis:

Hypothesis 1: The greater the individual's uncertainty about the candidate's policy positions, the lower their utility for the candidate and hence the lower their probability of supporting the candidate, all other things held constant.

Effects on Issue Voting

A second way in which uncertainty about candidate issue positions influences voter decision making concerns the ability of voters to employ issue preferences in their decision. Page, elaborating on Key's "echo chamber" notion, developed this relationship:

When ambiguity confuses perceptions, it necessarily interferes with policy voting as well, for citizens cannot vote their policy preferences with any confidence if they do not know where candidates stand. There is every reason to expect that ambiguity generally depresses the extent of policy voting (this, we have argued, is in fact the purpose behind candidates' ambiguity), and that policy voting is especially reduced on issues which the candidates are most ambiguous. (Page 1978, 186–87)

However, there have been no attempts to incorporate systematically this relationship between uncertainty about candidate policy positions and policy voting into theoretical or empirical work. This is one gap in the literature which the following discussion should fill.

In figure 3.3 I gave examples of how uncertainty can be conceptualized spatially, with a candidate's policy position represented as a probability distri-

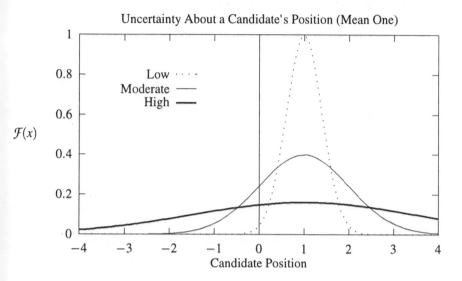

Fig. 3.3.   Voter uncertainty of a candidate's position.

bution in the issue space. What does this imply for a voter's ability to employ his or her preferences on this issue in evaluating this candidate? Assume first that the candidate's position is centered around zero, as in figure 3.3, and that the voter has a position of two on this particular issue. If the voter is relatively certain of the candidate's position on this issue, then the relative distance between the voter and the candidate can be employed by the voter in his or her calculus as predicted by the spatial voting model. However, if the voter has a high degree of uncertainty, then the voter really cannot discern whether the candidate's position is close to his or her position on this issue, or whether as shown in the figure, the candidate is an extremist on the issue. Under such conditions, it would be difficult for the voter to utilize this information in her decision.

A similar conclusion holds for the representation of the voter's perceptions shown in figure 3.3. Here, even though the candidate's position has been moved one unit towards the voter's, notice that if the voter has a low amount of uncertainty about the candidate's position, she still can discern a difference between her position and the candidate's. Again, though, under moderate and high levels of uncertainty, the voter will have a difficult time discerning exactly the differences between her position and the candidate's on the issue. And it would be difficult, under such circumstances, for the voter to use her issue preferences in her evaluation of the candidate.

So if the candidate gives great emphasis to an issue, the voter may know the candidate's position with relatively greater certainty, and accordingly the issue would factor more heavily in her decision making. But as the candidate talks less about the issue, all things held constant, the voter may be less certain of the candidate's position, and should place less weight on the issue in her evaluation of the candidate. Thus, when voters are extremely uncertain about the position of the candidate, that information will not be very useful in their evaluations of the candidate. In these conditions, voters might use more available and accurate information in their decision making. Voters should then rely more heavily upon the nonpolicy characteristics of the candidates (as encompassed in the c_{iJ} term in equation 3.8) and not as heavily on their policy preferences.

The impact of uncertainty on issue voting can be expressed formally. Beginning with the expected utility calculus for one candidate on one issue, consider:

$$E(U_{iJ}) = c_{iJ} - w_{iJ}(p_J - x_i)^2 - \sigma_{iJ}^2 \qquad (3.14)$$

where w_{iJ} is a weight on the issue distance component of the voter's expected utility calculus, and the other terms are as defined in the previous section.[9] It is easiest to assume that this weight is proportional to a voter's uncertainty about the candidate's position on the policy issue and that it is constrained so that $0 \leq w_{iJ} \leq 1$. This means that when $w_{iJ} = 0$, the voter is uncertain of the candidate's position on the issue—so uncertain that in her expected utility calculus, this issue is irrelevant to the voter's decision. Also, when completely uncertain of the candidate's position, the voter relies on only the nonpolicy characteristics and their uncertainty in determining her expected utility for this candidate. Conversely, when $w_{iJ} = 1$, the voter is now completely certain of the position of the candidate on this issue, and she can now confidently rely upon this information in her evaluation of the candidate.

As before, I write a similar expected utility function for the opposing candidate:

$$E(U_{iG}) = c_{iG} - w_{iG}(p_G - x_i)^2 - \sigma_{iG}^2. \qquad (3.15)$$

The voter will again choose the candidate who brings the greatest expected

---

9. Recall that c_{iJ} is i's evaluation of J's trait attributes, p_J is the position of J on the issue, x_i is the voter's position on the issue, and σ_{iJ}^2 is i's uncertainty about J's position on the issue.

utility. So, the voter chooses candidate J if $E(U_{iJ}) \geq E(U_{iG})$, or if:

$$c_{iJ} - w_{iJ}(p_J - x_i)^2 - \sigma_{iJ}^2 \geq c_{iG} - w_{iG}(p_G - x_i)^2 - \sigma_{iG}^2 \qquad (3.16)$$

Given this expanded decision rule, uncertainty plays a broader role in the voter's determination of which candidate to support. If $c_{iJ} = c_{iG}$ and $(p_J - x_i)^2 = (p_G - x_i)^2$ (implying that the voter evaluates the candidates equally on policy and nonpolicy dimensions), the voter's decision again hinges on the relative uncertainty about the positions of the candidates. If the voter is more uncertain of candidate G's position, then $\sigma_{iJ}^2 < \sigma_{iG}^2$ and $w_{iJ} > w_{iG}$. Thus, the voter will support J over G, since her greater uncertainty about candidate G reduces her expected utility for G in two ways: first by the direct risk aversion effect of uncertainty and second by the reduced weight placed on the issue distance term by the voter given her uncertainty of G's position on the issue.

Again, to better understand the effect of uncertainty on the ability of voters to employ their issue preferences in their voting calculus, as depicted here, I cast the final expression in equation 3.16 into probabilistic terms. First, for simplicity, assume that $E(U_{iG}) = 0$. This allows simplification of the expression in equation 3.16 as well as the notation:

$$-w_{iJ}(p_J - x_i)^2 + \sigma_{iJ}^2 + c_{iJ} \geq 0$$

which simplifies to:

$$-I_{iJ} + u_{iJ} \geq 0, \qquad (3.17)$$

where $I_{iJ} = -w_{iJ}(p_J - x_i)^2 + \sigma_{iJ}^2$, and $u_{iJ} = c_{iJ}$. And, by again assuming that u_{iJ} is distributed normally and independently of the terms contained in I_{iJ}, the expression in equation 3.17 can be written probabilistically,

$$P[-I_{iJ} + u_{iJ} \geq 0] = \int_{-\infty}^{wI} \frac{1}{\sqrt{2\pi}} \exp^{\frac{-u^2}{2}} du \qquad (3.18)$$

Thus the primary importance of equation 3.18 is that it can be used to simulate the effect of uncertainty on the ability of voters to employ their issue preferences in their decisions. Such a simulation, showing the relationship between the distance between the voter and the candidate on the policy issue and the probability that the voter would support the candidate, is presented in figure 3.4.[10] In figure 3.4 the probability of supporting the candidate is given

---

10. The probabilities in figure 3.4 were obtained as described earlier.

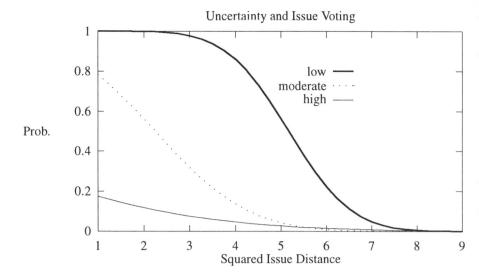

Fig. 3.4. **Simulated interactive effects of uncertainty on issue voting.**

on the y-axis. But the x-axis now expresses the squared distance between the candidate and the voter on the issue. Here, the dark line gives the effect of the relative distance between the voter and the candidate on the probability of supporting the candidate when the voter has a low degree of uncertainty about the candidate's position. The dotted line shows the same effect for a moderate level of uncertainty, and the thin line, for a high degree of uncertainty.

Note the slope of the probability curves in figure 3.4 and how they vary as uncertainty about the candidate's positions increases. The greater the uncertainty about the candidate's position, the less the impact of the relative distance between the voter and the candidate on the voter's probability of supporting the candidate. As the voter's uncertainty of the candidate's position increases, his or her ability to employ issue preferences in voting decisions decreases.

Consider two situations. First, assume that a voter has low uncertainty about the candidate. If we consider two possible positions of the candidate, one very near the voter (squared candidate issue distance = 2) and the other somewhat further from the voter (squared candidate issue distance = 5), it is clear that moving the candidate this distance from the voter decreases the probability of candidate support by approximately 50 percent. Now assume instead that the voter has a great deal of uncertainty about the candidate's position on the issue, relative to the voter. An identical examination (moving the squared position of the candidate relative to the voter from 2 to 5) produces just over a 10 percent reduction in the likelihood of candidate support. Thus, the model predicts that as uncertainty about a candidate's position increases, the policy issue becomes less relevant in the voter's calculus. This leads to the second hypothesis:

Hypothesis 2: The greater the individual's uncertainty about the candidate's policy positions, the lesser their ability to employ their issue preferences in their voting calculus, all other things held constant.

However, this argument has broader implications than merely predicting that the effect of policy issues on a voter's choice is conditional on their uncertainty of the candidate's position. For, if the voter is extremely uncertain of the candidate's position on the issue, that information will be difficult or impossible for the voter to employ, since she cannot know with much precision where the candidate stands relative to her own ideal point on the issue. Upon what grounds, then, can the very uncertain voter evaluate the candidate?

In such a situation, voters will rely upon information which was encompassed in the c_{ij} term in the spatial model developed above. Thus, they will bring to bear in their decision factors like the personal and professional characteristics of the candidate (Kinder 1986; Lau 1986; Miller, Wattenberg, and Malanchuk 1986; Rahn 1990; Rahn et al. 1990), partisanship (Campbell et al. 1960), or other nonpolicy information about the candidate. This leads to an additional hypothesis:

Hypothesis 3: The greater the voter's uncertainty about the candidate's policy positions, the more likely it will be that they will rely upon nonpolicy factors in their decision making, all other things held constant.

The Dynamics of Information and Uncertainty

The spatial model developed in the previous section allowed development of three theoretically driven hypotheses about the decisions made by voters under certain assumptions. However, it is a static model of voter decision making, since it assumes that the relevant elements of the voters' calculus, especially their uncertainty about the candidate's policy positions, are constant and unchanging. I relax this assumption in this section to examine theoretically how information made available to the electorate during a presidential campaign influences voters' uncertainty about a candidate's policy stands and, perhaps, also influences their preferences.

To examine the dynamic relationship between campaign information and voter perception and preference, I employ a simple Bayesian model of political information. The Bayesian learning model, like the spatial model of voting, is not a completely descriptive model of behavior. Instead, it provides an explicit, consistent, and systematic accounting of the way in which individuals might combine newly encountered information with their past understandings of the political world.[11] While Bayesian models are rare in the political science literature, their empirical applications have been successful (Achen 1989; Bartels 1993; Calvert and MacKuen 1985; Husted et al. 1995; Zechman 1978).

The intuition behind the Bayesian model is compelling. Basically, the model states that the voter has prior perceptions or information (called "priors"), and that these prior beliefs can be updated with the acquisition of new information, yielding revised, posterior beliefs. The Bayesian approach provides a particular mathematical framework for the formation of new perceptions. To express the Bayesian model formally, first define θ_{kt} to be candidate k's position on a particular issue at time t, γ_{kt} to be the voter's knowledge of the candidate's position, and η_{kt} to represent information received about the candidate k's position.

Then, assume that the beliefs (or perceptions of the candidate on issues in this case) are known imperfectly by the voter, and hence, are described by a series of probability distributions. The voter's prior probability distribution, the voter's calculation of the probability that the candidate will have a certain position once in office, conditioned on their knowledge of that position, is defined by:

$$P(\theta_{kt} \mid \gamma_{kt}) \sim N(\mu_1, \sigma_1^2) \tag{3.19}$$

This means that the voter's calculation of the candidate's position developed from past knowledge of that position is assumed to be normally distributed

---

11. Many believe the Bayesian model to be of little utility in the analysis of perceptual formation and change. But the Bayesian model actually complements the psychological learning models which have become popular in the political science literature. Where the cognitive-psychological models have presented very complete descriptions of the structures of past political information, whether they are termed scripts, schemas, stereotypes, or whatever else, these models have been less descriptive as to the processes by which new information is incorporated into these cognitive structures (some attempts have been made in this literature to overcome this tendency; see Conover and Feldman 1989; Lodge and Hamill 1986; Lodge, McGraw, and Stroh 1989). While the Bayesian model is less descriptive in the structuring of past information, it is more rigorous in the description of how newly encountered information can be combined with old knowledge for updated assessments of the political world. See Achen 1989 for additional discussion.

with a mean μ_1 and a variance σ_1^2. Similarly, the probability that the voter would actually observe the newly encountered information, η_{kt}, conditioned on the candidate's position and the voter's knowledge of that position, were the candidate in office, is defined as:

$$P(\eta_{kt} \mid \gamma_{kt}, \theta_{kt}) \sim N(\mu_2, \sigma_2^2) \tag{3.20}$$

And last, the voter's posterior distribution also has a similar definition, where the probability that the candidate is actually at the particular position is conditioned on the voter's knowledge of the position and the newly encountered information about the candidate:

$$P(\theta_{kt} \mid \gamma_{kt}, \eta_{kt}) \sim N(\mu_3, \sigma_3^2) \tag{3.21}$$

Now that these probability distributions have been defined, Bayes's theorem states that the posterior distribution is proportional to the product of the prior distribution and the distribution of the newly encountered information. That is,

$$P(\theta_{kt} \mid \gamma_{kt}, \eta_{kt}) \propto P(\theta_{kt} \mid \gamma_{kt}) * P(\eta_{kt} \mid \gamma_{kt}, \theta_{kt}) \tag{3.22}$$

This can be expressed in terms of the moments of these distributions.[12] The mean of the posterior is given by:

$$\mu_3 = \frac{\tau_1 \mu_1 + \tau_2 \mu_2}{\tau_1 + \tau_2} \tag{3.23}$$

The variance of the posterior is then:

$$\tau_3 = \tau_1 + \tau_2 \tag{3.24}$$

Note that $\tau_k = (\sigma_k^2)^{-1}$ for $k = 1,2,3$. The τ_k are termed precisions in the literature.

So what does this Bayesian learning model say about the dynamics of information and uncertainty? Where the voter perceives the candidate to stand on the issue, in light of some new information, is the weighted average of her past

---

12. Derivations of this step are in Zechman 1978, appendix A, as well as in Judge et al. 1988, chapter 4, and in most references on decision theory (Berger 1985; Jones 1977). The simplicity of this derivation is conditional on the normality assumption. Here I am seeking to develop a simple mathematical representation of campaign learning; future research should explore the use of different assumptions about the distributions of voter beliefs and campaign learning.

knowledge of the candidate's position and her newly obtained information. The weights, further, are simply the precisions of each piece of information, are proportional to the variances of the relevant probability distributions. The voter finds out something new about the candidate's position—from speeches, conventions, advertising, advertisement, the media, or whatever source—which alters her perception of this position in the direction of the new information. But, and of importance for this research, *the amount by which the voter alters her perceptions depends on the precision of the new information, relative to her past perceptions.*

In order to highlight the intuition behind the Bayesian model as presented in equations 3.23 and 3.24, the effects of newly obtained information upon both the mean and precision of the voter's posterior distribution regarding the position of the candidate on an issue are shown graphically. I performed two sets of simulations by setting all of the terms in equations 3.23 and 3.24 to the following simulated values. The voter's prior knowledge of the candidate's position (μ_1) is 0.5. The voter then receives new information that the candidate's expected position is changed to 1.5. To assess the effects of the precision of both the prior and new information on the voter's posterior knowledge, I then varied the precision of the new information about the candidate's position (τ_2), which takes a range of hypothetical values from zero (extreme imprecision) to 20 (extreme precision), and the precision of the voter's prior knowledge of the candidate's position (τ_1), which I varied across three values, low, moderate, and high. These simulations are given in figures 3.5 and 3.6, where the former gives the mean of the voter's posterior knowledge and the latter gives the posterior precision. In each figure, the lines represent one of the assumed levels of prior precision while the x-axis gives the precision of the new information.

What is interesting to notice in figure 3.5 is how the precision of the new information influences the rate of change in this voter's perception. When the precision of their prior knowledge is low, even relatively imprecise new information can induce a dramatic change in the posterior mean in favor of the new information. However, as the precision of the prior knowledge increases, the voter places more weight on her prior knowledge than on the new information, so the new information must be extremely precise to induce a change in the perception of where the candidate stands on the particular issue.

In figure 3.6 the y-axis represents the precision of the posterior distribution. Recall that the posterior precision is simply the sum of the precision of the prior knowledge and the new information, which accounts for the linear relationships seen in the figure. Not surprisingly, a positive relationship is observed in the figure for each level of prior precision, indicating that as the precision of the new information increases, so does the precision of the posterior. Also worth notice here is that new information in the model always

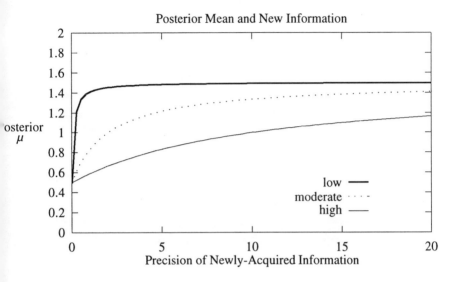

Fig. 3.5.   New information and the posterior mean.

increases posterior precision. Thus, the model predicts that if the voter has a very precise prior understanding of where the candidate stands on the issue and encounters very precise information which leads her to update her prior perceptions, the precision of her posterior knowledge will be greater, though not by a very large amount.[13]

This makes a great deal of sense as an explanation for how new information would affect voter beliefs. Say a hypothetical voter is very uncertain about the position of Bush on an issue in the 1988 election (as in the simulations in figs. 3.5 and 3.6 she believes initially that Bush's position is .5). And since she is very uncertain of Bush's position, she would be on the dark line in both figures. Now assume she receives new information about Bush's position, from a speech by Bush or some media coverage of his campaign—information which indicates very certainly that Bush is at a different position (1.5) on the issue. This new information would have a dramatic effect on this voter's beliefs about Bush's position, since she would shift her best estimate of Bush's position (the

---

13. Since the variances of these distributions are assumed to be positive, so are the precisions. Under such conditions, the precision of the posterior will never be less than the precision of the prior.

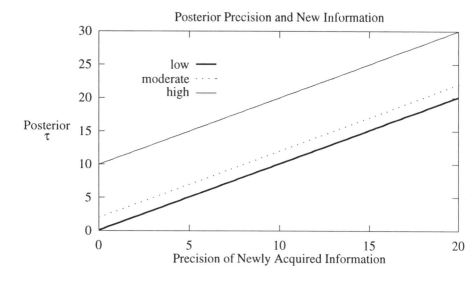

Fig. 3.6.   **New information and the posterior precision.**

mean of the distribution) much closer to where the new information says Bush stands on the issue. Since the new information is very precise, that would dramatically reduce the voter's uncertainty of Bush's position on the issue.

So far, I have demonstrated two aspects of the Bayesian model: the effects which newly obtained information has on each component of a voter's perceptions about candidate policy stands—the mean and precision (or variance) of that perception. The next step is to show the process by which such changes in voter perception of candidate issue positions are incorporated into their evaluations of the candidates. For this purpose, I return to the spatial model of voting as developed in the previous section.[14]

As in the spatial model above, assume that there are two candidates and that the preferences and utility functions of voters are such that the axioms of expected utility maximization apply. I also assume that there is only one policy dimension relevant to the voter and that the voter takes only information about their position and the candidate's position on this issue into account. The

_____

14. The incorporation of the updated knowledge of the candidate's position into the spatial model is relatively simple to demonstrate. More exhaustive discussions are in Calvert 1980 and Zechman 1978.

voter's expected utility from a particular candidate J is the utility the voter would anticipate, conditioned on their posterior distribution (Zechman 1978):

$$E(U(\theta_J) \mid P(\theta_J \mid \gamma_J, \eta_J)) \tag{3.25}$$

This leads to a decision-making rule for the voter, that is, vote for candidate J instead of G if:

$$E(U(\theta_J) \mid P(\theta_J \mid \gamma_J, \eta_J)) \geq E(U(\theta_G) \mid P(\theta_G \mid \gamma_G, \eta_G)) \tag{3.26}$$

Assume, as above, that the voter has a normally distributed posterior with a mean and a variance (proportional to the precision), and as in the earlier sections of this chapter, that the distance between the voter and the candidate can be written in terms of quadratic loss. This implies that the voter will prefer candidate J if $(\mu_{3J} - \omega_3)^2 \geq (\mu_{3G} - \omega_3)^2$, that is, if the posterior mean of candidate J is closer to their position (where the voter's position is denoted by ω) than the posterior mean of candidate G. By substituting from equations 3.23 and 3.24 for each candidate, this gives an amended decision rule, vote for candidate J if:

$$\left(\frac{\tau_{1J}\mu_{1J} + \tau_{2J}\mu_{2J}}{\tau_{1J} + \tau_{2J}} - \omega_3 \right)^2 \geq \left(\frac{\tau_{1G}\mu_{1G} + \tau_{2G}\mu_{2G}}{\tau_{1G} + \tau_{2G}} - \omega_3 \right)^2 \tag{3.27}$$

As complex as this might seem, interesting insights into the dynamics of voter preferences are obtained by analysis of the relationships between information, perceptions, and preferences in equation 3.27. A very easy way to gain intuition into these relationships is again through simulations. As in the earlier sections of this chapter, this model in equations 3.26 and 3.27 can be transformed probabilistically and rendered very tractable for simulation by assuming that the expected utility for candidate G is zero.[15] Four such simulations were carried out, with two in figure 3.7 and two in figure 3.8.

The x-axis in each panel of both figures gives the precision of the newly encountered information, and the y-axis gives the *change* in probabilities of supporting the candidate once the new information has been assimilated by the voter. The new information the voter receives is that the candidate is closer to the voter on the issue than was reflected in the voter's prior knowledge. Two lines are plotted in each figure, one for a situation where the new information

---

15. The probabilistic model is identical to the one in equations 3.13 and 3.18, except that here the systematic component of the model is given by the left-hand side of Equation 3.27 and the elements of the voter's evaluation of the candidate are distributed normally and independently of the systematic component.

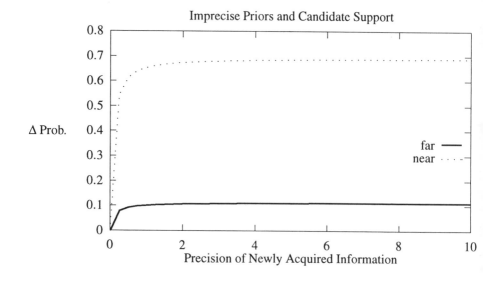

Fig. 3.7. New information and changes in imprecise preferences.

indicates that the candidate is much closer to the voter's position on the policy issue than the voter previously believed (dotted line), and one where the information states that the candidate is not much closer to the voter on the issue (dark line). Figure 3.7 presents these plots for a situation in which the voter's prior knowledge was imprecise, while figure 3.8 gives the plots for a scenario in which the voter's prior knowledge was precise.

Comparison of the results of these simulations produces some interesting conclusions. First, in figure 3.7 it is apparent that when the voter has an imprecise prior knowledge of the candidate's position and receives new information that the candidate is closer to the voter's ideal point, relatively large changes in the voter's probability of supporting the candidate occur across a wide range of precisions of the new information. Compare two scenarios: first, where the new information is very imprecise, with a precision near zero, and second, where the information is relatively precise, at a simulated value of approximately nine. In the first scenario, the probability that the voter supports the candidate does not change very much, no matter how close the candidate has moved to the voter's position, since their perception of the candidate's position is simply not very precise. However, in the second scenario, notice the wide di-

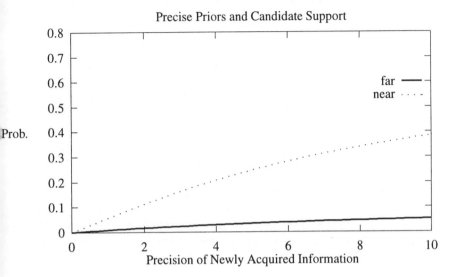

Fig. 3.8.   New information and changes in precise preferences.

vergence between the changes in probability of supporting the candidate where the candidate has moved much closer to the voter, compared to only slightly closer. As we might anticipate, when the prior information is imprecise, but the new information is precise, the voter adjusts her evaluation of the candidate heavily in the direction of the new information. This is evidenced by the large change in the probability of supporting the candidate, and these changes are greater when the information indicates that the candidate is closer to the voter on the issue.

But in figure 3.8, where the prior information is much more precise, a different conclusion is apparent. Again, compare two scenarios, the first in which the voter's new knowledge is very imprecise (near zero), as compared to a situation in which the information obtained is relatively precise (near nine). Interestingly, in the first scenario the voter is very unlikely to change her lack of support for the candidate—since her relatively precise prior states that they are not very near to the candidate on the issue, and very imprecise information does little to change this prior. Yet in the second scenario, there is a change in the likelihood that the voter would support the candidate (the difference in simulated probabilities is approximately 0.35 for the voter close to the candidate and around 0.05 for the voter further from the candidate), indicating that precise information can lead to a change in preferences when the new information is itself precise.

What is most interesting here, however, is the comparison between the figures. The conclusions when the new information obtained by the voter is very imprecise do not vary whether the candidate is near or far from the voter, or whether the priors are precise or imprecise. But when the new information is precise, we do see a good deal of variation depending on the relative location of the candidate *and* the precision of the prior knowledge. In the two simulations where the voter is closer to the candidate, she is more likely to support the candidate when she obtains new and precise information about the candidate's position.

But when the prior information is less precise, and the information reveals that the candidate is much closer to the voter, the changes in probabilities are much greater than when the prior information is more precise. New information—even relatively imprecise information—leads the voter to update prior information about the candidate's position is uncertain. However, when the voter's prior knowledge is more certain, new information—even relatively precise information—does not lead to greatly updated perceptions and does not result in relatively large changes in candidate evaluations.

The Bayesian model discussed in this section has revealed some very interesting implications for the way new information about a candidate's policy position might influence a voter's perception or misperception of the candidate's position, and his or her evaluation of the candidate. The following two hypotheses follow from the discussion in this section:

> **Hypothesis 4:** Voters should update their perceptions of candidate issue stands when they obtain new information about those stands; thus the perceptions of voters should respond when information about these stands becomes available during the campaign, all other things held constant.
> **Hypothesis 5:** New information will lead voters to change their evaluations of the candidate, especially when the prior information was very imprecise, all other things held constant.

Conclusions

In this chapter, I have developed a theoretical perspective that incorporates imperfect information into individual-level models of voter preferences and perceptions. This perspective shows that voter uncertainty about candidate policy stands has important implications for voter decision making. Voter uncertainty about a candidate's position influences directly the likelihood of candidate support; uncertainty also affects the extent to which, and the way in which, issues should matter in presidential elections. So the extent to which policy issues matter is expected to be contingent on the uncertainty which voters possess about the candidates.

Additionally, when presented with new information about the positions of the candidates on policy issues, voters should assimilate that information into their perceptions of the candidates' stands. This learning should occur on two levels: voters are expected to update, or change, their estimate of the candidate's position (the mean), as well as their uncertainty of the candidate's position (the precision). Therefore, when information is available, perceptual learning should occur in the electorate. Demonstrating this relationship, then, will show that campaigns do matter.

Yet the insights of the Bayesian learning model also extend to my criticism of the campaign literature in chapter 2. First, as I noted there, the effects of campaign learning should be most apparent in the perceptions or misperceptions of voters. Usually, in general elections at the presidential level, voters will have some, if not a great deal of prior knowledge of both candidates. In such a situation, the insights of the Bayesian model are that we expect to see new information have little effect on the expected value of the voters' perceptions, but perhaps a larger effect on the certainty of their perception; additionally we would rarely expect a substantial change in their preferences.

Therefore, to understand the effects that campaigns have on voters, it is necessary to look at voter perceptions—both the perception itself and the uncertainty of that perception—in addition to voter preferences. It may be very difficult for campaigns to change voter preferences; however, they may change perceptions and uncertainty and nonetheless have an impact on the electorate.

But different electoral contexts might produce different conclusions. For example, early in a presidential primary, when voter knowledge of the positions of the candidates is very uncertain, new information, even if it is also uncertain, can produce large changes in voters' perceptions of a candidate's position, their uncertainty of that position, *and even in their preferences*. This provides a theoretical account for the volatility witnessed early in the primary season in voter preferences and perceptions. Since they may have imprecise knowledge, learning new information in an uncertain situation can have dramatic consequences.

CHAPTER 4

Measuring Uncertainty

The problems of erroneous and unmeasured variables are becoming more apparent in the social sciences as researchers explore empirically new areas and subjects. Many of these new research areas concern theoretical variables where the measures are known to be faulty or where measures do not exist at all.

—Eric A. Hanushek and John E. Jackson, *Statistical Methods for Social Scientists*

To test the hypotheses discussed in chapter 3, accurate measures of perceptual uncertainty are necessary. Unfortunately, while uncertainty has been discussed in the theoretical literature on voting (Enelow and Hinich 1984; Page 1976, 1978; Shepsle 1972), it was, until very recently, absent from empirical models of voting behavior. The absence of measures of uncertainty, and their absence from empirical analyses of elections, is problematic if uncertainty is ubiquitous in the world of politics and public opinion. Also, the absence of measures of uncertainty has made it impossible to test models like those presented in the previous chapter.

There are two different approaches to measuring perceptual uncertainty in public attitudes. The first approach, the *aggregate* measurement of uncertainty, looks at aggregated variations in voter perceptions of candidate policy positions and therefore cannot directly measure individual-level uncertainty. This makes aggregate measures of uncertainty of limited utility for studying individual-level hypotheses about the effects of uncertainty on voter learning and decision making.

The other general measurement approach, though, looks for *individual-level* measures of uncertainty and is better suited for this research. However, the individual-level measures come in two classes: *inferential* and *di-*

rect. The inferential measures, while more suitable for testing the hypotheses developed in chapter 3, have unique flaws which plague their use in empirical research—their reliance on the vagaries of the estimation procedures used to infer individual-level uncertainty. This leaves only the direct measurement strategy, which I argue is the best way to develop measures of uncertainty for empirical research.

Yet direct measurement of perceptual uncertainty is difficult, and I devote much of this chapter to discussion of this measurement strategy. The first direct measurement strategy, the *direct survey question,* is probably the preferred approach. However, use of this approach requires the development of new survey questions about perceptual uncertainty and their inclusion in surveys of the American electorate. Below I discuss two different ways of measuring uncertainty via direct survey questions and present their relative merits. But, while direct survey questions are a good measurement strategy, questions probing uncertainty have only recently been included in some academic surveys.

The second measurement strategy forms the basis of the empirical work in this book. This approach, *direct operationalization* of uncertainty, is based on measuring the variation in voter perception of candidate issue positions, relative to the positions of the candidates on the issues. While perhaps not as accurate as asking respondents directly about the certainty of their perceptions, operational measures can be developed from existing survey data. Thus, survey data which has already been collected can be used to test the hypotheses of chapter 3.

In this chapter I argue that while direct survey questions should be used to study perceptual uncertainty in public attitudes, in the absence of direct questions, direct operationalization of uncertainty is the best measurement strategy. In the sections that follow I first discuss in detail the aggregate and the individual-inferential measures, arguing that they have serious defects. Then I turn to direct measures of uncertainty, both direct survey and operational measures, and provide empirical support for the validity of both measurement approaches. Thereafter, using data from the 1993 NES Pilot Study, I compare the different measures of uncertainty and demonstrate the power of direct relative to inferential measurement of uncertainty.

Inferential Measures of Uncertainty

All of the individual measures of candidate policy position uncertainty which have been proposed in the literature are derived from the spatial notion of uncertainty given in chapter 3. Recall that I assumed the perceptual uncertainty that voters have about candidate issue positions to be a random variable, with a central tendency p_{ij} and an error in perception v_{ij}. To reiterate, the interpretation is that under conditions of uncertainty, voters perceive candidate policy stands as being composed of a central tendency (e.g., an expected value of a distribution) and a variance about that central tendency.

The first attempt to measure this conception of uncertainty was developed by Campbell (1983). He developed an *aggregate* way to infer voter uncertainty. He said that "the principal variable in this analysis—the ambiguity of the candidate's issue positions—is estimated as the standard deviation of the public's perception of the candidate's position" (Campbell 1983, 285). But this is not an ideal measure of uncertainty because it seeks to infer *individual-level voter uncertainty* about the candidate's position from observations of the *fluctuations across voters* in their placements of the candidates on each issue. This approach could yield misleading results for at least two additional reasons. First, there is likely to be variation across voters due to projection, partisan biases, and measurement error. All of these systematic differences *across* voters in their candidate placements would inappropriately be labeled "uncertainty" by Campbell's approach. Second, at the extreme, all voters may be absolutely certain about a candidate's positions, yet they may differ among themselves over what position they are certain the candidate has taken. Even in less extreme cases, variance in responses across voters may have no relationship to the level of certainty held by an individual respondent.

Others, recognizing the problems with aggregate measurement of uncertainty, have attempted to estimate *individual-level* measures from voter and candidate attributes. One early measure was developed by the polling firm of Yankelovich, Skelly, and White, who used a multiple indicator approach to develop what they called the mushiness index. They combined measures of the respondent's position on an issue, the salience of that issue, and how much the respondent knew about it and talked with others about it, and how likely the respondent believed he or she was to change their opinion on the issue (Asher 1992; Keene and Sackett 1981). The mushiness index they estimated from this list of survey items revealed interesting heterogeneity across voters and issues (Keene and Sackett 1981).

Other researchers have used even more complicated procedures to measure individual-level uncertainty, with more success. Bartels (1986) assumed that an uncertainty threshold exists which is constant across voters, candidates, and issues. Respondents will place a candidate on an issue only if their certainty of the candidate's position exceeds this threshold; otherwise they refuse to place the candidate. His model is one of survey item nonresponse, since while we do not have data on the phenomenon of interest (in this case, direct observations of v_{ij}), we do observe whether the respondent answered a specific survey question, which is a dichotomous variable. The response dichotomy is the dependent variable, and with a set of right-hand side variables concerning the characteristics of the respondent, Bartels estimates the probability that a respondent provides an answer to an issue question. The parameters from this model are then used to estimate a measure of voter uncertainty, which corresponds under the assumptions of the model to v_{ij}, up to an unknown scaling factor.

This is a clever approach, since the frequency of item nonresponse in the National Election Studies candidate issue placement questions is often quite great. The novelty of this model is that the people who do not respond to the candidate placement questions are those we might expect to be the most uncertain about the policy placements of the candidates—and these individuals typically are excluded from empirical studies of voting behavior.

While clever, this approach is problematic. First, item nonresponse may indicate the voter is uncertain about the candidate's policy position; but it may also show that the person did not answer the question, the question was unclear, the respondent is ambivalent, or that they made a mistake by not answering the question.[1] Thus, sole reliance on "don't knows" may not correctly assess the uncertainty voters have about the positions of candidates. Second, this approach does not directly, or accurately, measure voter uncertainty about candidate placements. Instead, the indicator for voter uncertainty is a predicted value from the linear probability model Bartels employed to estimate item nonresponse. But as is apparent in table 1 of Bartels's article (and which has been demonstrated by others attempting to analyze the systematic variation in survey item nonresponse, e.g., Francis and Busch [1975] and Feick [1989]), the linear probability model, even after a weighing procedure to increase the efficiency of the estimates, does not accurately account for the variation in item nonresponse.[2] This suggests that the predicted probabilities are not accurate

---

1. "Don't Knows" have been shown to be due to survey item ambiguity (where the respondent simply did not understand the question, as discussed in Coombs and Coombs 1976 and Converse 1976), response errors by individuals (Rapoport 1982, 1985), nonattitudes (Bogart 1967; Bishop, Oldendick, Tuchfarber, and Bennett 1980; Bishop, Tuchfarber, and Oldendick 1986; Schuman and Presser 1981), as well as item or topic uncertainty or equivocation (Coombs and Coombs 1976 and Faulkenberry and Mason 1978). So relying on these particular survey responses to measure uncertainty introduces measurement error. This measurement error is particularly problematic when it is correlated with variables on the right-hand side of the response model, which produces inconsistent estimates of the parameters of the model, and hence, incorrect estimates of respondent uncertainty. Given that the survey response literature has found strong correlations between nonrespondents and variables like respondent education, an approach which relies solely on nonrespondents is not sufficient.

2. By the R^2 statistics presented for the two models estimated, approximately three-quarters of the variance in question nonresponse remains unaccounted for by the model. Of course summary statistics are not good indicators of measurement, because the lack of fit could be explained as the result of poor measures of the right-hand side variables in the model. Yet I will show in later chapters that it is possible to achieve better model fit with an alternative measurement strategy, em-

indicators of uncertainty and that this inferential approach is flawed.

The third approach used to measure uncertainty was developed by Franklin (1991). He used a two-equation model, applying his procedure to Senate election data. The first equation regresses the incumbent's perceived ideological position on the incumbent's office performance (roll call voting record), the respondent's ideological placement of the incumbent's party, and the respondent's own ideological placement. He uses the resulting error term (squared) from this equation as the indicator of voter uncertainty.[3] He then models uncertainty (the squared residual from this regression) as a function of campaign effects and voter education.

This approach is interesting in a number of ways. First, by studying Senate elections, Franklin readily obtains measures of campaign effects, which he incorporates in the uncertainty model. This by itself is an important contribution, since Franklin takes advantage of the variation in campaign effects across Senate campaigns in a particular election year, which provides more variation in campaign-related variables than is typically possible when studying presidential elections. Second, Franklin's model does provide an estimate for voter uncertainty about candidate ideological positions. This estimate of uncertainty is intuitively plausible, since it is an analogue of v_{iJ}, except that he employs a number of indicators which account for variation in the voters' perceptions of the senator's ideological position.

However, this approach is also inadequate, since it will not estimate consistently the uncertainty voters have about candidate ideological or policy positions. Note that all of the influences on the voter's perceived ideological placement of the incumbent not explicitly included on the right-hand side of the first equation of the model (the ideological placement equation) are relegated to the error term of this equation. Thus, this error term can have three components: the respondent's perceptual uncertainty in their placement of the candidate (δ_{iJ}), other systematic effects not included in the model (ζ_{iJ}), and a random component (ε_{iJ}).[4] Call the stochastic term in the first equation μ_{iJ}, and define it as a function of these three components:

$$\mu_{iJ} = \mathcal{F}(\delta_{iJ}, \zeta_{iJ}, \varepsilon_{iJ}) \tag{4.1}$$

ploying identical right-hand side variables. This provides prima facie evidence for the inaccuracy of the Bartels approach.

3. Here I discuss Franklin's two-stage regression-based method for estimating his model. It is somewhat more intuitive to understand. The maximum-likelihood model differs in that it allows for simultaneous estimation of the two equations, under the assumption that the errors have bivariate normal distributions.

4. Here i indexes voters, and J represents a candidate, as in chapter 3.

For this approach to estimate δ_{iJ} accurately, the first equation must be correctly specified so that ζ_{iJ} and ε_{iJ} are of trivial magnitude and are uncorrelated with any of the independent variables in the model.

Are these assumptions appropriate? I argue that they are not appropriate and that the failure of these assumptions yields an inaccurate estimate of voter uncertainty about candidate placements. Most problematic, we cannot consider ζ_{iJ} to be nonexistent nor uncorrelated with independent variables included in the model. There are a number of other effects which have not been accounted for in the ideological placement equation which voters would rely upon to infer the ideological or policy placements of candidates: the policy stands and statements of the candidates, more explicit personal or professional criteria, the position of the other candidate in the race, and the issues and information revealed in the process of campaigning by the candidate. Since none of these other influences on ideological placements are included in the model, they are relegated to this stochastic term, and their presence makes this an inconsistent estimate of uncertainty. Also troubling, but less problematic, is the presence of ε_{iJ} in this measure of uncertainty. It is likely that there is some random variation across respondents in their ideological placements of the candidates—due to inattentiveness, distractions, interview effects, misunderstandings of the question, and perceptual differences in understandings of the seven-point scales. These sources of random variation across respondents further reduce the accuracy of this estimate of uncertainty.

Direct Uncertainty Measures

Few survey instruments directly incorporate indicators of voter uncertainty. Why haven't survey-based measures of voter uncertainty been developed and employed earlier? Only recently has imperfect information been incorporated into the theoretical and empirical literature on voter decision making. So the empirical relevance of including imperfect information in models of campaigns and voter behavior has not been understood. On a practical level, it is very difficult and costly to experiment with new survey questions. Instead of focusing on survey question development, it is far easier for most to concentrate on using the existing questions in widely available academic surveys.

But there are at least two ways in which we could assess respondent uncertainty directly from the survey instrument. First, existing question formats could be redesigned to directly probe respondent uncertainty during the interview. Second, using the survey data at hand, we can find ways of obtaining direct measures of uncertainty which closely follow the theoretical definition of perceptual uncertainty provided in chapter 3.

Survey Questions about Uncertainty

Most major academic surveys tend to follow the NES format when asking respondents to place themselves or the candidate on the various policy issue scales, in which the respondents are encouraged to choose a number from one to seven to represent their (and the candidate's) position on each policy issue. These existing seven-point scale questions could be altered in two minor ways to obtain measures of uncertainty during the survey interview. Thinking back to how perceptual uncertainty was defined in chapter 3, recall that uncertainty can be thought of as the spread or range of possible positions taken by a candidate on a particular issue. Typically, in most surveys using issue scales, respondents are asked to pick only one point along the scale to represent where they believe the candidate stands on that issue. Interviewers are usually instructed to persuade respondents to give only single-point responses to the issue scale questions, if the respondent provides some range of points as an initial reply. And if the respondent refuses to give a single-point response even after attempts to dissuade them, the coding instructions tell interviewers to record only the midpoint of the range responses.

Clearly one direct measurement approach could involve asking respondents to give a range of points as possible positions, and that range would then indicate their uncertainty of the candidate's positions. This approach toward the direct measurement of uncertainty has been examined in two academic surveys, the 1980 NES Pilot Study (analyzed in Aldrich et al. 1982 and Alvarez 1992) and in a survey I conducted with Franklin in 1991 (Alvarez and Franklin 1994). A second direct measurement approach could simply ask respondents about their uncertainty of a particular placement. This approach has figured in my recent work as well (Alvarez and Franklin 1994) and has been studied in a series of recent national surveys from 1991 to 1994. Both of these approaches to direct measurement deserve close scrutiny.

Range Responses as Direct Survey Questions

In the 1980 NES Pilot Study two issue placement questions—regarding relations with Russia and government efforts to help minority groups—were designed to allow respondents to provide range responses for their own positions and for the positions of Carter, Reagan, Ford, Kennedy, and current government policy. The National Election Studies abandoned these experimental issue question formats, mainly because preliminary analysis of these two questions found little worth reporting (Aldrich et al. 1982).

The range questions were posed to each of the 280 Pilot Study respondents on the first wave of the panel study. These questions were positioned next to each other in the survey, included in a long series of issue questions. For each issue question, the respondent was shown a card with the seven-point scale and asked to place themselves, and other political stimuli, at some point or range of points. Either type of response was coded.

The two questions were dissimilar in one regard, however. The Russian relations question had a lengthy introduction in which the interviewer noted that an individual who "is sure" about his or her placement would give a point response, while an individual who "isn't exactly sure" would give some range of points. The minority aid question, which immediately followed, did not include the extensive example, but it did probe for a possible range of points along the scale.[5]

In our 1991 survey, we followed a different procedure. Of the 979 respondents to our telephone interviews, 424 (53.2 percent of the sample) were randomly assigned to receive range questions (Form A respondents), with the remaining half of the sample serving as a control group (Form B respondents), receiving nonrange issue questions of the type normally seen in the National Election Studies. These issue questions asked about the respondent's own position and the positions of their sitting senators on abortion, tax increases, and ideology and were worded and posed to the respondents as they were in the 1980 NES Pilot Study. For example, the tax increase question was posed to our Form A respondents:

Here is an example of a scale on which three persons have placed themselves. Person 1 is sure he is at point 3. Person 2 feels he is between

---

5. Here is how the questions were worded:

Relations with Russia
Here is an example of a scale on which three persons have placed themselves. Person 1 is sure he is at point 3. Person 2 feels he is between 5 and 6. Person 3 knows he is somewhere between points 2 and 4, but isn't sure exactly where. On the next couple of questions you might wish to place yourself and others at one point, as did Person 1, or at a range of points, as did Person 2 and 3. Here's the first of these questions. Some people feel that it is important for us to try to maintain relations with Russia. Others feel that it is a mistake to try too hard to get along with Russia. At which point or points would you place yourself on this scale, or haven't you thought much about this?

Minority Aid
Some people feel that the government in Washington should make every possible effort to improve the social and economic position of blacks and other minority groups. Others feel that the government should not make any special effort to help minorities because they should help themselves. At which point or points would you place yourself on this scale, or haven't you thought much about this?

5 and 6. Person 3 knows he is somewhere between points 2 and 4, but isn't sure where. On the next few questions you might wish to place yourself and others on one point, as did Person 1, or at a range of points, as did Person 2 and 3.

Some people feel that the federal government should not raise taxes under any circumstances. Others feel that a tax increase is required to reduce the deficit and to pay for needed programs. At which point or points would you place yourself on a scale from one to seven, where 1 means you feel taxes should not be raised under any circumstances and 7 means you feel that a tax increase is required to reduce the deficit and pay for needed programs?

The Form B respondents were presented with the usual question format:

Some people feel that the federal government should not raise taxes under any circumstances. Others feel that a tax increase is required to reduce the deficit and pay for needed programs. Where would you place yourself on a scale from one to seven, where 1 means you feel taxes should not be raised under any circumstances and 7 means you feel that a tax increase is required to reduce the deficit and pay for needed programs?

The first question is what proportion of study respondents used the range formats in the two studies. In table 4.1 I give the percentages and sample frequencies for three types of responses to the seven–point scale questions in both surveys—range responses, scale point responses, and nonresponses to these questions from the two studies.

First, note that a sizable percentage of respondents provide range responses when probed in some cases—between 20 and 25 percent on relations with Russia. The fact that this many respondents indicated their uncertainty through the range response provides prima facie evidence that there are significant proportions of survey respondents for whom a point estimate of a candidate's position on these issues may not reflect their perceptions. Somewhat lower percentages of respondents provide range responses on the minority aid questions in the 1980 Pilot Study data, but still, between 9 and 18 percent of respondents in that study give range responses.

However, it is interesting to compare the distributions of range responses and nonrespondents across the four political figures in the 1980 data. It is apparent that the proportion of nonrespondents varies across the political figures in a predictable manner: the number of item nonrespondents is lowest for the incumbent president, somewhat higher for a salient national politician (Kennedy) and a past incumbent president (Ford), and the highest for the least salient political figure among this group in 1979—Ronald Reagan. But this pattern is reversed for the relative distributions of range responses, with Carter having consistently the highest proportion of range responses, and with Reagan having at least the same proportion of range responses as the other political figures (and even the fewest on minority group aid).

This might be considered counterintuitive. I expected that the relative proportions of nonrespondents and range responses would have some correlation for each political figure, since the proportions of each should be related to the salience of the figures or the amount of information we might expect the electorate to possess about these politicians. Yet, there is a systematic pattern in these percentages. Of these four political figures, Carter should be the best known and Reagan the least known in 1979. When the percentages of nonre-

TABLE 4.1.   Range Responses in the 1980 and 1991 Studies

	Range	Scale Point	Nonresponse
1980 ANES			
Russian relations			
Self	24.6(69)	69.3(194)	6.1(17)
Carter	23.2(65)	64.6(181)	12.1(34)
Reagan	19.3(54)	46.1(129)	34.6(97)
Ford	19.6(55)	60.0(168)	20.4(57)
Kennedy	18.9(53)	52.5(147)	28.6(80)
Minority groups			
Self	18.2(51)	75.0(210)	6.8(19)
Carter	15.7(44)	70.0(196)	14.3(40)
Reagan	8.9(25)	57.5(161)	33.6(94)
Ford	12.9(36)	63.2(177)	23.9(67)
Kennedy	13.2(37)	62.9(37)	23.9(67)
1991 Alvarez-Franklin			
Tax increase			
Self	6.4(27)	87.1(365)	6.4(27)
Senators	6.7(28)	48.7(204)	44.6(187)
Abortion			
Self	5.3(22)	91.4(383)	3.3(14)
Senators	3.1(13)	35.6(149)	53.5(257)
Ideology			
Self	8.4(35)	87.4(366)	4.3(18)
Senators	6.2(26)	55.5(233)	38.2(160)

Note: Entries are percentages of respondents, followed by sample frequencies.
Total sample size (all respondents) is 280 for 1980 and 419 for 1991.

Respondent nonresponse includes those who could not place themselves on the scale.
Candidate nonresponse includes both individuals who could not place themselves and those who could not place the candidate.

spondents and range respondents for these two political figures are compared, what is apparent is that most respondents knew enough about Carter to place him on these two scales, but that *many felt sufficiently uncertain about his position to avoid pinning him to a specific point* and hence replied that his position was a range of points. For Reagan, however, the pattern is reversed: roughly a third of respondents had so little information about Reagan that they could not place him on the scale, while far fewer had enough information to state that he had a position across some range of points. Therefore, there does seem to be a very interesting, and explicable, pattern in the relative percentages of nonrespondents and range responses in table 4.1.

Last, note that there is a 6 to 11 percent difference in the percentages of range responses given for each candidate on the two issues in the 1980 data and that the percentages of range responses are always greater on the relations with Russia question. This could be accounted for by a difference in the actual amount of information these respondents had about the political figures on these two issues—they may have been more certain about the positions of these political figures on the minority groups question. For example, many have argued that respondents are often less informed about foreign affairs than domestic affairs (Almond 1960; but see Aldrich et al. 1989; Alvarez and Gronke 1995; Holsti 1992; Hurwitz and Peffley 1987; Page and Shapiro 1992). Additionally, minority treatment by the federal government might have been a more salient issue in early 1979 than Russian relations, which may have dramatically changed by the fall of 1979, after the Soviet invasion of Afghanistan. Unfortunately, the pattern of nonrespondents across the two issues provides little insight into this puzzle.

This difference in the percentage of range responses across the two questions in 1980 could also be accounted for by considering the placement and question-wording of the two issue placement questions. Recall that the Russian relations question was positioned before the minority groups question, and that the former had a rather lengthy example designed to prompt uncertain respondents to give range replies. The minority groups question did not contain the lengthy example and prompt, suggesting two possible survey response phenomena. First, the lengthy example and prompt in the Russian relations question might have marginally inflated the proportion of range responses—it may have encouraged respondents to believe that a range response was expected by the interviewer. Second, the lack of a similar example or prompt in the wording of the minority groups question may have removed a necessary stimulus for a number of respondents, and without this stimulus they reverted to point or "don't know" responses.

But notice the dramatic differences between the 1980 Pilot Study and the 1991 Alvarez-Franklin study. Uniformly, across three issues and two different political objects (selves and senators), few respondents availed themselves of the range response option in the 1991 study. As few as 3 percent (senators on abortion) and only as many as 8 percent (self placement on ideology) of the respondents in this study provided range responses.

And the evidence is quite mixed as to whether the range response seems to vary in an understandable pattern across the issues and objects being placed in the Alvarez-Franklin study. For one, I would expect to find that senators are less visible than prominent national politicians and that their issue positions would be less well known. This is reflected in the percentages of nonrespondents in the Alvarez-Franklin data, where from 40 percent (ideology) to 54 percent (abortion) of the respondents could place neither themselves nor the senators from their state on the respective scales. These rates of nonresponses are significantly greater than those seen in the 1980 Pilot Study data. What happens is that the range responses for the senators do not seem to pick up the reduced visibility expected for the senators, but instead more people simply do not answer the placement questions for the senators. Thus, the range responses do not seem to elicit the additional uncertainty expected for less visible political figures, since more respondents opt for the "don't know" option.[6]

This large difference in the use of the range option by respondents could also be an artifact of the survey instrument. The 1980 NES Pilot Study used face-to-face interviews; the respondents were physically shown a card with a seven-point issue scale on it and asked to provide a scale point or a range response for the particular issue–object pairing. However, the 1991 Alvarez-Franklin study used telephone interviews, and the questions were read to respondents over the phone. It is possible that the lack of the visual aid in the latter study makes the range response a difficult option for respondents to understand (Groves and Kahn 1979). While this is a strong explanation for the differences in use of the range responses across these two studies, the results for the 1991 Alvarez-Franklin study still undermine the utility of range responses as direct measures of uncertainty, if the format can only be used in expensive face-to-face survey interviews.

Therefore, simply on the basis of the responses presented in table 4.1, it is hard to make a strong case for range response measures as strong candidates for direct-survey measures of uncertainty. First, there are few respondents who are willing to provide range responses, even in a face-to-face interview.

---

6. Or, these results on the frequency of use of the range responses in the 1991 data could be interpreted as showing that senators are distinct from prominent national political figures since the former are significantly less visible. Thus respondents either do or do not know the positions of these less-visible political figures. Below I present evidence which indicates that this is an incorrect interpretation of the frequency of range response usage in the 1991 data; additional evidence is in Alvarez and Franklin 1994.

And these range responses do not provide much information about the actual uncertainty individuals may have about the position of a political figure on an issue. Only between 25 to 65 respondents gave range responses on any particular candidate placement in the 1980 Pilot Study, and the overwhelming majority of these were only one-point differences. On the Russian relations question, for example, 77 percent, 81 percent, 82 percent, and 81 percent of the range responses for Carter, Reagan, Ford, and Kennedy, respectively, were one-point differences. Virtually all of the remaining responses were two-point differences. This evidence indicates either that range response questions do not produce good measures of uncertainty or that uncertainty is not an important aspect of public attitudes.

The Direct Uncertainty Questions

The second way of directly probing for respondent uncertainty about issue placements is to ask respondents, after giving an issue placement, about their certainty of that placement. This is the approach I have used in joint work with Charles Franklin (1994). Here, after each seven-point placement of their own position, respondents were asked: "Are you very certain of where you stand on this, pretty certain, or not very certain?" Then, they were asked about the placement of a political figure on the same issue; afterward they were asked a similar question: "How certain are you of (figure's name) position on this? Very certain, pretty certain, or not very certain?" We included these questions in our 1991 survey and in another survey we did in 1992. Additionally, they were carried on the 1993 NES Pilot Study and the 1994 Election Study conducted by the NES. These questions were asked about a variety of political issues and figures across these studies, with abortion, tax increases, and general ideology as issues, and senators, House incumbents, Clinton, and Perot as political figures.

We analyzed extensively these uncertainty questions from the 1991 survey and found "that they appear to be valid measures of uncertainty, since they yield explicable response patterns and are related systematically to individual information costs and objective aspects of perceptual objects" (Alvarez and Franklin 1994, 686). Unlike the range responses from the same study, these uncertainty questions revealed substantial uncertainty in the issue perceptions of the American public.

For example, consider the response marginals from the 1993 NES Pilot Study given in table 4.2. Here a series of regularities can be seen. First, concentrating on those respondents who answered both the placement and the uncertainty questions, 7 percent said they were uncertain of their own ideological position while most said they were certain (36 percent) or somewhat certain

(30 percent). So most respondents are relatively certain of their ideological positions.

But contrast that to the other political figures included in the survey. Of those who were uncertain of their placements for these political figures, 22 percent were uncertain about Clinton's ideological position, 27 percent of Perot's, and 31 percent of their House incumbent's position. And notice the dramatically lower percentages who are certain of their ideological placements of the political figures: 19 percent were certain of Clinton's position, 11 percent of Perot's, and 8 percent of their House incumbent's position.

So respondents are more certain of their own placement than they are of political figures like Clinton, Perot, or House incumbents. This result has important implications for the analysis of public opinion. First, these percentages show that uncertainty is an important component of the political world. Respondents are quite willing to reveal the fundamental uncertainty in their perceptions, even in their attitudes about prominent political figures. That 22 percent of the respondents in the 1993 NES Pilot Study felt they were "not certain" about the ideological position they had just given for the *current* president and 41 percent said they were "somewhat certain" provides strong evidence of the empirical relevance of uncertainty in American politics. If 63 percent of the respondents in a national sample one year into a presidential term, after almost two full years of exposure to Clinton and his policy beliefs, are not certain of his ideological position, uncertainty must be considered an important aspect of American politics.

Second, respondents are not absolutely inhibited by a lack of attitudes about issues or by inherent cognitive limitations when thinking about political

TABLE 4.2.   Uncertainty Responses, 1993 Pilot Study

Response	Self	Clinton	Perot	House
Certain	35.6	18.7	11.3	8.2
	266	140	112	82
Somewhat certain	29.9	41.2	30.7	23.1
	223	308	305	230
Not certain	6.8	22.3	26.8	30.9
	51	167	266	308
Don't know	27.7	17.8	31.3	37.8
	207	133	311	377

Note: Data from the 1993 NES Pilot Study.
Entries are percentages followed by sample frequencies.
The don't know percentages include respondents who were unable to place themselves or the candidate on the seven-point scale.

issues. If respondents were so inhibited in their opinions, we should see little difference in levels of uncertainty about their own positions on issues and in the positions of candidates on issues. That we do observe large differences in reported uncertainty when moving from the respondent to the various political figures does strongly suggest that when armed with information about an issue a respondent can report with confidence an opinion about a political issue. But when faced with ambiguous candidates and imperfect information about the positions of these candidates on the same issues, confidence in their perceptions drops considerably.

Last, uncertainty varies across the political figures in direct proportion to their visibility one year after the 1992 elections: Clinton's position is known with the most certainty, Perot's with less, and the House incumbents with the least certainty. This serves as one confirmation of the validity of these survey questions. Additionally, this points toward the substantive conclusion that voter uncertainty is a potent strategic variable for candidates, as has been argued in the theoretical literature (e.g., Shepsle 1972). That the level of reported uncertainty varies across the political figures, and that it varies simply by their political visibility, implies that uncertainty is an important and understandable component of the political world.

A more rigorous way of validating these survey questions comes by showing that they are correlated in expected ways with carefully chosen explanatory variables (Cook and Campbell 1979). In the 1993 Pilot Study data, I culled explanatory variables for demographic attributes of each respondent, their levels of political information, attention to political affairs in the media, and ideological extremity. In general, the expectations for the relationship of these variables with the uncertainty questions follows the logic laid out by Downs (1957), where individuals with lower information costs should be better informed about their political perceptions. Those respondents with higher levels of political information, education, and media attention should express lesser uncertainty about their perceptions. Ideological extremists, those who express strong ideological perceptions, may feel more certain of their beliefs. Last, information costs may be higher among certain demographic groups (minorities, women, and the elderly), given their often more peripheral social and political positions.

Table 4.3 shows ordered probit estimates from models relating this set of explanatory variables with the responses to each uncertainty equation. Ordered probit was used in this case since the responses to these survey questions are discrete and ordered categories, ranging from very certain (1) to not certain (3) (McKelvey and Zavoina 1975). These models do not include respondents who did not respond to a particular uncertainty question, and the substantive results presented in Table 4.3 do not depend upon the inclusion of these nonrespon-

TABLE 4.3. **Ordered Probit Models of Uncertainty Responses, 1993 Pilot Study**

Independent Variables	Self Uncertainty	Clinton Uncertainty	Perot Uncertainty	House Uncertainty
Constant	1.3**	1.9**	1.4**	2.3**
	.28	.25	.22	.25
Education	−.09**	−.04	−.02	.007
	.04	.03	.03	.03
Media attention	−.22	.02	−.11	−.17
	.21	.18	.17	.18
Political information	−.76**	−1.2**	−.75**	−.43*
	.30	.27	.25	.27
Age	.001	.00	.003	−.01**
	.004	.003	.003	.003
Minorities	.18	−.23*	−.02	−.45**
	.20	.17	.16	.16
Gender	.29**	.24**	.11	.14*
	.11	.10	.10	.10
Ideological extremity	−.38**	−.41**	−.10**	−.24**
	.06	.05	.05	.05
σ_1	1.4**	1.6**	1.3**	1.2**
	.09	.08	.07	.07
% Correct	57.2	56.9	51.5	50.0
Model χ^2	163.6#	243.9#	164.6#	145.9#
Sample n	488	446	461	429

Note: Entries are maximum-likelihood probit estimates, with their standard errors below.
* indicates statistically significant estimates at the $p = .10$ level, one-tailed tests.
** indicates statistically significant estimates at the $p = .05$ level, one-tailed tests.
# indicates a statistically significant model χ^2, with 7 degrees of freedom.

dents.[7] Last, operationalizations of all variables are in appendix A.

First, note that these four ordered probit models all fit the data reasonably well. Each correctly classifies at least 50 percent of the cases, and all have model χ^2 statistics well above the $p = .05$ threshold of significance. Second, most estimates have the anticipated signs, and many reach standard levels of statistical significance. In particular, political information (those who are more informed have a higher probability of a more "certain" response) and ideolog-

---

7. Identical ordered probit models with the "don't knows" included do not produce substantively different results, and neither did they in the earlier analysis of this question format for the 1991 data (Alvarez and Franklin 1994). There we did both ordered probits and tobit models, thus operationalizing the nonrespondents as a substantive phenomenon and as a missing data problem; neither approach yielded substantively different results.

ical extremity (extremists are more certain) are both consistently significant predictors of the individual's response to these questions. In general, women are more likely to reveal uncertainty about their ideological placements, while minorities are less certain of the placements of all three political figures (significantly so for Clinton and House incumbents). These results provide confirmation that the uncertainty questions seem to tap into the factors which should be related to respondent uncertainty. They are also in line with the results we obtained for similar models using the 1991 survey data (Alvarez and Franklin 1994).

Thus the direct uncertainty question seems to provide a valid measure of respondent uncertainty (Alvarez and Franklin 1994). Unfortunately, it has two major drawbacks for testing the hypotheses laid out in the previous chapter. First, in terms of using existing data from recent presidential elections, these uncertainty questions have not yet been carried on a national survey during a presidential campaign. This is certainly a serious limitation. Second, in terms of future surveys, the problem with the uncertainty questions is that they add to the length of survey questionnaires. In a time when response rates to surveys are plummeting (Brehm 1993), it may be difficult to add a new battery of questions to major academic surveys like the NES without sacrificing other important survey questions. For example, a full battery of issue and ideology uncertainty questions in a typical presidential election survey could add at least twenty-one new questions, by probing for uncertainty following placements on one ideology and six issue questions for the respondent and for two presidential candidates. This makes it important to search for other ways of measuring voter uncertainty which do not rely on survey questions unavailable in previous academic survey data nor on indirect estimation strategies.

Direct Operationalization of Uncertainty

So how can voter uncertainty about candidate policy positions be measured? If direct indicators are not available in the existing academic survey data, and if the use of inferential approaches is inadequate, where can reliable indicators be obtained? Recall that in the previous chapter, this uncertainty was defined as v_{iJ}, which theoretically is a dispersion of points around some placement of the candidate's position. It is possible to obtain measures of such a dispersion around points, under a few assumptions.

In statistical theory, the "spread" of points around a central tendency is commonly defined for a mean as $\sigma^2 = \frac{1}{n} \sum_{n=1}^{N} (x - \bar{x})^2$, where x denotes the n points in the sample, and $\bar{x}$ represents the mean value, or the central tendency, in x. With this representation in mind, consider:

$$v_{iJ} = \frac{1}{k} \sum_{k=1}^{K} (P_{iJk} - T_{Jk})^2 \tag{4.2}$$

where v_{iJ} represents the uncertainty of voter i in their placement of J, P_{iJk} gives the placement of J on each of the relevant k policy dimensions, and T_{Jk} indicates the position of candidate J on policy dimension k.

Less technically, this is a representation of the voter's uncertainty about the candidate's position across the policy space, in terms of the net dispersion of the voter's perception of the candidate's position and the candidate's true position. The greater the dispersion of their perceptions of the candidate's position from the candidate's true position, the more uncertain they are about the candidate's position on the policy issues; the tighter this dispersion of points, the less uncertain they are about the candidate's position.

This representation of voter uncertainty is appealing for three reasons. First, unlike the measures of uncertainty advanced in the literature, this representation directly operationalizes uncertainty from the survey data and does not infer an uncertainty measure from ancillary information about respondents. Second, this measure meshes closely with the theory of uncertainty discussed in chapter 3, which allows for rigorous tests of the hypothesis advanced there. Third, this measure can be applied to existing survey data, particularly the historical data from the National Election Studies, where there have been questions asking respondents to place candidates on policy scales.[8]

---

8. In chapter 3 (equation 3.3) I defined a voter's perceived position of a candidate's position on an issue as $P_{iJ} = p_J + v_{iJ}$, where p_J is the true position of the candidate on the issue and v_{iJ} is the variance of the voter's perception. There has been some work which argues that different survey respondents conceptualize the NES issue scales in different ways, and this introduces a perceptual error in their placement of the candidate which adds another possible term into the above relation: $P_{iJ} = p_J + v_{iJ} + d_{iJ}$, where d_{iJ} is the individual distortion introduced by this effect (Aldrich and McKelvey 1977; Brady 1989, 1990; Brady and Ansolabehere 1989; Brady and Sniderman 1985; Palfrey and Poole 1987). Aldrich and McKelvey (1977) examined data from 1968 and 1972, and used an econometric procedure (elaborated by Palfrey and Poole 1987) which used the placements of each individual respondent across a set of candidates and parties to estimate a model of how each respondent maps their perceptual issue space on the NES seven-point scales. In general they found that *between 7 percent and 30 percent of the error in perceptions might be due to this individual-level distortion.* So there is evidence that this d_{iJ} effect might exist for a minority of respondents—but what does it imply for this measure of uncertainty? If the d_{iJ} term is random over individuals, it will produce inefficiency; if it is systematic over individuals, it will produce bias. There is no empirical evidence in this literature which indicates that d_{iJ} varies systematically over survey respondents, and thus there is no reason to believe this measure is biased. Inefficiency could be a problem, though, since a small component of random error might be introduced into the measure; but this only makes it more difficult for my subsequent analyses to find substantial

As in the previous section, the 1993 Pilot Study data provides an opportunity for the validation of this approach to measuring voter ideological uncertainty. Here, I used this approach to estimate respondent uncertainty about their placement of Clinton, Perot, and their House incumbent. For Clinton and Perot, this operationalization was based on the squared deviation of the respondent's placement of each political figure on the ideology scale relative to the mean positions of each in the entire 1993 Pilot Study sample (3.15 for Clinton and 4.68 for Perot). Respondents who did not place the candidate on the particular scale were coded as maximally uncertain of the position of the candidate on the ideology scale. For the House incumbent, I estimated the "true" positions using the mean position for each House member using only respondents from their district. Unfortunately, this means that there are many districts for which these estimates are based on only a handful of cases. Again, respondents who did not place the incumbent on the scale were coded as maximally uncertain.[9]

To validate this measurement strategy, I regressed these three measures of ideological uncertainty on the same set of independent variables as in the previous section: political information, media attentiveness, ideological extremity, and demographic information. Again, the expectations are that those with higher information costs ought to be more uncertain of their placements of these political figures on the ideological dimension. The results of these regressions are given in table 4.4.

The regression results show that the Clinton uncertainty measure is relatively well predicted by this set of explanatory variables (adjusted-R^2 = .24). But the Perot and House uncertainty measures are not as well predicted by these variables, as seen by their substantially lower adjusted-R^2s. Across the three equations, though, the explanatory variables do tend to perform as expected. Both higher political information levels and greater educational attainment are related to lower levels of information (both results statistically significant for Clinton and House incumbents but only marginally significant for Perot). Also, ideologically extreme respondents have significantly lower levels of uncertainty about these three political figures than ideologically moderates. Last, minorities and the elderly both are significantly more uncertain about all three political figures.

---

and statistically significant effects. In later chapters I present strong empirical results in support of my theoretical expectations, which implies that this is a valid measure of uncertainty.

9. I also estimated the true position of each House incumbent by regressing the perceived position of the incumbent on the ACA score for the incumbent, which produced the equation: true incumbent position = 3.88+.01*ACA. The squared deviation of this "true" position from each respondent's perceived position gives another measure of ideological uncertainty. The correlation between the uncertainty measure this produced and the one described in the text is .87.

TABLE 4.4.   Estimates of Alvarez Uncertainty Measures

Independent Variables	Clinton Uncertainty	Perot Uncertainty	House Uncertainty
Constant	8.3**	3.7**	4.4**
	.86	.77	.87
Education	−.56**	−.14*	−.26**
	.13	.11	.13
Media attention	.20	−.46	−1.2**
	.67	.61	.68
Political information	−6.7**	−1.1	−1.5*
	1.0	.92	1.0
Age	.06**	.03**	.03**
	.01	.01	.01
Minorities	1.0**	1.0**	.77*
	.60	.55	.61
Gender	−.07	.43	−.04
	.38	.35	.39
Ideological extremity	−.87**	−.54**	−.28*
	.20	.18	.21
Adjusted R^2	.24	.05	.04
Sample n	677	668	651

Note: Entries are maximum-likelihood probit estimates, with their standard errors below.
* indicates statistically significant estimates at the $p = .10$ level, one-tailed tests.
** indicates statistically significant estimates at the $p = .05$ level, one-tailed tests.

These results compare favorably with those for the direct uncertainty questions presented in table 4.3 which shows that Clinton uncertainty was more predictable than Perot or House incumbent uncertainty (similar to the patterns of model fit seen in table 4.4). Also, the patterns of coefficient signs and statistically significant coefficients are similar between the different uncertainty measures. Consistently, political information, ideological extremity, education, and age have similar effects in the different models for each uncertainty measure. The only major difference is in the estimated effects of minority group membership on uncertainty; in the direct question results, minority group members were generally less uncertain about the ideological placements of Clinton, Perot, and their House incumbent, while in table 4.4 they are significantly *more* uncertain of these same placements. While the results in table 4.4 help to validate this approach to measuring uncertainty, they also indicate that the two different measures seem to tap similar components of perceptual uncertainty.

Comparing the Uncertainty Measures

However, comparing only my operationalization of uncertainty, as discussed in the last section, with the Alvarez-Franklin direct survey measure of uncertainty is not the sole purpose of this section. In addition, the 1993 Pilot Study gives me the opportunity to compare how these two measures of uncertainty perform relative to the two indirect measures of uncertainty—the Bartels and Franklin measures.

Accordingly, I estimated the Bartels measure of uncertainty for Clinton, Perot, and for House incumbents. The details of the probit models used to estimate the Bartels measure are in appendix A; here it is sufficient to say that I followed the operationalization of the model as discussed in Bartels (1986), with the major departure being that I used a probit model instead of the linear probability model used by Bartels.

The Franklin measure was more difficult to develop, since it is designed to estimate uncertainty for congressional incumbents, who have an established voting record. Franklin (1991) modeled an individual's perception of his or her Senate incumbent's position as a function of the incumbent's ACA rating, the respondent's perception of the party position, the respondent's own position, and the interaction between the respondent's position and thermometer rating of the incumbent. Here, I replicated that model for House incumbents using the 1993 Pilot Study data and obtained:

$$\text{Position} = 2.12 + .006 * \text{ACA} + .36 * \text{Party Position}$$
$$- .10 * \text{Respondent's Position} + .003 * \text{Interaction}$$

which had an adjusted-R^2 of .39, indicating a good fit to the 368 observations (each of the estimated coefficients are statistically significant at the $p = .05$ level, one-tailed tests). The squared residual from this regression provides the Franklin estimate of respondent uncertainty for the ideological position of their House incumbent.[10]

The easiest way to contrast the direct with the indirect measures of uncertainty is to examine their correlations. If they exhibit strong correlations, that is evidence that they are measuring similar perceptions. If, as I asserted

---

10. I regressed these squared residuals on the same explanatory variables used to validate the direct survey and direct operationalizations of uncertainty discussed in the previous two sections of this chapter. The adjusted-R^2 from that regression (343 observations) is .004. In that regression, political information was statistically significant and correctly signed, with the estimate for gender being negative and significant (implying that women have smaller error variance in their perceptions of House incumbent ideological positioning). Also, media attention was positive and significant.

TABLE 4.5.   Correlations of Uncertainty Measures

	Clinton Uncertainty (Survey)	Perot Uncertainty (Survey)	House Uncertainty (Survey)
Clinton (Alvarez)	.60	.27	.13
	748	738	740
Perot (Alvarez)	.24	.66	.55
	738	994	989
House (Alvarez)	.17	.13	.47
	715	709	717
Clinton (Bartels)	.53	.27	.18
	678	669	674
Perot (Bartels)	.35	.24	.12
	678	669	674
House (Bartels)	.28	.15	.22
	678	669	674
House (Franklin)	−.02	.003	−.07
	369	365	369

Note: Entries are Pearson correlation coefficients, followed by the number of observations for a particular correlation.

earlier, the indirect measures do not correlate highly with the direct measures, that should provide some evidence about the greater reliability of the direct measurement strategy.

And unsurprisingly, that is what the 1993 Pilot Study data confirm. In table 4.5 I give the bivariate Pearson correlation coefficients, first for the direct measures of uncertainty (where "Alvarez" denotes direct survey operationalization and "Survey" the Alvarez-Franklin measures) and then for the indirect measures with the direct survey measure. First, notice the high degree of correlation between the direct survey measures of uncertainty. For Clinton the uncertainty correlation is .60, for Perot it is .66, and for House incumbents it is .47. These indicate that across individuals, these two measures vary in a close manner.

However, the Bartels uncertainty measures are not nearly as highly correlated with the direct survey measures. The Clinton uncertainty correlation is .53, the Perot is .28, and the House incumbent is .21. Especially for Perot and House incumbents, these are substantially lower than the correlations between the direct measures. And at an even lower degree of correlation is the Franklin measure for the House incumbents. At −.07, this correlation is in the right direction (as the indicator of the residual variance increases so does an individual's stated uncertainty about a House incumbent's ideological position), but it is clearly close to zero.

This is compelling evidence for the validity of the direct approach for measuring uncertainty. That the direct measures are highly correlated and the indirect measures are relatively uncorrelated with direct survey measure indicates that both of the direct measures are measuring respondent uncertainty, even though they do so in very different manners.

Conclusion

To conclude this chapter, I have carried the fundamental argument of this book one step further. In the previous chapter, the theoretical importance of voter uncertainty about candidate policy positions was established, and hypotheses about the effects of this uncertainty were specified. Here, I have made one basic argument—given that the political environment is clearly one of rampant uncertainty and imperfect information, it is time that this uncertainty be taken into account in empirical models of elections. But taking this uncertainty into account and obtaining reliable estimates of the effect uncertainty has in elections are dependent in turn on valid empirical indicators of the concept.

Only a few attempts have been made in the literature to measure the uncertainty voters have about candidates for office. I discussed these approaches and noted that they are inferential in nature, since they attempt to *infer* the amount of uncertainty a voter might have from some demographic or attitudinal information available to the researcher. But inference can provide, at best, only a very crude approximation of the phenomenon at hand.

Thus, I have made the case for direct measurement of uncertainty. This can be done in two ways: by the use of direct questions to respondents about how certain their perceptions of candidate policy positions are, or by the operationalization of uncertainty indicators from existing survey data. Most of this chapter was devoted to an analysis of data from a recent academic survey which attempted to measure uncertainty directly with questions in the survey instrument—the 1993 NES Pilot Study. The results from this analysis have been provocative and should lead to further development of other such questions in academic surveys.

CHAPTER 5

Modeling Uncertainty and Voting

The science of politics, however, like most other sciences, has received great improvement. The efficacy of various principles is now well understood, which were either not known at all, or imperfectly known to the ancients.

—Alexander Hamilton, *Federalist 9*

Die Politik ist keine exakte Wissenschaft. (Politics is not an exact science.)

—Prince Otto von Bismark, December 18, 1863

To test the hypotheses advanced in chapter 3, using the operationalization of voter uncertainty discussed in chapter 4, requires rigorous statistical methodologies to overcome a number of hurdles. The first obvious hurdle is correctly specifying the statistical models, since controlling for the influences of other independent factors on voter perceptions and behavior will ensure that I estimate correctly the effects of voter uncertainty in presidential elections. The second hurdle is the accuracy of these estimates, and my ability to test the hypotheses statistically.

I begin by discussing the survey data which figures prominently in the remainder of this book. Then I turn to a discussion of the statistical models. First is the theoretical development of the model of uncertainty and candidate evaluation. I argue that there are good reasons to suspect that voter uncertainty regarding the candidates, and the preferences of voters for the candidates, are endogenous. Next I discuss the statistical models which can cope with this simultaneity. The models I use, limited-information models for mixtures of dichotomous and continuous endogenous variables, have only recently seen discussion in the political science literature. I discuss briefly the properties of these estimators in this chapter—interested readers can turn to appendix B for additional information.

The remainder of the chapter considers two additional statistical problems.

One of these problems concerns modeling the 1980 and 1992 elections, in which relatively strong independent candidates ran. Multicandidate elections present problems for the assumptions of the empirical models normally used to understand voter decision making. They call for the use of multiple choice models, and I discuss these models in this chapter as well.

The other problem concerns testing the interactive relationship between uncertainty and issue voting posited in chapter 3. The models I employ of voter preferences are nonlinear, and the parameters are dependent upon each other by assumption, which poses certain problems for the estimation of interactive relationships. Following the arguments of Nagler (1991), I discuss the approach I use in subsequent chapters to estimate the necessary interactive models.

Survey Data from the 1976–92 Presidential Elections

In the chapters which follow, I examine the five presidential elections from 1976 to 1992. These five elections were selected for both theoretical and practical reasons. On the theoretical front, employing data from before 1976 would be problematic since it is only then that the "rules of the game" following the many electoral reforms of the 1960s and 1970s were established. Two of the most important of these reforms occurred between 1968 and 1976: a dramatic change in the process of selecting the nominees of the major parties, and substantial alterations in the provision and documentation of campaign finance (Ceaser 1979; Polsby and Wildavsky 1988). Additionally, significant changes in the two-party system before 1976, coming under the broad heading of the "decline of parties," altered how candidates conducted their campaigns as well as how voters perceived candidates (Aldrich 1995; Wattenberg 1990). Thus, given that structural changes in the presidential election process preceded the 1976 election, including these elections in my analysis would confound any attempts to compare and contrast the empirical results across elections.

But even these five elections have significant, and theoretically interesting, differences. They vary, unfortunately, on too many dimensions for rigorous empirical analysis. One important source of variation involves incumbency, since there is one election without a sitting incumbent (1988), one election with a nonelected incumbent (1976), and three elections with sitting incumbents (1980, 1984, and 1992). Another distinction comes in the nature of the challengers, given that there was one election with a little-known governor as challenger (1976), two with former vice presidents, and two with better known governors (1988 and 1992). A third way in which these elections vary is the ideological or issue positioning of the candidates, with relatively extreme polarization occurring in 1984 and extreme moderation in 1976. Thus, by studying multiple presidential elections, I am able to probe how contextual differences across each election may have influenced voter uncertainty and voter decision making.

But practically, these five elections are the only ones with consistent and reliable measures which are required for this analysis. The measure of uncertainty discussed in the last section of the previous chapter relies on the availability of survey data in which respondents are asked to place the candidates on various policy dimensions. In the National Election Studies presidential election series, only the post-1976 elections possess the required data, especially the seven-point policy scales, which I use extensively. These scales were originally developed in the 1968 NES study and were examined extensively in the split-sample frame of the 1972 NES study.[1] But only thereafter have they been included in a consistent manner in the NES surveys.

However, in my analysis I rely heavily on the 1976 panel study collected by Thomas E. Patterson in addition to the NES samples. The data in this panel study provide an excellent arena for analysis of the impact of uncertainty on voter decision making. The data is a panel study of voters in Erie, Pennsylvania, and Los Angeles, California, designed primarily to analyze the effects of the mass media on voting attitudes and behavior, as the presidential campaign progressed. There are five major panels in this study, conducted in February, April, June, August, and October, with most respondents being reinterviewed following the election.

Below, when I examine the first two hypotheses from chapter 3, I employ data from the October wave of this 1976 panel. This makes the time period of data collection comparable to the NES studies. Additionally, this data set has a large number of policy issue placements (nine) that were asked for each candidate. The 1976 Patterson panel study also factors heavily in my examination of the hypotheses generated by the Bayesian learning model in chapter 3. Here I use the earlier waves of the panel study to analyze which voters learned about the candidates and how this learning occurred. Also, with the use of other data collected by Patterson, I can document the flow of information during the campaign. During the 1976 election Patterson conducted a content analysis of the news media coverage of the campaign in the major television and print news sources, and he randomly selected almost 7,000 political news stories for analysis (Patterson 1980). Each story was elaborately coded, and in the last chapter of this analysis, I make use of this unique data to make inferences about the information available to the electorate during the 1976 election. However, I also use the 1980 NES Panel Study when I look at voter learning in chapter

---

1. There were many seven-point scales in the 1972 survey, but they were posed in a split-sample format. Unfortunately this makes the use of this survey data impossible for the purposes of this analysis.

10. I undertook a content analysis of the *Los Angeles Times* coverage of the 1980 campaign following the sampling and coding guidelines Patterson used in collecting his 1976 media data. The 1980 election provides an interesting comparison for the 1976 election, since the dynamics of media coverage of the campaigns and candidates differed markedly.

The 1980–92 NES surveys were very similar in the format of the questions, with the only major variation in the survey instrument coming in which policy issue questions were placed in each survey. However, one significant difference in these presidential pre- and postelection surveys must be noted: the 1980 survey was based on a sampling frame of *congressional districts*, not of *the national voting-age population* as in most NES presidential studies. These sampling differences should not influence the empirical results in the next chapters. The only limit involved in use of the 1980 NES study is the population that I can make inferences about, which in this case involves the population of voters in the congressional districts, not necessarily in the nation at large.

Measuring Candidate Positions

An initial concern with estimating the voter uncertainty variable discussed in the previous chapter is the measurement of the actual position of each candidate on each issue. Recall that the uncertainty measure is defined as the variation in the voter's placement of the candidate relative to the candidate's true position on the particular policy dimension. In the empirical work reported in the following chapters, I rely on the simple strategy of utilizing the sample mean placement for each candidate on each policy issue in the analysis. Obviously, this approach can be justified on the grounds of simplicity and ease of measurement, since information about the candidate's position is readily available and is on identical scales. This approach is widely employed in the literature and has been shown to give quite reasonable estimates of the true positions of the candidates (Aldrich, Sullivan, and Borgida 1989; Markus and Converse 1979; Page 1978).[2]

---

2. Two very different approaches to measuring the true positions of candidates have appeared in the literature. One, the Aldrich and McKelvey (1977) scaling procedure, uses a very clever set of data manipulations to eliminate one potential problem with the use of the seven-point scales (also see Palfrey and Poole 1987). They argued that when one respondent maps their perceived issue spaces onto seven-point scales, the difference between a 4 and a 6 for this respondent may not be equal to the same difference for another respondent, even though they give identical responses to the survey question. I did not use this procedure to obtain estimates of candidate positions in this study for a number of reasons. First, a number of strict assumptions are required by the scaling procedure, and it is quite complicated and computationally intensive since it involves a unidimensional scaling step, followed by a regression, for each respondent. Second, the procedure requires

Additionally, assumptions must be made about respondents who answered "don't know" to some of the policy placements. One approach would be to eliminate them entirely from the analysis, but because there are systematic patterns in which respondents are likely to say they "don't know," deletion of such respondents would involve selection bias (Achen 1986; Dubin and Rivers 1990; Francis and Busch 1975). Basically, elimination of nonrespondents would dramatically attenuate the effects of uncertainty, since many of these respondents might simply be uncertain about the positions of the candidates on these policies (Alvarez and Franklin 1994). Therefore, I opted for a second approach, in which I assume that if a respondent answered "don't know" to a placement question, they should be considered maximally uncertain about the candidate's position on the policy issue.

The last issue involves only the 1992 election. Unfortunately, the NES only asked seven-point issue placement questions for Clinton and Bush but not for Perot. However, the NES did ask ideological placement questions for all three candidates. So, the measurement of the uncertainty variable for the 1992 election will follow a different strategy than that for the other four elections; it will be based only on the voter's placement of the candidate relative to the mean position of each candidate on the seven-point ideological scale.

---

list-wise deletion of missing data, since otherwise data matrices are singular and impossible to invert. This forces the number of available observations down to a very small number of cases and would obviously produce an exceptionally biased sample. Aldrich and McKelvey have suggested estimating the relevant parameters first for the respondents for whom complete information is available, then using these to estimate the parameters for respondents who have missing data on one or more of the information scales. However, the statistical properties of such a procedure are not known, nor is it clear that the statistical properties claimed by Aldrich and McKelvey for their procedure would still hold. Palfrey and Poole (1987) choose a different course; they estimated the scaling model for respondents who placed themselves and the candidates on a subset of questions (at least three of the nine placements available in the 1980 data they employed). However, since different policy issue information is utilized for different voters, as well as different amounts of information, it is not clear whether they are recovering estimates of the same phenomenon across respondents.

The other procedure has been developed by Brady and Sniderman (1985) and was expanded by Bartels (1988). This model assumes that when respondents place candidates on issue scales, they engage in a simultaneous minimization strategy—they try to minimize their error in the placement of the candidate on the respective policy issue, and the difference between their placement and the placement of the candidate. Bartels's expansion of this procedure involves including indicators for information and interest in this presumed minimization routine. This approach appears to also produce reasonable estimates of candidate positions, but I did not employ this procedure since it is nonlinear and also requires strict assumptions for estimation, and since the estimates of the voter's perceived placement of the candidates are often very imprecise (Bartels 1988).

The Statistical Model

Before testing the first hypothesis—the direct effect of voter uncertainty about candidate policy positions on their evaluation of the candidate—I examine the determinants of voter uncertainty. This is important theoretically, since unraveling the processes which drive voter perceptions is one of the primary concerns of this book. This is also important empirically, since if the measure of uncertainty is influenced by certain exogenous variables as expected by a theory of voter knowledge, that greatly increases my confidence in this particular measure of voter uncertainty.

As was introduced in chapter 4, three factors account for voter uncertainty of the candidate's policy positions: their personal information costs, their exposure to information, and the flow of information during the campaign. To recapitulate, the more costly it is for a voter to obtain, process, and store information, the more uncertain they should be about the candidate's position; the less exposed to information, and the less attentive and interested the voter is, the greater their uncertainty about the position of the candidate; and the greater the amount of information available about the candidates, the less the uncertainty a voter will have regarding the positions of the candidates. With these variables a model of uncertainty can be constructed, under certain assumptions about the relationship between these independent effects and voter uncertainty.

Then, as discussed in chapter 3, this uncertainty should directly influence the voter's evaluation of the candidate, controlling for other policy and nonpolicy factors relevant to the voter's calculus. The uncertainty measure is thus an important explanatory variable in the determinants of candidate evaluation and choice, as well as an important endogenous variable. This causal process relating uncertainty to candidate evaluation and choice is usually depicted in the literature as a hierarchical model (Bartels 1986; Franklin 1991). This hierarchical model can be shown as two equations:

$$v_{iJ} = \beta_1 + \beta_{11}X_{1i} + \beta_{12}X_{2i} + \tau_{11}u_{iJ} + \xi_{1iJ} \tag{5.1}$$

$$u_{iJ} = \beta_2 + \beta_{21}X_{1i} + \beta_{23}X_{3iJ} + \tau_{21}v_{iJ} + \xi_{2iJ} \tag{5.2}$$

where v_{iJ} is the uncertainty of voter i about candidate J, X_{1i} are demographic variables, X_{2i} are variables measuring information costs and exposure to political information, X_{3iJ} are variables relating to the voter's evaluation of candidate policy and nonpolicy attributes, u_{iJ} is the utility or evaluation of the voter for candidate J, the β's and τ's are parameters to be estimated, and ξ's are error terms in each model.[3]

---

3. The demographic variables (X_{1i}) are in the first equation since I expect that two demo-

Past research regarding voter uncertainty of candidate policy positions has assumed that τ_{11} is zero, implying that a voter's evaluation of the candidate does not influence their uncertainty of the candidate. Under this assumption, there is no reason to suspect a correlation between ξ_{1ij} and ξ_{2ij}, and therefore, the estimates of the parameters of each model have the usual properties under certain other assumptions. But if τ_{11} is *not zero*, then the two error terms are likely to be correlated, and the error term on each of the equations is likely to be correlated with right-hand side variables in each equation. As a consequence of this endogeneity, the estimates of the parameters in this model are likely to be biased.

But are there theoretical reasons to suspect that a voter's evaluation of a candidate might influence the amount of uncertainty they have about the candidate? Assume for a moment that the situation is the typical two-candidate presidential race—under what conditions might we expect that voter uncertainty about the candidates is conditional on their respective evaluations of the two candidates? Downs, in his chapter "The Process of Becoming Informed," argues:

> Three factors determine the size of his planned information investment. The first is the value to him of making a correct decision as opposed to an incorrect one, i.e., the variation in utility incomes associated with the possible outcomes of his decision. The second is the relevance of the information to whatever decision is being made . . . The third factor is the cost of the data. (Downs 1957, 215–16)

Take a voter to whom the value of making a correct decision is quite high, and to whom the relevance of the available campaign information is quite high, but the cost of obtaining and utilizing this information is quite low. It is reasonable to argue that such a voter would attempt to minimize the uncertainty associated with both candidates, regardless of prior evaluations of each candidate, since the value of being correct is high and the costs are low.

But what of a voter to whom the value of being correct is quite low, but the costs of information are high and relevant information is quite difficult to obtain? It is reasonable to argue that such voters might be attentive to, or process, only information about their preferred candidate, and avoid or ignore information about the other, less preferred candidate. This is similar to information

---

graphic groups, minorities and females, might be more uncertain than others. It is possible that other demographic groupings might be useful, like income and socio-economic status, but these are concepts that surveys are not well-suited to measure. These same variables are in the second equation to control for nonpolicy and candidate variations across individuals in their candidate preference.

processing strategies discussed in the political cognition literature—termed "top-down" or "theory-driven" processing by Rahn (1990), or schema-based processing by Fiske and Pavelchak (1986), or those described in the literature on how the media influences voter information processing (Graber 1988; Lazarsfeld, Berelson, and Gaudet 1944; Patterson 1980). In any case, there are strong theoretical reasons to believe that the uncertainty voters possess about candidates might be contingent not only on their information costs, awareness, and attentiveness, and the information made available by the campaign, *but also upon their existing evaluations of the candidates.*

Thus, there are theoretical reasons to suspect that τ_{11} might be nonzero and that a simultaneous relationship exists between candidate evaluations and voter uncertainty. This means that independent estimation of equations 5.1 and 5.2 is inappropriate and would lead to incorrect estimates of the coefficients in each equation. Rather, the endogeneity between these two variables must be appropriately modeled so that consistent empirical results can be obtained.

The terms in the model can be expanded to clarify the general statistical model of uncertainty and evaluations:

$$v_{iJ} = \beta_1 + \beta_{11}X_{1i} + \beta_{12}X_{2i} + \tau_{11}u_{iJ} + \xi_{1iJ} \tag{5.3}$$
$$u_{iJ} = \beta_2 + \beta_{21}X_{1i} + \beta_{23}X_{3iJ} + \beta_{24}X_{4iJ} + \tau_{21}v_{iJ} + \xi_{2iJ} \tag{5.4}$$

where v_{iJ} is the voter's uncertainty of the candidate's policy positions, X_{1i} is a vector of demographic variables measuring information costs, X_{2i} is a vector of variables expressing the voter's exposure and depth of political information, X_{3iJ} is a vector of variables for policy-specific information about the candidate, X_{4iJ} are variables for nonpolicy information about the candidates, and u_{iJ} denotes the voter's utility for the candidate.

In chapter 3, the decision rule in a situation of two-candidate competition was developed, and it was shown that they voted for the candidate with the greatest expected utility. Two changes need to be made in the model given in equations 5.3 and 5.4 to reflect this. First, the voter's uncertainty for the other candidate (G) must be modeled. This is accomplished by simply adding another equation to the model for v_{iG}. To express comparative candidate evaluations, however, I denote whether the voter prefers candidate J to the other G by u_i and add this term the voter's evaluation of candidate G to the equation for comparative candidate utility.[4]

---

4. In the empirical models below, we observe only a dichotomous indicator for the preference of each voter for the Democratic candidate relative to the Republican candidate, where Democratic preference is coded one. Other measures of evaluation and preference are possible to operationalize from the survey data, but the use of the "thermometers" is suspect, and "thermometer" ratings were not available in the 1976 panel data. For the 1980 and 1992 models, the choice

These two changes yield the model:

$$v_{iJ} = \beta_1 + \beta_{11}X_{1i} + \beta_{12}X_{2i} + \tau_{11}u_i + \xi_{1iJ}$$
$$v_{iG} = \beta_2 + \beta_{21}X_{1i} + \beta_{22}X_{2i} + \tau_{21}u_i + \xi_{2iJ}$$
$$u_i = \beta_3 + \beta_{31}X_{1i} + \beta_{33}X_{3iJ} + \beta_{34}X_{4iJ} + \tau_{31}v_{iJ} + \beta_{35}X_{3iG}$$
$$+ \beta_{36}X_{4iG} + \tau_{32}v_{iG} + \xi_{3i} \qquad (5.5)$$

where v_{iJ} is the voter's uncertainty for candidate J, v_{iG} is their uncertainty of candidate G, X_{3iJ} and X_{3iG} are vectors of variables for policy-specific information about each candidate, X_{4iJ} and X_{4iG} are variables for nonpolicy information about the candidates, and u_i comparative utility for whether i prefers candidate J to candidate G. Also, as before, the β's and τ's are parameters to be estimated and the ξ's are error terms.

Given that the structural model here is nonrecursive, estimation of this uncertainty and evaluation model must be carefully considered. First, there must be enough information in the data matrix to obtain a unique set of parameter estimates—in other words, the structural model must be identified. Given that there are actually a number of restrictions in the structural model, the equations are overidentified; and, given overidentification, instrumental variables procedures could be employed to produce consistent estimates of the parameters in the structural model.[5]

There is a further complication involved in the estimation of the structural model. Since we observe comparative utility variable as a discrete variable—representing whether the voter stated preferring one candidate to the other—straightforward application of two-stage least squares, the typical solution to the problem of simultaneous equations, is rendered inappropriate.[6] Instead, a mixed estimation strategy has been developed for cases such as this, where some endogenous variables in the structural model are continuous and some are discrete (Achen 1986; Alvarez 1995; Amemiya 1978; Heckman 1978; Lee 1981; Maddala 1983; Rivers and Vuong 1988). An excellent summary

---

variable takes three values, with the comparison category being the incumbent candidate.

5. Later, when this structural model is operationalized for each election, verification of the identification status of each equation is apparent through checking the order condition, which is a necessary but not sufficient condition for identification of recursive systems (Hanushek and Jackson 1977). The order condition states that the number of exogenous variables excluded from each equation must be at least as great as the number of endogenous variables included in each equation.

6. Thus, this model is similar to the model discussed by Nelson and Olsen (1978). Maddala (1983, 242–45) presents the reduced-forms and one two-stage estimation procedure for this model; Amemiya (1979) also discussed this model, and derived the asymptotic covariance matrix for the two-stage estimator.

of one approach, which I call two-stage probit least squares (2SPLS), is given in Maddala (1983), where he summarizes the estimator discussed by Amemiya (1978). This estimator has seen limited applications in the political science literature (Alvarez 1995; Fiorina 1981; Franklin and Jackson 1983).

The two-stage probit least squares (2SPLS) methodology involves first estimating reduced-form equations for each endogenous variable. The reduced form equations for the uncertainty terms are estimated in the usual fashion, using ordinary least squares regression, while the reduced form equation for the preference variable is estimated via probit analysis. The parameters for the reduced form equations are then used to generate a predicted value for each endogenous variable, and these predicted values are then substituted for each endogenous variable as they appear on the right-hand side of the respective equation.[7] Then the equations are estimated, with the predicted values from the reduced forms serving as instruments on the right-hand sides of the equations, and the estimates obtained in this second stage are consistent (Achen 1986; Amemiya 1978).[8]

But the estimated standard errors of the 2SPLS are likely to be biased. For the uncertainty equations, since these are continuous variables being estimated by two-stage least squares, the standard errors are easily corrected by multiplying the estimated standard errors by an appropriate weighting factor, as summarized in Achen (1986, 43).[9] However, for the probit preference equation, the standard errors cannot be easily corrected (Achen 1986, 49). The asymptotic covariance matrix of the probit estimates has been derived by Amemiya

---

7. Note that the predicted value from the probit reduced form is the linear predictor, βX_i, not a transformed probability for each voter.

8. The use of two-stage, or limited-information models, instead of full-information models, is justified on two grounds. First, limited-information models are easier to estimate and interpret than their full-information counterparts. Derivation of a full-information likelihood function for the model posited in the text yielded an exceptionally complex function, which made estimation computationally difficult. Second, full-information models, while theoretically more efficient since they utilize information in the data more fully, can be quite problematic if even one of the equations in the model is misspecified since the biases associated with specification errors will be distributed throughout the model. Limited-information models are not problematic in this regard, since they ignore information about the joint distribution of the error terms across the equations, which leads to a loss of potential efficiency.

9. The weighting correction is easy to implement. Define the variance of the residuals from the second-stage least-squares regression as $\sigma^2_{\xi_1}$. Then compute a slightly different residual variance, using these same second-stage least-squares coefficients, but after substituting the actual value of the endogenous right-hand side variable for the instrumental values obtained from the reduced-form model. Define this second residual variance as $\sigma^2_{\xi_2}$. The weighting factor, which should be multiplied by each standard error in the second-stage least-squares regression, is $\sqrt{\sigma^2_{\xi_1}/\sigma^2_{\xi_2}}$. These standard errors are more efficient than the unweighted errors (Achen 1986; Alvarez 1995).

(1978), but it is exceptionally complex and computationally difficult. Indeed, those in the political science literature who have utilized the 2SPLS methodology have settled for consistent estimates and possibly incorrect standard errors due to this problem (Fiorina 1982; Franklin and Jackson 1983).

Yet it is important to be able to estimate reliable standard errors so that statistical tests of the hypotheses from chapter 3 can be conducted. Since correcting the standard errors in the 2SPLS probit equation is exceptionally difficult, I use an additional estimation strategy. Rivers and Vuong (1988) developed what they term a two-stage conditional maximum likelihood (2SCML) approach to obtaining consistent and asymptotically efficient estimates for the probit equation. By estimating the two-stage probit model in typical fashion, producing consistent but perhaps incorrect standard errors, and estimating the same model again using the 2SCML approach, I can better evaluate the second-stage probit results. If the two methodologies produce similar results, my confidence in the validity of the results, for both methodologies, will be greatly enhanced.

The 2SCML approach assumes that I am primarily interested in recovering the structural parameters for the probit equations. This assertion is not problematic, since it is possible using the usual 2SPLS method to obtain consistent and efficient estimates of the coefficients in the uncertainty equations. Then, to estimate the probit coefficients and their variances in the 2SCML method, I first estimate the reduced forms for the uncertainty equations, obtain the residuals for the reduced forms, and add these residuals to the probit equation as two additional variables with corresponding parameters to be estimated. Rivers and Vuong demonstrate that this method produces consistent and asymptotically efficient estimates.[10] Rivers and Vuong also demonstrate an additional property of this model, which is that a test of the joint statistical significance of the parameters on the reduced form errors is a robust exogeneity test.[11]

Unfortunately, little is known about the statistical properties of these two-

---

10. They show that the 2SCML estimators are clearly asymptotically efficient when in the probit equation, the right-hand side endogenous variables are actually exogenous, or when the probit equation is just identified. However, their Monte Carlo evidence shows that the 2SCML estimator is more efficient than the other classes of simultaneous probit estimators even if these conditions are not met.

11. Rivers and Vuong show that a number of exogeneity tests can be constructed for the 2SCML model. In particular, the likelihood-ratio test is easy to implement and is computed as: $LR = -2(\ln \widehat{L}_R - \ln \widehat{L}_U)$, where $\widehat{L}_R$ is the log-likelihood function evaluated at the restricted estimates (a probit model without the regression reduced-form errors on the right-hand side) and $\widehat{L}_U$ is the log-likelihood computed at the unrestricted estimates. Rivers and Vuong show that this test has a χ^2 distribution with degrees of freedom equal to the number of endogenous variables in the binary choice equation. This provides a simple and useful diagnostic test for exogeneity in the two-stage model.

stage estimators in real world data applications, especially when used in small data sets. A detailed comparison of these estimators is in Alvarez (1995), where I present extensive Monte Carlo results. These simulations show that if non recursive relationships are suspected in a model like that presented here, the estimates obtained from recursive models will be seriously biased. Also, I show there that both two-stage models produce consistent estimates. Additional discussion of these statistical issues is in appendix B.

For the 1976, 1984, and 1988 elections I use both the 2SPLS and 2SCML techniques to estimate the model of candidate evaluations and uncertainty presented in equation 5.5. These three elections involve two major party candidates, so the binary choice models are appropriate. However, the 1980 and 1992 elections saw serious challenges from third-party or independent candidates. Methodologically the Anderson and Perot candidacies could be handled empirically in at least three ways. First, I could simply ignore the third-party or independent candidates and estimate models of binary choices between the two major party candidates using the techniques just discussed. Second, I could estimate an ordered probit or logit model, which would include the third-party or independent candidates. Third, I could estimate multinomial logit models which would also include Anderson in 1980 or Perot in 1992 as third choices.

The first two approaches are badly flawed, and even multinomial logit has potential problems in this application (Alvarez and Nagler 1995). The first approach ignores the choices of significant shares of the American electorate (Anderson received 6.6 percent of the popular vote in 1980, just over 5.7 million votes; Perot obtained 18.9 percent of the general election vote in 1992, which was 19.7 million votes.) Also, ignoring the third-party or independent candidate and estimating binary-choice models on the remaining candidates is selecting on the dependent variable, which produces inconsistent estimates (Manski and Lerman 1977). For example, to treat Perot supporters in 1992 as "missing data" and assume that they would have behaved as others of similar socioeconomic status and issue preferences behaved—on the few issue preferences we have measures of—is to ignore something striking about these voters: they did not behave as the Clinton or Bush voters behaved, since they voted for Perot. That Perot voters behaved differently from Clinton and Bush voters has been demonstrated elsewhere (Alvarez and Nagler 1995).

The second approach, using ordered probit (McKelvey and Zavoina 1975), cannot be applied, either. The ordered probit model assumes that the choices can be ordered on the same unidimensional continuum for all voters. Since there is no necessary unidimensional ordering of these candidates, the use of ordered probit in this situation is incorrect.

The third approach, multinomial logit, assumes that the random disturbance terms associated with each of the three candidates are independent. This is equivalent to making the strong behavioral assumption of "Independence of Irrelevant Alternatives" (IIA) with regard to the random disturbances in the model. This assumption implies that the ratio of the probability of choosing the first candidate to the probability of choosing the second candidate is not altered by the availability of the third candidate. Since I do not have strong prior beliefs about the relationship between the disturbances for the candidates, there is no reason to make such strong and restrictive assumptions about those disturbances. In the next section I outline an alternative approach—the multinomial probit model—which can flexibly alleviate all of these problems (Alvarez and Nagler 1995; Hausman and Wise 1978).

Modeling Multicandidate Elections

Following Hausman and Wise (1978) and Alvarez and Nagler (1995, 1997), I define the random utility of each voter over each of the three candidates in both the 1980 and 1992 election:

$$U_{ij} = a_i \psi_j + X_{ij}\beta + \varepsilon_{ij} \tag{5.6}$$

where a_i is a vector of characteristics unique to the voter i, X_{ij} is a vector of characteristics unique to candidate j ($j = 1,2,3$) with respect to voter i, ψ_j and β are vectors of parameters to be estimated, and ε_{ij} is a disturbance term. I assume that the three error terms (ε_{i1}, ε_{i2}, ε_{i3}) have a multivariate normal distribution, and as in Alvarez and Nagler (1995) I allow the errors to be correlated across the candidates, but be homoskedastic. This formulation is quite flexible since with the multinomial probit model I can estimate the error correlations across the utility functions without being forced to make strong and restrictive assumptions about the error process.

Using the multinomial probit model, only one coefficient is estimated per characteristic of the alternatives. For characteristics that vary by individuals I estimate $(M - 1)$ coefficients per characteristic, where M is the number of choices. So in the 1980 and 1992 elections I estimate two coefficients per individual characteristic. Both these models will be estimated so that one vector of coefficients will estimate the effect of a change in the variable on the voter's utility of voting for the independent candidate relative to the incumbent, while the second vector will express the effect of a change in the variable on the utility of voting for the major-party challenger relative to the incumbent. In appendix B I give more details about the multinomial probit model.

The only extra wrinkle, then, involves the uncertainty component of the model for 1980 and 1992. The full, nonrecursive estimation model for both these elections will be similar in form to that given above in equation 5.5, with two exceptions. First, in the multinomial probit voter choice equation, since each parameter vector produces coefficients expressing the relative effect of a variable on the choice between two candidates, each parameter vector will contain uncertainty instruments only for the two candidates being compared. So, for the 1992 voter choice equation, the first parameter vector will include uncertainty variables for Bush and Perot, while the second will include uncertainty terms for Clinton and Perot. Second, I will estimate three uncertainty equations, one for each candidate. The multinomial probit model, in reduced form, will produce three linear predictors, one for each candidate. Thus, each uncertainty model will have a linear predictor—an estimate of the voter's utility for that candidate—on the right-hand side to control for the effects of candidate preference on uncertainty.

Modeling Uncertainty and Issue Voting

One last methodological topic is considered in this chapter: how to model the interaction between uncertainty and issue preferences in voter decision making. The argument advanced in the last chapter was that the greater the voter's uncertainty about the candidate's policy positions, the less the voter's ability to take that information into account in their decision making.

The crux of the problem, however, is that this interaction is to be analyzed in a nonlinear model. The vote choice models used in this book are either binary or multinomial probit models, and both are inherently nonlinear. One way to understand the problem is to think of the binary probit model in the general context of the "link function" (McCullagh and Nelder 1983). The probit model is written:

$$P(Y_i = 1) = \pi_i = g(\beta x_i) \tag{5.7}$$

where the cumulative normal distribution is substituted for g. The cumulative normal distribution is not a linear function across the range of the linear systematic component of the model so the impact of a change in a component of X_i depends upon the point on the curve from which the comparison begins. Thus, in these nonlinear models, assessing the impact of a change in an exogenous variable upon the variable being modeled is dependent on where we start on the appropriate curve—in other words, what the values of the other exogenous variables are.

This nonlinearity has led some to argue that interactions between right-hand side variables are *assumed by the model*. Since these interactions are assumed, so this argument goes, it could be possible to study the interaction of uncertainty and issue voting by simple manipulation of different configurations of values of the independent variables in the model. Such an approach to studying interactions in probit models has been employed in a number of prominent studies, including the analysis of turnout by Wolfinger and Rosenstone (1980) or the diffusion of policy innovations across state governments by Berry and Berry (1990, 1991).

Yet, this is a flawed approach to modeling interactions in nonlinear models (Frant 1991; Nagler 1991, 1992). Assume that the systematic component of the model has two variables, X_1 and X_2, and their corresponding parameters. If we were interested in the influence of X_1 on the $P(Y_i = 1)$, it would depend upon where we began on the curve of the distribution, that is, on the linear combination $(\beta_1 X_1 + \beta_2 X_2)$. And the influence of X_1 will be the greatest when this linear combination is close to zero, or in the case of the cumulative normal distribution, when the $P(Y_i = 1)$ is near 0.5 (Nagler 1991).

There are two alternative strategies to modeling the interaction in nonlinear models. One is to disaggregate the data set into subsets based on the variable believed to be producing the interaction and to assume that the parameters of the model vary across different levels of this particular variable. This explicitly allows for heterogeneity in the parameters of the model, but it reduces the size of the dataset, which can dramatically erode estimation efficiency. The other approach is to include interaction terms in the model. This approach allows direct estimation of the effect of a variable on another in a nonlinear model using all of the available data. Unfortunately, there is a cost associated with modeling the interactions directly. This cost is the risk of severe multicollinearity, since we would be adding more variables which are simply the products of variables already in the model.

In chapter 8, I primarily use the second approach and disaggregate the data sets for the 1976, 1984, and 1988 presidential elections by different levels of the uncertainty variables. Unfortunately, given the use of instrumental variables in the two-stage models, multicollinearity is a looming risk in the uncertainty and evaluation models. This risk precludes the addition of variables to the model. But the stratification of the sample by the levels of uncertainty the voters have about the candidates allows all of the coefficients of the preference equations to vary. This provides the opportunity to examine not only the influence of voter uncertainty about candidate policy positions on issue voting, but its influence on the use of other information by the voters in their decision making as well. For the 1980 and 1992 models, I use the second approach and directly estimate the interaction between uncertainty and issue distance. The multinomial probit models do not perform well in small samples, so for these two elections I chose not to divide the samples.

Conclusion

Discrete choice models in political science are an underutilized methodology. All too often, researchers make incorrect assumptions about how to model a discrete choice process, ranging from using ordinary least-squares regression on binary choice variables to using restrictive multiple choice techniques like multinomial logit instead of multinomial probit. Given the advances in computational power and in understanding of maximum-likelihood techniques (e.g., King 1989), it is clear that this is an area of political methodology that will see substantial development in coming years.

This chapter has outlined two important discrete choice methodologies for political research. The first, two-stage estimation techniques for systems of equations with continuous and discrete dependent variables, provides an introduction to some of the trade-offs associated with these techniques. Even though both the 2SPLS and the 2SCML models are very easy to estimate (see appendix B for more details about estimation), they are rare in political science. One of the important points I discuss elsewhere is that the nonlinear nature of discrete choice models makes the biases caused by endogeneity more problematic than in the usual linear models (Alvarez 1995). Thus, if endogeneity is suspected in a discrete choice model, two-stage techniques to eliminate the bias are required.

The second new methodology is the multinomial probit model. The only other application of the multinomial probit model in political science research has appeared in my work with Nagler (1995). In the chapter, I echo the arguments we made in that paper for the multinomial probit model. The multinomial probit model is the most flexible multiple choice technique, since it does not require the assumption of the "independence of irrelevant alternatives" as does the multinomial logit model. Nor does it require any assumptions about the structuring of the choice process like the nested logit or general extreme-value models. With the rising popularity of methods-of-moment and simulation-based estimation techniques (Keane 1994) the computational hurdles often associated with the multinomial probit model will become less problematic.

From here, the book moves directly to testing the hypotheses advanced in chapter 3. In the next two chapters these two techniques will be successfully used to examine what factors influence how uncertain voters are about the policy positions of presidential candidates. Then I use these techniques to demonstrate that voters do hold candidates accountable for uncertainty about their issue positions. Through these substantive applications I show the importance of these techniques for political research.

CHAPTER 6

The Causes of Uncertainty

I know of no safe depository of the ultimate powers of the society but the people themselves; and if we think them not enlightened enough to exercise their control with a wholesome discretion, the remedy is not to take it from them, but to inform their discretion by education.

—Thomas Jefferson, Letter to William Charles Jarvis, September 28, 1820

In this chapter, I present the first set of empirical results from the two-stage uncertainty and evaluations models—the models for voter uncertainty of the presidential candidates, 1976–92. The purpose of these models is twofold. The primary purpose of these models of voter uncertainty is substantive, since it is imperative to understand the processes at the individual level which drive this uncertainty. Basically, these models answer substantive questions about the determinants of voter uncertainty; that is, which voters are more uncertain than others? By answering this question, I can move to the next and more important question—what might be done to better inform voters?

Also, these models justify the measurement approach to voter uncertainty which is the basis for the empirical work in this book. Recall that the measure for voter uncertainty is the variation in voter placement of each candidate across a number of issues, representing the difference between the voter's perception of the candidate's position and the candidate's actual position across different issues. Here, by demonstrating that this uncertainty measure is correlated with a set of independent variables across voters in theoretically expected patterns, I increase confidence that this measure taps the uncertainty voters actually possess about the policy stands of presidential candidates (Alvarez and Franklin 1994; Cook and Campbell 1979).

A good deal of the theoretical discussion of individual-level determinants of uncertainty is in chapter 4. The first section of this chapter returns to that

93

discussion and presents the theoretical expectations for the individual level determinants of uncertainty. The second section gives the models and discusses the results. Appendix C contains details of the operationalizations of the independent variables in the models, and the reduced-form model results for the candidate preference instruments.

Theoretical Expectations

In chapter 4, I argued that three factors are related to voter uncertainty about the policy positions taken by political figures: *the flow of information in the political environment, the voter's personal information costs,* and *the voter's attachment to the political world and their exposure to information about politics.* Since the first, information flow in the presidential campaign, is a dynamic concept, it will be impossible to include in these static models of voter uncertainty, estimated with one set of survey data (typically from October) from each election year. The influence of the campaign's information dynamics will be discussed in great detail in subsequent chapters. However, the latter two factors can be operationalized from available survey data in each of these presidential elections. I discuss these two factors in turn.

As both those working in the rational choice and political cognition fields have discussed in the literature, the voter bears considerable costs in gathering, analyzing, and evaluating information. This leads me to expect that those voters to whom the costs of obtaining, processing, and recalling information about presidential candidates are the lowest should be systematically *more certain* about the policy positions of the presidential candidates. Correspondingly, those who have greater information costs should be *more uncertain* of the policy positions of the presidential candidates.

A number of variables can be operationalized to account for differential information costs across voters. The first measure of information costs is the voter's education, since the better educated the voter, the better their ability to utilize information about the candidate's policy positions. The second variable is the voter's store of objective political information, which is a direct representation of how much a voter knows about political affairs (Zaller 1989). Thus the more politically informed and the better educated the voter, the less uncertain I expect him or her to be of candidate policy positions.

Two other variables are included in these models to account for additional social and demographic factors that might lead some voters to be more uncertain about candidate policy positions than others. These are the race and gender of the voter. Given the impediments that have often been placed in the paths of both minorities and women in American society and political life, it is likely that these two social groups might be less certain of the positions of the presidential candidates.[1] The other set of independent variables which should influence voter uncertainty of candidate positions are the voter's attachment and exposure to the political system. Voters who are more exposed to political coverage in the mass media, those who are more politically efficacious, and those with stronger affiliations to the party system, should be the most heavily exposed to information about the policy stances of presidential candidates (Campbell et al. 1960; Converse 1962; Fiorina 1981; Hamill, Lodge, and Blake 1985; Rahn 1990; Zaller 1989). And those with the most information should be the most certain of the presidential candidate's policy positions.

Lastly, following the discussion in chapter 5 of the endogeneity of voter uncertainty and candidate evaluation, an indicator for the voter's relative preference for the Democratic to the Republican candidate is included in these models. Note that this indicator for preference in these models is an instrument taken from a reduced form probit model of candidate preference.[2] The preference indicators for the 1976, 1984, and 1988 models are coded so that a high score indicates Democratic preference and a low score indicates Republican preference. Therefore, in the uncertainty equations for the Democratic candidates, the sign of the preference indicator should be negative (the more likely they are to prefer the Democrat, the less uncertain the voter should be); and for the Republican candidates, the sign should be positive (the more likely they are to prefer the Republican, the more certain they are about the Republican). The preference indicators for the 1980 and 1992 elections are coded so that a high score shows a stronger preference for the particular candidate. The signs of the estimated coefficients should also be negative—the stronger a voter's preference for the candidate, the less uncertain she should be of the candidate's issue positions, all things constant. The operationalizations for all of the variables for each election year are in appendix C.

---

1. Certainly, these two sociodemographic variables are not the only factors which might lead some voters to be less certain than others. For example, broader indicators of income levels or socio-economic status would have been useful to include as well. However, there tends to be very poor measurement of socio-economic status in attitudinal surveys, since respondents often refuse to answer such questions, or they give incorrect answers. Past empirical work on uncertainty has provided support for the expectation that some social groups are systematically less informed about candidate issue positions (Alvarez and Franklin 1994; Bartels 1986; Franklin 1991).

2. The reduced-form probit models are in appendix C. The instrument from the reduced form models is the linear predictor from the probit model, βX_i, for each voter. Also, the standard errors in these two-stage models have been corrected when necessary as suggested by Achen (1986).

Empirical Results

Carter and Ford: 1976

The first set of uncertainty models is from the 1976 campaign, which pitted Jimmy Carter against Gerald Ford. The models are presented in table 6.1, which gives the independent variables in the first column, the estimates and standard errors for the Carter uncertainty equation in the second column, and similar statistics for the Ford uncertainty equation in the third column. The data used to estimate these models came from the October wave of the 1976 Patterson panel study.

First, note that the models fit the data reasonably well. Both equations have similar R^2's and standard errors, which indicate that the two-stage models do account for a good deal of the variance in the voter's uncertainty of Carter and Ford in 1976. Additionally, almost all of the estimates are in the anticipated direction and have standard errors sufficiently small that the estimates are reliable indicators of the population parameters at reasonable levels of statistical significance.

The indicators of voter information costs in these models, the first four variables in the table (education, political information, gender, and race) are all in the expected direction. That is, better educated and informed voters were less uncertain of the policy positions of Carter and Ford in 1976, while both women and racial minorities were more uncertain of the positions of these two candidates. And only the estimate for racial minorities fails to reach statistical significance in these models.

The rest of the variables in these two models, besides the relative candidate preference indicator, measure various dimensions of voter attachment to the political world and their exposure to political information. Unlike the National Election Studies, however, the 1976 Patterson data contained a useful set of questions that allowed me to incorporate three additional variables into these two models, which indicated whether the respondent watched either or both of the televised debates or recalled seeing some advertisement from the particular candidate's paid media campaign. So the estimates for watching the debates or allow examination of two specific types of exposure to campaign information.[3]

---

3. The debate and advertisement questions were included in the October wave of the Patterson study, just after the two presidential debates (September 23 and October 6). However, in the NES surveys (except for 1992), questions about viewing advertisements are not included, and the debate questions, when included in the survey instrument, are in the postelection instrument and hence are not very reliable measures of exposure to debate or advertising information. Consequently, I do not include the NES debate recall questions in the 1980–92 uncertainty models.

TABLE 6.1.   Two-Stage Uncertainty Results, 1976 Election

Independent Variables	Carter Uncertainty	Ford Uncertainty
Constant	5.5**	5.1**
	0.91	0.87
Education	−0.28**	−0.29**
	0.15	0.14
Political information	−0.28**	−0.25**
	0.04	0.04
Gender	0.65**	0.78**
	0.25	0.24
Race	0.24	0.46
	0.51	0.49
Partisan strength	0.12	0.06
	0.15	0.15
Media exposure	−0.14**	−0.22**
	0.06	0.06
Political efficacy	−0.06**	−0.03*
	0.03	0.03
First debate	0.004	−0.25*
	0.18	0.17
Second debate	−0.22*	−0.13
	0.17	0.16
Candidate advertising	−0.17	−0.49*
	0.38	0.35
Candidate preference	−0.08**	0.02
	0.03	0.03
Adjusted R^2	0.23	0.27
Model S.E.	2.5	2.7
Uncertainty mean	3.9	3.8
Number of cases	464	464

Note: Entries are two-stage least squares estimates and their associated adjusted standard errors.

* indicates a $p = 0.10$ level of statistical significance, one-tailed tests.

** indicates a $p = 0.05$ level, level of statistical significance, one-tailed tests.

The standard errors have been corrected as discussed by Achen (1986).

Of all of these variables, only the estimates for partisan strength and the first debate indicators are incorrectly signed, but they are not statistically significant. All of the rest have the predicted sign, and most do reach reasonable levels of statistical significance. The first two indicators—media exposure and political efficacy—both show that the more exposed and efficacious voters are statistically more certain of the policy positions of the two candidates in this election. Also, voters who watched the first debate were more certain of Ford's policy positions, while those who watched the second debate were more certain of Carter's positions. What is fascinating about these results is that they comport with both the information made available by these two debates in 1976, as well as popular perceptions concerning which of the two candidates had more effectively presented themselves and their campaign positions in each debate. Most observers concluded that in the first debate, Ford had articulated his positions on unemployment and the economy quite forcefully and had put Carter on the defensive. Then, while Carter began to respond, the debates were interrupted by technical difficulties which most believed damaged Carter's ability to get his arguments across (Witcover 1977). During the second debate, both candidates attacked their opponent's foreign policy positions, which might account for the negative effect watching this debate appears to have had on the policy uncertainty for both candidates in the models. But the second debate was marred by Ford's "no Soviet domination of Eastern Europe" comment, retracted within the next five days—which might account for the only marginal reduction in Ford uncertainty for voters who watched the second debate.[4]

Last, the candidate preference indicator is signed as predicted for both candidates, but it is statistically significant in only the Carter equation. The signs of these estimates indicate that the greater the likelihood of Carter support, the higher a respondent's uncertainty about Ford's policy positions and the lower their uncertainty about Carter's positions, all things constant. But the magnitude of this effect is interesting, since it is significant for only the challenging candidate. This suggests that while voters do engage in selective information processing about presidential candidates, such strategies may not be necessary for incumbent candidates: voters may have already obtained enough information about incumbents to make selective processing unnecessary.

Carter, Reagan, and Anderson: 1980

As discussed in chapter 5, the modeling of uncertainty and candidate evaluations in the 1980 election is complicated by Anderson's independent campaign for the presidency, since his candidacy complicated the choice process for voters (turning a usually two-candidate choice into a three-candidate choice). The results for the Carter, Reagan, and Anderson two-stage uncertainty models are in table 6.2. Here, the first column gives the independent variables, the second column the two-stage least squares estimates and their adjusted standard errors for the voter's uncertainty about the policy positions taken by the three

---

4. In the second debate during the 1976 race, Ford responded to a question about relations with the Soviets: "There is no Soviet domination of Eastern Europe, and there never will be under a Ford Administration." This was heavily covered in the mass media, and Ford was forced to campaign heavily to diminish the impact of this campaign mistake.

TABLE 6.2.   Two-Stage Uncertainty Results, 1980 Election

Independent Variables	Carter Uncertainty	Reagan Uncertainty	Anderson Uncertainty
Constant	4.9**	7.6**	9.4**
	.69	1.0	1.1
Education	−.13	−.33**	−.34**
	.12	.16	.17
Political information	−.28**	−.46**	−.54**
	.05	.06	.07
Gender	.56**	1.1**	1.5**
	.21	.30	.31
Race	.63**	−.03	−.57
	.35	.49	.52
Partisan strength	.06	.06	.23*
	.11	.15	.16
Media exposure	.03	.05	−.08
	.06	.08	.09
Political efficacy	−.32**	−.34**	−.31*
	.14	.19	.20
Candidate preference	−.16**	−.74**	.19
	.09	.15	.16
Adjusted R^2	.13	.24	.23
Model S.E.	2.2	3.0	3.2
Uncertainty mean	2.5	3.3	4.7
Number of cases	469	469	469

Note: Entries are two-stage least squares estimates, and their associated adjusted standard errors.

* indicates a $p = 0.10$ level of statistical significance, one-tailed tests.

** indicates a $p = 0.05$ level of statistical significance, one-tailed tests.

The standard errors have been corrected as discussed by Achen (1986).

candidates.

First, the models for Reagan and Anderson fit the data reasonably well, with adjusted-R^2 values of .24 and .23, respectively. However, the Carter uncertainty model does not fit as well. Even so, most of the variables in the uncertainty models across the three candidates are correctly signed, and a number do have important influences on voter uncertainty in the 1980 race.

Beginning with the information cost indicators, notice that education and information both continue to be strongly related to voter uncertainty. All have the predicted sign, and all but one (education in the Carter uncertainty model) are statistically significant: voters with higher education and more information were clearly more certain of candidate positions in 1980. Also, as was true for the 1976 election, women were statistically more uncertain about candidate policy positions than were men in this election. Notice that the effect of gender on uncertainty was almost three times greater for Anderson uncertainty than for Carter uncertainty. Last, race is statistically significant only in the Carter uncertainty model, where it was positive.

Of the variables measuring a voter's relationship to the political system, the most important in 1980 was political efficacy. Across the three models, the more efficacious a voter, the less uncertain he or she was about each candidate. The strength of a voter's partisan affiliations is estimated to have a positive impact in these models—implying that the stronger a voter's partisanship, the greater their uncertainty about each candidate. But the effect of partisan strength is statistically significant in only the Anderson uncertainty model; given Anderson's independence from the two established political parties, this means that self-proclaimed independents were *more certain* of Anderson's issue positions than were strong partisans.

There is evidence that in the 1980 election, voters practiced selective information processing about the two major party candidates. For Carter and Reagan, the candidate preference instruments are negatively signed and statistically significant, which demonstrates that voters who preferred either candidate were more certain of the candidate's position, all things constant. Notice that the effect of candidate preference is stronger for Reagan (the challenger) than for Carter. Again, just as in 1976, it appears that selective information processing for challengers is of more importance for uncertain voters than for incumbents. However, the same is not true for the 1980 independent candidate, John Anderson. Selective information processing is not seen in the Anderson uncertainty models, where the effects of Anderson preference cannot be discerned from zero.[5]

Mondale and Reagan in 1984

The 1984 election pitted the incumbent Ronald Reagan against his vice presidential opponent from the last election, Walter Mondale. The models of policy uncertainty for each of these candidates are given in table 6.3, and are virtually identical in terms of their operationalizations and functional form to the models presented for the major party candidates in the 1980 election.

First, among the information cost variables, the estimated effects of both education and political information are as expected. Better educated and more knowledgeable voters were more certain of the policy positions of both Rea-

---

5. The incorrectly signed and statistically insignificant estimate on the Anderson preference instrument is quite likely caused by the inability of the reduced-form model (presented in appendix C) to discriminate Anderson voters from Carter and Reagan voters. The model only correctly classifies 1 of the 44 Anderson voters in this sample (2.3 percent).

TABLE 6.3.   Two-Stage Uncertainty Results, 1984 Election

Independent Variables	Mondale Uncertainty	Reagan Uncertainty
Constant	6.1**	5.1**
	0.49	0.45
Education	−0.35**	−0.20**
	0.09	0.08
Political information	−0.47**	−0.38**
	0.04	0.03
Gender	0.21*	0.03
	0.15	0.14
Race	−0.14	0.50**
	0.29	0.26
Partisan strength	0.19**	0.20**
	0.08	0.07
Media exposure	0.04*	0.03*
	0.03	0.02
Political efficacy	−0.15**	−0.16**
	0.07	0.06
Candidate preference	−0.21**	0.20**
	0.03	0.03
Adjusted R^2	0.25	0.23
Model S.E.	2.3	1.9
Uncertainty mean	2.7	2.3
Number of cases	856	856

Note: Entries are two-stage least squares estimates, and their associated adjusted standard errors.

* indicates a $p = 0.10$ level of statistical significance, one-tailed tests.

** indicates a $p = 0.05$ level of statistical significance, one-tailed tests.

The standard errors have been corrected as discussed by Achen (1986).

gan and Mondale, and these estimates are clearly statistically reliable. Also, women were more uncertain of the positions of both candidates, especially for Mondale. But racial minorities were significantly more uncertain only of Reagan's positions, while the estimate for the influence of racial status on Mondale policy uncertainty was both negatively signed and statistically insignificant.

Second, among the political attachment and exposure indicators, the political efficacy coefficients are positive, as expected, and are significant in both models. Thus more efficacious voters were more certain of both candidates in 1984. The media exposure estimates, however, are positive and significant, as are the estimates of the effects of partisan attachments. These estimates imply that the less attachment a voter had to the party system in 1984, the more certain they were of the positions of Reagan and Mondale; yet the more exposed they were to the media the more uncertain they were.

Last, the candidate preference instruments were statistically significant in both models, underscoring the implication that voter certainty of the positions of these candidates was influenced by which candidate the voter supported. The coefficients are virtually identical, with a negative sign in the Mondale uncertainty model and a positive sign in the Reagan uncertainty model. Thus, Mondale supporters were more certain of Mondale's policy positions and less certain of Reagan's; while Reagan supporters were statistically more certain of Reagan's positions, but less certain of Mondale's. Note that in the 1984 results, there is no indication of any differential effect in the use of selective information processing strategies across the two major party candidates, unlike the patterns discovered in the 1976 and 1980 data where selective information processing appeared to have been more prevalent for the nonincumbent candidates.

Dukakis and Bush in 1988

The next set of two–stage uncertainty models concern voter uncertainty of Michael Dukakis and George Bush in 1988. These models follow directly the lines of the 1980 and 1984 models in terms of model specification and variable operationalization. The models are given in table 6.4, which is organized as the previous tables in this chapter were.

The uncertainty models in table 6.4 fit the data well, as seen in the summary statistics for the models. Additionally, all of the coefficients in each equation are in the anticipated directions (except for the partisan strength indicator), and almost all reach reasonable levels of statistical significance. The political information variables all perform as anticipated, and all coefficients except the racial status indicator in the Bush uncertainty model are statistically significant. Thus, it is clear that in 1988 those voters who had the highest levels of education and who were the best informed about political affairs were the most certain of the positions of Bush and Dukakis on policy issues. Also, as expected, women and racial minorities were less certain of the positions of the candidates in 1988.

Both the political efficacy and media exposure variables are significant in each model and have the expected sign. That is, those more exposed to media coverage of politics, and the more efficacious voters, tended to be more certain of the candidates' policy positions. However, the partisan attachment variable is not significant and is not signed as predicted—which, if any weight is attached to the coefficient, implies that the less attached a voter was to the party system, the more certain they were of the candidate's positions on the policy issues.

TABLE 6.4.   Two-Stage Uncertainty Results, 1988 Election

Independent Variables	Dukakis Uncertainty	Bush Uncertainty
Constant	7.7**	6.2**
	0.55	0.51
Education	−0.39**	−0.21**
	0.10	0.10
Political information	−0.46**	−0.44**
	0.04	0.04
Gender	0.70**	0.43**
	0.20	0.18
Race	0.70**	0.12
	0.35	0.32
Partisan strength	0.09	0.06
	0.11	0.10
Media exposure	−0.07**	−0.04*
	0.03	0.03
Political efficacy	−0.10**	−0.06*
	0.05	0.04
Candidate preference	−0.38**	0.09**
	0.05	0.04
Adjusted R^2	0.29	0.24
Model S.E.	2.7	2.3
Uncertainty mean	3.6	2.9
Number of cases	691	691

Note: Entries are two-stage least squares estimates, and their associated adjusted standard errors.
  * indicates a $p = 0.10$ level of statistical significance, one-tailed tests.
  ** indicates a $p = 0.05$ level of statistical significant, one-tailed tests.
  The standard errors have been corrected as discussed by Achen (1986).

The last coefficient in these models concerns the relative candidate preference instrument. Here, the estimated impact of relative candidate preference is significant and signed as predicted in each equation. That is, if a voter preferred Dukakis to Bush, they were more certain of Dukakis's positions on the issues, but less certain of Bush's. Additionally, if the voter supported Bush, they were more certain of Bush's positions, but less certain of Dukakis's. While both are clearly significant, the coefficient in the Dukakis model for the candidate preference instrument is almost twice the magnitude, which implies that which candidate the voter preferred had a larger influence on Dukakis uncertainty than on Bush uncertainty, all things constant. Or, again it appears that selective information processing in 1988 was more prevalent for knowledge of Dukakis's policy positions and less influential for certainty of Bush's positions.

Bush, Clinton, and Perot: 1992

The uncertainty models for 1992 are given in table 6.5, which is organized as the previous tables in this chapter were. Before moving further into my discussion of these results, however, I'd like to point out that these models have a different dependent variable than the previous candidate uncertainty models. The models for 1976–88 used the operationalization of uncertainty across multiple issues, while for 1992 I evaluated uncertainty only on the ideological dimension, since that was the only Perot placement asked in the 1992 NES survey.

TABLE 6.5.   Two-Stage Uncertainty Results, 1992 Election

Independent Variables	Clinton Uncertainty	Bush Uncertainty	Perot Uncertainty
Constant	4.3**	4.3**	5.4**
	.74	.76	.84
Education	−.10	−.40**	.17
	.13	.13	.14
Political information	−1.1**	−1.2**	−1.6**
	.12	.12	.14
Gender	.55**	.72**	.39*
	.22	.22	.25
Race	1.2**	2.0**	−.05
	.44	.38	.49
Partisan strength	.27**	.15*	−.03
	.12	.12	.13
Media exposure	−.09	.07	.22**
	.09	.09	.10
Political efficacy	.06	.03	−.04
	.05	.05	.05
Candidate advertisement	−.14	.18	−1.2**
	.26	.23	.36
Candidate preference	−.37**	−.13*	−.31**
	.11	.08	.12
Adjusted R^2	.12	.17	.16
Model S.E.	3.3	3.3	3.7
Uncertainty mean	2.2	2.2	4.0
Number of cases	937	937	937

Note: Entries are two-stage least squares estimates, and their associated adjusted standard errors.

* indicates a $p = 0.10$ level of statistical significance, one-tailed tests.

** indicates a $p = 0.05$ level of statistical significance, one-tailed tests.

The standard errors have been corrected as discussed by Achen (1986).

With that in mind, it is important to note that these models do fit the data reasonably well. The Bush and Perot uncertainty models fit slightly better than the Clinton model (adjusted-R^2 of .17, .16, and .12, respectively). Moving to the information cost variables, they continue to perform as in the other models from previous elections. Political information is correctly signed and statistically significant in each model, while education works relatively well in the Bush and Clinton models. In general, gender and race also perform as expected, with both being positive and significant with only one exception (race in the Perot uncertainty model). However, other than partisan strength, none of the political connectedness variables performs well in these models. But partisan strength is again positive and significant (Clinton and Bush uncertainty), which indicates that partisan independents are *more certain* of the positions of the two major party candidates.

As in the 1976 data, the 1992 NES survey asked a series of questions which allowed respondents to state whether they recalled up to five advertisements aired by each presidential candidate. The most surprising result in the 1992 candidate uncertainty models is that I obtain a statistically significant result for recollection of candidate advertisements only in the Perot model. And the estimated effect is negative, which means that recalling advertisements by Perot *lowers the voter's uncertainty of Perot's ideological position.* This result may indicate that the long, "infomercial" nature of Perot's television advertisements, with the candidate and his succession of charts, did inform voters about Perot's ideological position.

Last, there is again clear evidence of selective information processing in the 1992 results. As in virtually all of the previous elections, here the candidate preference instrument is negative and statistically significant. There are some important differences to note about the candidate preference results in 1992, though. The effects of candidate preference on uncertainty are slightly stronger for Bush (the incumbent) than for either Clinton or Perot. This is similar to one of the results from earlier elections, since the general result was that uncertain voters appear to practice selective information processing more for challengers than for incumbents. Notice that unlike the 1980 results, the candidate preference coefficient in the Perot uncertainty equation is correctly signed and statistically significant. On the whole, the 1992 election was like the other elections in that voter preferences influenced their relative certainty of the candidate's ideological positions.

Voters and Candidate Uncertainty

This chapter has two major themes. The first is primarily substantive—what are the determinants of voter uncertainty? What factors appear to cause some voters to be more uncertain about the policy positions of presidential candidates, while other voters are very certain of the positions taken by the candidates? The theory posited in the first section, and in chapter 3, stated that the variation between voters in their uncertainty about candidate policy positions is caused by differences in information costs between voters, by differences in their exposure to political affairs and their attachments to the political system. Voters with lower information costs, and greater exposure and attachment to the political world, are more certain of the policy positions of the presidential candidates.

The two-stage models provided strong support for these theoretical expectations. Across the various candidates in each election, and across five presidential elections, I have shown that voter uncertainty about the candidates positions on issues is influenced by these three factors. Almost without exception, I demonstrated that voters with greater levels of education and political information are more certain of the candidates' positions in each election, while female and minority voters typically are less certain of these positions. Additionally, the more exposed a voter is to political coverage in the mass media, and the more she perceives herself to be effective in the political world, the more certain she is of the candidate's positions. Last, and somewhat surprisingly, the less the voter's attachment to the political party system—the *greater her political independence*—the more certain she is of the positions of each candidate.

These results have implications for many aspects of the voting behavior literature and for normative understandings of presidential elections. Two of the implications for the voting behavior literature I feel are especially important to note. First, this chapter shows quite clearly that information, and the costs of obtaining and processing that information, form the basis of what voters know of candidate policy positions. The importance of voter information and information costs has not received enough attention in the literature. It is clear from the models presented here that how much voters know about political affairs, how much information they are exposed to, and how easy it is for them to process and utilize this information, have important consequences for what they know of candidates in a particular election. Therefore, these results have clear normative implications for the conduct of presidential elections.

If the uncertainty voters have about presidential candidate policy positions has ramifications for their decisions—the subject of following chapters—the results just presented above provide a guidepost to some of the changes necessary to reduce voter uncertainty. Basically, the models demonstrate that to reduce the amount of uncertainty voters have about the presidential candidates, we must work toward decreasing the cost of obtaining and processing information, and we must also change voter attachments to the political system. Thus, as Thomas Jefferson argued in the quotation at the beginning of this chapter, to increase the quality of voter decision making, the solution is not to take important choices away from the voter, "but to inform their discretion."

This can be done in a number of ways. First, the results in this chapter indicate that any changes in the political system which serve to lower voter information costs reduce uncertainty—so increasing the level of political knowledge, education levels, and enhancing the opportunities for minorities to learn about political candidates will all serve to make voters more certain of the positions of presidential candidates on issues. Additionally, increasing exposure to the news media and enhancing the effectiveness of the individual in the political system will also work to reduce issue uncertainty. I have also presented some evidence which indicates that candidate debates and advertising—often despised by pundits and political commentators—may serve to better inform the electorate about candidate issue positions.

Yet the findings about the effects of political independence strike to the heart of a lasting debate in the literature concerning the nature of partisan attachments and independence. Campbell et al. argued that partisan attachments provide a set of mechanisms by which voters could evaluate, process, and structure their political thinking; and voters without such attachments (independents) would have more difficulty evaluating and structuring their knowledge of the policy positions of presidential candidates (1980, 132–33). But recent research, especially regarding partisan independence, has shown that many independent voters are actually more knowledgeable and participate more actively in politics than expected by Campbell et al. (Keith et al. 1986; Valentine and Van Wingen 1980).

The results in this chapter provide some support for the revisionist portrait of partisan independence. For, instead of being *less certain* of the positions of the presidential candidates on policy issues, the models in this chapter have instead shown that the weaker a voter's partisan ties, the *more certain* they are of a candidate's positions on the issues. This supports the recent research on partisan independence since it indicates that, indeed, partisan independents appear to be better informed about candidate policy positions than strong partisans.

Thus, instead of being a tool used by voters to reduce their costs of processing and obtaining political information, the results here imply that partisanship instead might be an impediment to how informed voters become of candidate positions on the issues. In this sense, partisanship might be used by poorer-informed voters as a simple information processing tool, but the use of this information filter might actually lead these voters to be less informed about the policy positions of the candidates. For example, a poorly informed voter who is a strong partisan identifier might avoid negative information about their party's candidate or focus only on negative information about the positions of each candidate, compared to the more independent voters, who do not process information about the candidates through a partisan filter. Therefore, partisan information processing, while a reasonable shortcut in the face of looming information costs, can actually lead those same voters to be *more uncertain.*

The results in this chapter also provide consistent support for my claim that voter evaluations of the candidates, or their preferences for the candidates, do in fact influence the amount of certainty they have about the candidates' positions. Consistently, the models supported the argument that the greater the likelihood that the voter supported a particular candidate, the more certain they were of that candidate, and the less certain they were of the opponent. This lends credence to the theoretical claims that one strategy voters might employ to cope with the flow of information during a campaign is selective processing based on prior candidate preferences. That is, the evidence here implies that voters are more likely to process and store information about the candidate they support, but not necessarily the opponent.

The second theme of this chapter is primarily methodological. I have shown that the measure of voter uncertainty based on the variation in voter placement of candidates on policy issues has empirical validity. I even employed a slightly different operationalization of uncertainty in the 1992 NES data, but obtained results for that measure (based only on ideological placements of the three candidates and not on any specific issue placements) that were consistent with the results from the previous elections. Thus, the candidate uncertainty models presented in this chapter have consistently shown that this operationalization of voter uncertainty of candidate positions is statistically related to a set of independent variables in theoretically expected manners. This is one way of demonstrating measurement validity (Cook and Campbell 1979). Thus, since the evidence supports this measure of voter uncertainty, I can confidently move to models employing this measure as an independent variable.

CHAPTER 7

Information, Issues, and Candidate Evaluations

You can fool some of the people all of the time, and all of the people some of the time, but you cannot fool all of the people all of the time.

—Abraham Lincoln, Clinton, Illinois, September 2, 1858

My first hypothesis about the effect of voter uncertainty about candidate policy positions is that the more uncertain a voter is about the candidate, the less likely they are to support the candidate. Whether this uncertainty is rooted in deliberate attempts by presidential candidates to present vague and ambiguous positions—to systematically fool the electorate—or is based on imperfections in information transmission and processing, it should decrease support for candidates. In short, voters are predicted to prefer the devil they know more about to the devil they know less about.

Testing this hypothesis is the primary concern of this chapter. Here I present the voting equations from the two-stage models and discuss the findings from these models. Two themes emerge in this chapter. First, as expected, voters clearly discount candidate policy uncertainty in their evaluations. But second, and of extreme importance, in each of the presidential elections under examination, *policy issues have had a significant impact in voter decision making*.

In the spatial model developed in chapter 3, the probability that a voter would support one candidate over the other (or that the voter would have *positive differential utility* for one candidate) was dependent on three factors: the squared distance between the voter and the candidate on one or multiple policy dimensions, a set of nonpolicy aspects of the voter's evaluation of the candidates, and the voter's uncertainty of the candidate's positions on the policy issues. In the evaluation models presented in this chapter, these three aspects of a voter's evaluation will be used as variables to understand the relative proba-

109

bility that the voter supported the Democratic candidate in the 1976, 1984, and 1988 elections, or the probability the voter supported the incumbent president in the 1980 and 1992 elections.

Here, the effects of policy issues are included as the sum of squared distances between the voter's position and each candidate's actual position on all of the policy issues, with the latter measured as the average position of the candidate in the survey data. The only exception to this operationalization of policy issues in the vote choice models arises in the context of the 1992 election. Given the absence of issue placement questions for Perot, I use ideological placements of the three candidates instead. The voter's uncertainty of the positions of the candidates is measured by the indicator discussed at length in chapter 4 and employed successfully in the previous chapter. To account for nonpolicy characteristics of the candidates, indicators for the voter's partisan identification and their evaluation of the leadership and personal qualities of the candidates are included. And last, two control variables are included in the models—gender and education—to help account for social and demographic influences on candidate evaluation not included in the model.[1]

Uncertainty and Issue Voting

The Politics of Conformity in 1976

The 1976 election is an excellent starting point for testing my hypotheses about the effects of voter uncertainty on candidate evaluation. Carter had been a little-known governor before the spring of 1976; and before being appointed to serve the remainder of Nixon's term, Ford was a low-key House Minority Leader. Neither candidate was a long-established national figure, and neither was very well-known at the beginning of the campaign. Partly as the result of their relative obscurity, but also partly caused by lingering memories of Watergate, both the candidates and the mass media were largely preoccupied during the general election with the character of the candidates. Yet this does not imply that matters of "substance," like their positions on policy issues like abor-

---

1. As noted in the previous chapter, these two demographic control variables are on the right-hand side of this equation to alleviate specification biases. That socio-demographic factors are important influences on candidate preferences and voting behavior, even after controlling for explicit political attitudes, is currently under considerable debate (for examples, see Achen 1992 and Leege et al. 1991). Unfortunately, other variables which might help to further reduce specification biases (race, income, socio-economic status) are difficult to employ in the model due to problems with their inaccurate measurement in the survey (socio-economic status), missing data (income), or extremely skewed distributions (very few minorities typically prefer Republican candidates).

tion, foreign affairs, or the domestic economy, were ignored. The statements of the candidates were covered widely in the press (Patterson 1980; Witcover 1977). But Ford and Carter were extremely moderate in most of their positions, and typically there was little which differentiated them on public policy.

Therefore, this could be an election in which voter uncertainty over the candidates' policy positions was exceptionally great, given two moderate and relatively poorly known candidates. Accordingly, it is reasonable to expect that this uncertainty may have strongly influenced voter evaluations of the candidates. Given that the campaign was focused on character questions, it would also not be surprising to see these nonpolicy aspects of candidate evaluation looming large in voter assessments of the candidates. This might have been further exacerbated by the difficulties associated with distinguishing between two relatively proximal candidates. But policy differences between the candidates might also have had an effect, since policy issues were discussed in the campaign, especially in the two fall debates.

Not surprisingly, these expectations are borne out in the evaluation models. The results are presented in table 7.1. Recall that the dichotomous dependent variable here is coded so that support for the Democratic candidate is the high category, and for the Republican candidate is the low category. Thus the parameter estimates express the relative effect of the particular variable on the probability of Carter support. I expect that the closer a voter is to Carter on the policy issues, the greater the voter's support for Carter (negative sign); the closer a voter to Ford on the issues, the lesser their support for Carter and the greater their support for Ford (positive sign). The more uncertain a voter is about Carter, the less likely they are to support Carter while greater uncertainty about Ford should lead to a greater likelihood of Carter support: thus I expect the uncertainty parameters to be negative for Carter and positive for Ford. The better a voter's evaluation of Carter's personal and professional characteristics, the more likely they should be to support Carter (positive sign); and likewise for Ford, where a higher evaluation of his character leads to greater probabilities of Ford support (negative sign). Last, Democratic identifiers should support Carter, and Republican identifiers Ford (negative sign).

In table 7.1, the first column gives the names of the independent variables in the model. The second column gives the parameter estimates and associated standard errors as estimated by the 2SCML model, and the third column gives estimates and standard errors from the 2SPLS model. The operationalizations and codings of the variables, a table giving descriptive statistics, and the reduced-form models used to correct for endogeneity in these two equations are discussed in appendix D.

Both models fit the data very well. Each correctly predicts slightly over 95 percent of the cases in the sample, and the χ^2 statistic for each model shows

TABLE 7.1.   Two-Stage Voting Models, 1976 Election

Independent Variables	2SCML Estimates	2SPLS Estimates
Constant	1.58**	1.71**
	.91	.91
Ford issue distance	.18**	.18**
	.08	.08
Carter issue distance	−.10*	−.11*
	.07	.07
Ford uncertainty	.66*	.68*
	.51	.51
Carter uncertainty	−.75*	−.77*
	.55	.55
Ford traits	−.40**	−.39**
	.05	.05
Carter traits	.33**	.33**
	.06	.06
Party identification	−.29**	−.29**
	.07	.07
Education	−.40**	−.39**
	.18	.18
Gender	−.35	−.34
	.31	.30
Ford error	−.61	
	.53	
Carter error	.64	
	.56	
% Correct	95.3	95.7
χ^2	699.8	697.6
Number of cases	464	464

Note: Entries are maximum-likelihood estimates, and their associated asymptotic standard errors.

* indicates a $p = .10$ level of statistical significance, one-tailed tests.

** indicates a $p = .05$ level of statistical significance, one-tailed tests.

2SCML is the River-Vuong conditional-maximum likelihood model; 2SPLS is the limited-information probit and least squares model. Candidate uncertainty in the 2SPLS model are instruments from a reduced form regression; the Ford and Carter error indicators are the error terms from the same regression.

that the models do perform vastly better than a null, intercept–only model.[2]

---

2. Neither of these goodness-of-fit statistics, however, is strong indicator of fit. The percent correctly predicted is strongly influenced by the distribution of high and low cases—when there are many high cases (say 80 percent of the cases are in the high category), the model will "correctly" predict better than when there are roughly similar frequencies of high and low cases. An alternative

Furthermore, the variables of interest are all correctly signed and statistically significant at reasonable levels.

First, in both models, the effects of uncertainty are correctly signed and are estimated relatively precisely. That is, the more uncertain a voter was of Carter, the lower the probability they would support Carter; the more uncertain a voter was of Ford, the lower the probability they would support Ford. This finding directly supports the first hypothesis advanced by the spatial model in chapter 3.

Worth additional notice, though, is the observation that the effects of policy uncertainty were greater for Carter uncertainty than for Ford uncertainty. In other words, the voter's uncertainty for Carter's positions had a greater effect on which candidate the voter supported than the voter's uncertainty of Ford's positions. These differential effects are probably the result of greater uncertainty about the positions of Carter, who was somewhat less visible before the general election began and who did not have the tools of an incumbent president to make his policy positions known to the electorate.

Relatedly, the estimates for the effects of policy issues upon candidate support in 1976 support this argument. Both squared issue-distance terms are correctly signed, yet the estimate for Carter issue distance is statistically significant at only the $p = .10$ level, while the similar estimate for Ford issue distance is estimated more precisely ($p = .05$). But the effect of issues is greater for Ford than for Carter, as witnessed by the relative sizes of the coefficients for Ford issue distance. With more uncertainty about Carter's positions, and with Carter uncertainty having more of an effect on candidate support, it is not surprising that Carter's positions on the issues had less of an influence on voter evaluations of the candidates in 1976.

---

criterion is the "proportional reduction in error" (Hildebrand et al. 1976). Here, a simple PRE measure would be the model's prediction rate relative to a naive prediction rate, the percentage falling into the modal category. In the 1976 data, the modal category was Carter support (53.9 percent). By this criterion, the 2SCML model predicts 41.4 percent better and the 2SPLS model predicts 41.8 percent better than the naive model. Of course, the PRE measure depends on what the naive prediction model is chosen to be by the researcher. The χ^2 statistic reported here is twice the difference between the log-likelihood of a naive model (with only an intercept included) and the log-likelihood of the actual models, often called the model's "deviance function" (McCullagh and Nelder 1983). The difference between log-likelihoods is often claimed to be distributed as a χ^2, with degrees of freedom equal to the number of restrictions. In the 2SCML model there are 11 degrees of freedom, and 9 in the 2SPLS model, making the χ^2 for each model highly significant. But the claim that the difference in log-likelihoods is approximated by a χ^2 is contingent upon the observations being distributed independently according to the binomial distribution and upon the number of observations being small. Thus as n increases, the approximation breaks down, and large differences will be observed (McCullagh and Nelder 1983). With these caveats in mind, I report the percent correctly predicted for all models, and the log-likelihood ratios for the binary probit models.

The other two sets of parameters of interest—the nonpolicy dimensions of candidate evaluations—are all correctly signed and precisely estimated. That is, the partisan affiliations of the voters clearly influenced their evaluations of Ford and Carter. Also, voter assessments of the characters of the candidates influenced their evaluations, with higher evaluations of a candidate's personal and professional characteristics leading to greater support for that candidate. But it is interesting to see that the effect of candidate characteristics on candidate support is greater for Ford than for Carter. Perhaps the decision by Ford and his advisors to focus on the character issue and to employ the Rose Garden strategy had some effect on the electorate, leading to more positive assessments of his character than for Carter.

Last, there are the two parameters from the reduced-form regressions for both Ford and Carter uncertainty (detailed in appendix D), presented for the 2SCML model. Recall the discussion of these two parameters from chapter 5: Rivers and Vuong (1988) demonstrate that these parameters give a robust test of exogeneity. The two parameters are larger than their standard errors, but the relative magnitudes of the parameters to their standard errors are not great enough for the parameters to be considered statistically significant. However, the likelihood-ratio test for the 2SCML model versus a similar model without these two parameters yields a χ^2 of 10.88, which is larger than the critical value of 5.99 at 2 degrees of freedom. Therefore, endogeneity between candidate evaluation and voter policy uncertainty is evident and needs to be accounted for in these models.

However, what is the magnitude of the estimated effects of these variables upon candidate evaluations in 1976? As discussed in chapter 5, the parameters in the evaluation models cannot be interpreted directly, since the models are nonlinear and the effect of any particular variable on the probability of supporting one candidate is dependent on the values of the other variables and parameters in the model. To give a more intuitive feel for the magnitude of two of the effects in the models (candidate uncertainty and squared policy issue distance upon candidate support), I utilize graphical methods (King 1989; McCullagh and Nelder 1983).[3] The results for the candidate policy uncertainty parameters are graphed in figure 7.1, and those for policy issue distance

---

3. Graphical methods involve simple simulations using the parameters of the model and some combination of values of the independent variables. Here, I set all but one of the independent variables to their mean values in the sample of voters used to estimate the model (the descriptive statistics are in appendix D). Then, I vary the one variable of interest across a range of values the variable takes in the actual data. This produces an estimate of the linear predictor for each value of the variable of interest, which is then transformed into a probability by the use of the appropriate link function. In each of the graphical interpretations for the 1976, 1984, and 1988 elections, I use the parameters from the 2SPLS model. For the 1980 and 1992 elections, I use the parameters from the multinomial probit models.

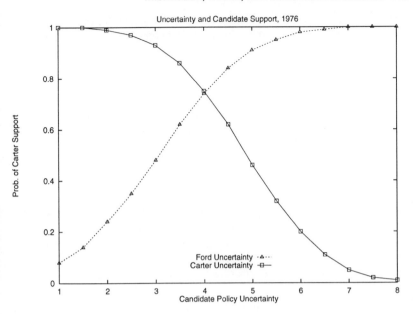

Fig. 7.1.   Effects of uncertainty, 1976.

in figure 7.2.

In figure 7.1 the voter's uncertainty about each candidate's policy positions is graphed along the *x*-axis, and the probability that the voter would support Carter on the *y*-axis. The dark line gives the effect of Ford policy uncertainty on probability of Carter support, while the light line gives the effect of Carter policy uncertainty on the probability the voter would support Carter (holding the other variables constant at their sample mean values). The strong effect of uncertainty on candidate evaluation is clear in this graph. Take two identical voters, with mean values on all the variables, but one is very certain of Carter's positions on the issues (1) and the other is uncertain of Carter's positions (5). The graph indicates that the certain voter has a very high probability of supporting Carter, while the uncertain voter is much less likely to support Carter. Thus, by changing the relative uncertainty of the voter from very certain to relatively uncertain, the probability of supporting Carter in 1976 changes by over .50.

To examine the relative impacts of these two variables, note that both Ford and Carter uncertainty had roughly similar distributions; the uncertainty means were 3.96 for Ford and 4.08 for Carter while the standard deviations were 3.03 for Ford and 3.07 for Carter. Under the assumption that these two variables are normally distributed, we would expect that 65 percent of the sample would have had uncertainty for both candidates within one standard deviation of the mean, ranging approximately from 1 to 7.[4] Across this range, it is apparent that Carter uncertainty does have a marginally larger impact of candidate evaluation than Ford uncertainty; there is a .95 change in probability of Carter support across this range of Carter uncertainty and a .92 change in the same range for Ford uncertainty.

Next, consider the influence of policy issues in the 1976 election. As was widely discussed in both the popular and academic press following the 1976 election, many believed that the election was predominantly concerned with the characters of the candidates, not their policy positions. Additionally, it is apparent in both table 7.1 and figure 7.1 that policy uncertainty about both candidates had substantial effects in this election. Thus, I expect to find the magnitude of the effects of policy issues in this election to be relatively small. But consider figure 7.2, which is similar to figure 7.1, except here the squared distance between the voter and the particular candidate is given on the x-axis. Thus, the dark line gives the effect of the squared distance between the voter and Ford's position on the issues on the probability of supporting Carter, while the light line gives the influence of the squared distance between Carter and the voter on the probability of Carter support.

The influence of policy issues in the 1976 election is striking. Across the full range of the squared distance between the mean voter and Ford, there is a .61 change in probability. Likewise, there is a .43 change in probability of Carter support across the full range of the squared distance between an average voter and Carter's positions on the issues. The relative magnitude of the effect of issues on candidate support is quite different for each candidate, with the distance between the voter and Ford having .18 greater change than the similar distance between the voter and Carter.

Therefore, the 1976 election supports the first hypothesis: voter uncertainty does have a strong effect on voter evaluations of presidential candidates. The greater a voter's uncertainty of a candidate, the less likely the voter is to support that candidate. Additionally, I have shown that in an election characterized as "candidate-focused" rather than "issue-focused," and where policy uncertainty had large effects, that policy issues still had a strong impact on voter evaluations of Ford and Carter.

---

4. As I will show in subsequent chapters, though, the distributions of uncertainty for the presidential candidates examined in this book are not normally distributed. In fact, they are by definition bounded on the left by zero (a variance or standard deviation is, by definition, positive), with a long tail to the left. I only mention the normal distribution in this context for convenience.

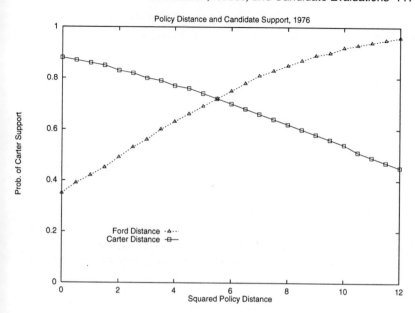

Fig. 7.2. **Effects of policy issues, 1976.**

Carter, Reagan and Anderson in 1980

The contest between the two major-party candidates in 1980 had both similarities with and differences from the 1976 election. The similarities with the 1976 elections were that much of the discussion by the candidates and the mass media in 1980 concerned the leadership and managerial abilities of the candidates, and also the vastly different signals the two campaigns sent concerning these aspects of the candidates' characters. Cavanagh and Sundquist argued, "One must concede the stark difference between the leadership and managerial images projected by Jimmy Carter and Ronald Reaga—the one seemingly overwhelmed by events and forces outside his or the nation's control, the other confidently articulating and pursuing a vision of national restoration" (1985, 50).

Another similarity was that despite the focus on dimensions of candidate characte, the campaign was also about the record, primarily economic, of the incumbent administration. In both the 1976 and 1980 elections, inflation and unemployment were of importance in the campaign. Indeed, it was during the 1980 debates that Reagan asked, "Are you better off than you were four years ago?" (Drew 1981, 325). Additionally, domestic and foreign policy issues were widely discussed, from social issues to defense policy. Therefore, while popular and academic opinion again pointed to the primacy of character concerns in the 1980 election, it is clear that policy issues were also very prominent.

But one major difference was apparent between 1976 and 1980. Both Carter and Reagan by the time of the 1980 general election were quite prominent national figures, well-known throughout the national electorate. Of course, Carter had been the incumbent president for the previous four years. But Reagan was a prominent Republican, having been a long-term activist in the right wing of the Republican party and a two-time presidential candidate. Also, Reagan's conservative affiliations were a much greater contrast to Carter's ideological and policy positions than were Ford's.

The plight of the domestic economy in 1979 and 1980, and the constant concerns about American foreign policy, caused many to wonder about Carter's competence and leadership abilities. However, for many voters searching for an alternative to Carter, Reagan may not have been wholly satisfactory. This became especially apparent toward the end of the primary campaigns, as it grew increasingly clear that Reagan would become the Republican nominee. A strategic opportunity thus arose, which John Anderson exploited, who on April 24, 1980 announced that he would run as a third-party alternative to Carter and Reagan.

But a candidate running for president outside of the two major political parties faces an uphill fight. Without the resource base of a major political party—financial and organizational—Anderson's problem was remaining visible to the national electorate. To the extent that he could succeed at remaining visible, Anderson could get his message across to those constituencies dissatisfied with both Carter and Reagan: younger, better educated, urban, affluent, and professional voters (Kessel 1984). The messages of Anderson's campaign for "National Unity" were picked to appeal to these groups of voters, with emphasis placed on investment in urban infrastructure and on improving civil rights and liberties. And since Anderson was a moderate Republican, positioned ideologically and on most major policy issues between Carter and Reagan, getting this message to these potential supporters (many of whom were in the ideological center themselves) clearly was an imperative for the "National Unity" campaign.

Success as a third-party candidate lacking substantial resources requires a carefully constructed and implemented campaign strategy. The Anderson campaign quickly developed their plan of attack in 1980:

> John Anderson's ultimate goal was to become the second candidate so that voters would think of Reagan versus Anderson, or Carter versus Anderson,

rather than Reagan versus Carter with Anderson being considered only in case the first two were unsatisfactory . . . They recognized that they had to fight Carter first in order to get the voters to eventually think of Reagan and Anderson as alternatives. Carter was the immediate tactical opponent. If all went well, Reagan would be the ultimate strategic opponent. (Kessel 1984, 183)

This plan was followed through late October, with Anderson focusing primarily on Carter and showing some success with his attacks. Anderson demonstrated enough support, furthermore, that the League of Women Voters decided to include Anderson in the debate scheduled for October 21.

This was a make-or-break moment for Anderson's candidacy. The Carter campaign decided not to participate in this debate, so as to avoid giving legitimacy to the Anderson campaign. But Reagan agreed to the debate, and both candidates engaged in showing the differences in their personalities and on many of the policy issues. While many polls showed that voters thought Anderson did well in the debate, it was apparent that he had not done well enough to swing many Reagan voters his way. This conclusion by the "political elite" did not lead to an increase in free media coverage of Anderson's campaign after the debate. Without a big increase in free media coverage Anderson's campaign was in an impossible situation since the "National Unity" effort did not have sufficient resources to make many major media buys.

Thus, Anderson's candidacy presents an interesting possibility to examine the effects of voter policy uncertainty on candidate evaluations and is a second major difference between the 1980 and 1976 elections. In spite of his efforts to get his "National Unity" message across to potential supporters, Anderson had great difficulty remaining visible especially in the fading weeks of the race, so it is likely that many voters were very uncertain of Anderson's position on the issues. This policy uncertainty should have dramatically influenced Anderson support.

Also it will be interesting to see if Anderson's strategic efforts had any payoff among the electorate. Two aspects of his campaign can be examined with the data available from the 1980 election. One is the effects of policy issues on Anderson support. Anderson attempted to articulate a set of policy positions, carefully crafted to appeal to a certain constituency. To the extent he was able to get these positions across to the electorate clearly, his positions on the issues should have influenced whether voters supported his candidacy. The other is the temporal aspect of Anderson's strategy—attacking Carter first and then following up on Reagan. In the period before the October 21 debate, Anderson focused his campaign on Carter, intending to turn his guns on Reagan after he had established his base among the Carter constituencies. But

Anderson faded *before he had this opportunity.* That is, while the October 21 debate with Reagan could have constituted the beginning of Anderson's move to claim Reagan supporters, his rapid move from the headlines to the back-pages obviated this strategy (Kessel 1984).

Testing these hypotheses using the 1980 NES data, however, is complicated by the presence of three candidates in the race and by the paucity of Anderson voters in the survey data. The econometric implications of these problems have been discussed in chapter 5. Briefly, the evaluation models used to test these hypotheses differ from the models discussed in the previous sections of this chapter in two ways. First, with three candidates in the race, the use of a binary vote choice model is inappropriate, which makes the use of the multinomial probit model necessary. Second, the multinomial probit model with three candidates requires a different set of normalizations than the binary choice model. The most important of these is the estimation of parameters which give the effect of a variable on the relative likelihood of supporting Anderson to Carter, and Reagan to Carter; thus there are two vectors of parameters to be estimated and presented. Additionally, the issue distance parameters are estimated here as choice-specific coefficients, not individual-specific coefficients (Alvarez and Nagler 1995).

The multinomial probit estimates for 1980 are given in table 7.2. The estimates for Anderson-Carter are in the second column and those for Reagan-Carter in the third column. At the bottom I give the estimated error correlations between the three candidates' utility functions. In general, the multinomial probit model fits the 1980 data reasonably well, since it correctly classifies 78.7 percent of the votes for the three candidates. Yet, this classification statistic is somewhat misleading, since it obscures the fact that most of this predictive power is for Reagan (87.3 percent of Reagan voters are correctly classified) and Carter (85.0 percent of Carter voters are correctly classified). Unfortunately, in the data set used to estimate this model, there are only 469 voters for whom complete information is available, and only 44 of these were Anderson voters. And only 2 of these Anderson voters are correctly predicted by the model to have voted for Anderson (4.5 percent). The model, given that there is so little information in the sample about Anderson voters, does a poor job of predicting Anderson support.[5]

Despite the inability of the model to predict Anderson voting accurately, most of the coefficient estimates are correctly signed and statistically significant. Recall from my discussion above that the 1980 campaign is thought to have revolved around discussions of candidate character. This is reflected in

---

5. Of the incorrectly classified Anderson voters, the model predicts that 26 would vote for Reagan (59.1 percent of the Anderson voters in the sample) while 16 (36.4 percent of the Anderson voters) would vote for Carter.

TABLE 7.2.   Two-Stage Voting Models, 1980 Election

Independent Variables	Probability of Voting For:	
	Anderson/Carter	Reagan/Carter
Issue distance	−.25**	
	.05	
Constant	.18	.09
	.88	1.1
Reagan uncertainty		−.48*
		.35
Anderson uncertainty	−.23*	
	.17	
Carter uncertainty	.40*	.97**
	.29	.58
Reagan traits		.07*
		.06
Anderson traits	.03	
	.02	
Carter traits	−.14**	−.18**
	.06	.05
Party identification	.18**	.55**
	.10	.12
Education	.26*	−.03
	.16	.14
Gender	.10	−.24
	.26	.31
σ_{AR}	−.04	
	.68	
σ_{AC}	.62**	
	.34	
% Correct	78.5%	
Number of cases	469	

Note: Entries are maximum-likelihood estimates, and their associated asymptotic standard errors.

* indicates a $p = .10$ level of statistical significance, one-tailed test.

** indicates a $p = .05$ level of statistical significance, one-tailed test.

the estimated effects of candidate traits in 1980. While both Anderson and Reagan trait assessments positively influenced the probability a person would vote for one of those two candidates relative to Carter, it seems that Carter trait assessments had a stronger influence on the vote in 1980. Partisanship also mattered for voters in 1980, all else constant, serving to more strongly distinguish Reagan and Carter than Anderson and Carter.

Notice next the estimated effects of candidate policy uncertainty in the

1980 election. Recall that the expected pattern of coefficients in the multinomial probit model would be that both Anderson and Reagan uncertainty should have negative signs, while Carter uncertainty should be positively signed. That is exactly what is observed in the multinomial probit results, and each of the uncertainty term estimates are statistically significant at the $p = .10$ level (one-tailed test). The estimates indicate that candidate policy uncertainty mattered in the 1980 election, and it mattered just as the theoretical model predicted.

Also notice that the issue-distance coefficient is negative and statistically significant. This implies that the farther a voter was from one of the candidates across the various issues in the model, the less he or she preferred the candidate, holding nonpolicy and uncertainty constant. So despite the common wisdom that the 1980 election focused on candidate characteristics, it seems that issue-position information about the three candidates was available to the electorate and that this information influenced which candidate voters chose in this election.

The last aspects of the multinomial probit results are the estimated error correlations. Of the two error correlation estimates, one is statistically significant, the positive error correlation for Anderson-Carter. The other error correlation estimate is close to zero, and is not statistically significant. However, these results imply that the IIA assumption is violated in this case.

This pattern of error correlations indicates that voters saw Anderson and Carter as relatively similar choices (significant and positive estimated error correlation). What is interesting about these error correlation estimates is that they imply that Anderson's strategy—to establish his differences with Carter first, and then to turn his attention to Reagan—appears to have backfired. The error correlation estimates indicate that, if anything, voters saw Carter and Anderson as similar. By focusing his campaign on Carter while he was a visible presidential candidate, Anderson may have simply attracted attention to his similarities with Carter, not their differences.

Of course, the multinomial probit results are difficult to interprete directly, so I again turn to a graphical presentation of the two important sets of coefficients—the effects of candidate uncertainty and issue positions on candidate choice. Again, I examine the effects of uncertainty first, by examining the effect that changing the level of uncertainty that an "average" voter has on the likelihood the voter would support the candidate. In figure 7.3 I present these results.

Each line in figure 7.3 traces the effect of voter uncertainty for each candidate on the likelihood that this "average" voter would support the candidate. The most important information in figure 7.3 is the slope of each of these lines. All are negative, which verifies the key prediction about the effect of candidate uncertainty on candidate choice: holding all of the other effects in the model

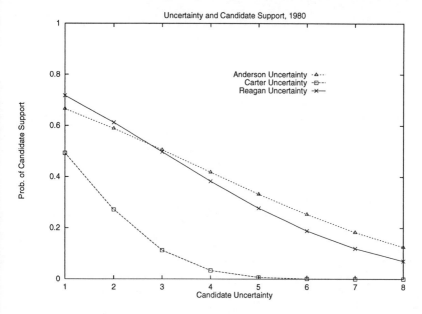

Fig. 7.3.   Effects of uncertainty, 1980.

constant, the more uncertain a voter was of the positions of these three candidates on the issues, the less likely the voter was to support the candidates.

But the magnitude of the effects varies between the three candidates in an interesting way. For Reagan, there is about a .70 shift in probability of Reagan support over the entire range of the graph; that is, if this voter was very certain of Reagan's positions on the issues she would be very likely to vote for Reagan (with probability of almost .80), but if this voter was very uncertain of Reagan's positions, she would be quite unlikely to vote for Reagan (probability of around .10). The change in probability of Carter support is also quite large across this range of Carter uncertainty, at approximately a .60 point change. But the change in probability of Anderson support is less, at around .40 points. Thus, issue uncertainty had the least effect on Anderson support, but the most effect on Reagan support.

What about the effect of issue distances in 1980? Earlier I argued that there were competing expectations for the role of issues in the 1980 election; however, the multinomial probit results indicated that issues did matter to voters in this election. To see how much they mattered, I again use graphical methods to examine the influence of candidate issue distance on candidate support for an average voter. These results are shown in figure 7.4

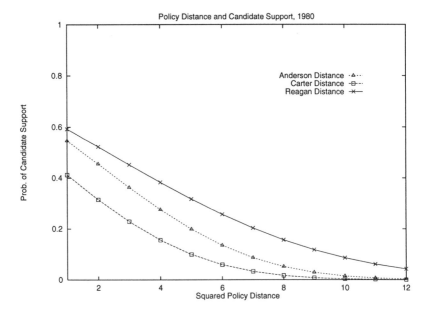

Fig. 7.4.   Effects of policy issues, 1980.

Each line in figure 7.4 gives the probability that this average voter would support the particular candidate dependent upon the distance between the voter and the candidate. Again, despite the arguments to the contrary, *issues did matter strongly in the 1980 election*, controlling for uncertainty and nonissue effects. So even though the 1980 campaign seemed to be about candidate character, or Carter's performance, issue information was available and exploited by voters.

Again, the effects of issues differed across the three candidates. Across the range of issue distances for this representative voter, issue distances had roughly the same impact for Reagan and Carter. By moving the position of Reagan or Carter from near this voter to far from this voter, there is a .60 or .50 change in the likelihood the voter would support Reagan or Carter, respectively. Thus, for the two major party candidates, their issue positions mattered greatly to voters, controlling for other factors.

But the same is not true for Anderson. Across this range of issue distance, there is only about a .30 change in probability the voter would support Anderson, which is almost half of the effect that issue distances had on voting for Reagan or Carter. Thus, either Anderson did not effectively get issue information across to the electorate through his "National Unity" campaign, or voters did not use issues in their evaluation of Anderson as a presidential candidate.

Where Was the Beef in 1984?

The 1984 contest is perhaps most interesting in terms of what it might have been, instead of what it actually was. In 1983 the prospects for a Democratic victory looked promising, with the economy edging out of recession and with Reagan's popularity relatively low. Yet by early fall, this scenario had abruptly changed, with a booming economy, falling unemployment and inflation, and with a corresponding 15 percent increase in Reagan's approval rating. All of these factors may have produced a virtually insurmountable lead for Reagan by August 1984 (Kiewiet and Rivers 1985).

This allowed the Reagan campaign to mimic the Rose Garden strategy: keep the candidate out of uncontrolled media and campaign events, and craft all presidential appearances and pronouncements to keep Reagan looking presidential. The robust economy and approval ratings, however, also allowed the Reagan campaign to avoid speaking about policy positions. Instead, and understandably, the theme of the campaign centered on Reagan's leadership abilities, revolving around the slogan "Leadership That's Working" (Kernell 1985).

Mondale, a former vice president who did not suffer greatly from a lack of visibility, turned to the strategy that had served him well before his rise to national prominence in 1976: pull together the many coalitions of the Democratic party and win the election on the back of the party organization. But this coalition-building approach had two implications for Mondale's election chances. First, it led the Mondale campaign into a peculiar media and advertising strategy. Mondale perceived his strengths to be pulling together coalitions and striking bargains between conflicting constituencies—not appearing often in either paid or free media spots. The result of this strategy was that the Mondale message did not get across to the electorate.

And second, it was not clear to the electorate (or even to the campaign) what the Mondale message was: "The coalitional strategy also failed the candidate by leaving him without a message . . . with which to appeal to voters beyond the core of the Democratic constituency" (Kernell 1985, 131). And on balance, whatever the voters might have heard of the Mondale message, its appeal among many of the potential "swing" constituencies in 1984 may have been tempered by the negative publicity surrounding the coalition-building approach—the claim that Mondale was the puppet of Democratic special interests.

Therefore, while Mondale and Reagan were perhaps the most ideologically distinct pairing of presidential candidates since 1976, the campaign never placed a great focus on the ideological or policy differences between these two candidates. And neither candidate desired to focus on these differences, with Reagan campaigning on his leadership abilities from the Rose Garden, and with Mondale presenting no consistent policy- or ideologically-based information to the electorate. Last, both candidates shunned uncontrolled media and campaign exposure, which could have served to further attenuate the possibility of a campaign based on policy issues.

Thus, there are competing expectations about what the evaluation models will reveal. On one hand, with two candidates from polar ends of the ideological spectrum, one might expect that the amount of issue voting would be high in 1984, and that the effects of voter uncertainty about candidate positions would be relatively low. Alternatively, since the campaign was not focused on policy issues and the flow of information to the voters through paid and free media sources may not have been as extensive or as substantive as other elections, the expectation might be that uncertainty was high, issue voting low, and that voters based their decision more on nonpolicy aspects of the candidates—their party or character traits.

Table 7.3 gives the results of the evaluation models for the 1984 election. These two models both fit the data very well. Both the 2SCML and 2SPLS models predict 91.5 percent of the cases in the sample correctly, and they have highly significant χ^2 statistics. Additionally, the relevant variables are all correctly signed, and most are highly significant.

However, both of the candidate uncertainty terms are statistically insignificant, with neither of the estimates being larger than their standard errors. This implies that the uncertainty voters had of these two candidates had very little estimated impact in this election. Whatever impact uncertainty may have had in 1984, moreover, may have been slightly greater for Reagan than Mondale.

There are two possible explanations for this result, one methodological and one substantive. The methodological question concerns the extent of endogeneity in this data between uncertainty and evaluation. Neither of the two reduced form error coefficients in the second column are statistically significant. Yet, the likelihood-ratio test recommended by Rivers and Vuong (1989) yields a χ^2 value of 6.84, which is greater than the critical level at $p = .05$ of 5.99, with two degrees of freedom. Therefore, it does appear that even though the uncertainty estimates are statistically insignificant, there is sufficient endogeneity to justify the use of the two-stage models.

Note, however, that the issue distance estimates are certainly significant. Also, they express almost identical effects of Reagan and Mondale issue distance on the voter's probability of supporting Mondale. The same is true of the candidate trait estimates, which are statistically significant and of identical magnitude.

The graphs in figure 7.5 present the effects of policy uncertainty on Mon-

TABLE 7.3.   Two-Stage Voting Models, 1984 Election

Independent Variables	2SCML Estimates	2SPLS Estimates
Constant	.60	.61
	.74	.74
Reagan issue distance	.08**	.09**
	.03	.03
Mondale issue distance	−.11**	−.11**
	.04	.04
Reagan uncertainty	.31	.28
	.39	.39
Mondale uncertainty	−.22	−.19
	.29	.28
Reagan traits	−.15**	−.15**
	.03	.03
Mondale traits	.15**	.15**
	.04	.04
Party identification	−.29**	−.28**
	.07	.07
Education	−.03	−.04
	.10	.10
Gender	.06	.06
	.16	.16
Reagan error	−.27	
	.39	
Mondale error	.22	
	.30	
% Correct	91.5	91.5
χ^2	1506.0	1504.4
Number of cases	856	856

Note: Entries are maximum-likelihood estimates and their associated asymptotic standard errors.

* indicates a $p = .10$ level of statistical significance, one-tailed tests.

** indicates a $p = .05$ level of statistical significance, one-tailed tests.

dale support, following the procedures used above. These graphs tell a different story than did the model estimates. Here the curves indicate that uncertainty about each candidate had a strong effect on the probability of candidate support. Mondale uncertainty, across the entire range of values in the graph, shows a .37 change in probability of Mondale support. Uncertainty about the policy positions of Reagan, however, has a .67 change in probability of supporting Mondale, across the entire range of uncertainty about his position for an average voter. These graphs, in addition to the results in table 7.3, suggest

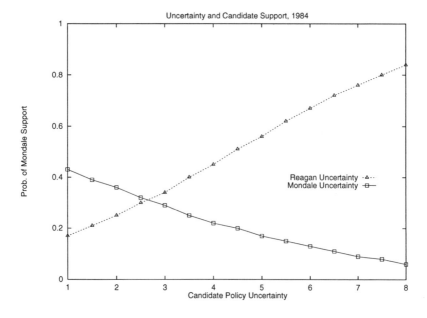

Fig. 7.5. Effects of uncertainty, 1984.

that voter uncertainty about the positions of both candidates mattered in 1984 and that Reagan uncertainty may have had a greater effect on voter evaluations than Mondale uncertainty. However, the estimates of this uncertainty are not very precise, with large standard errors.

Figure 7.6 presents graphical interpretations of the estimated effects of distances between the candidates and the voters on the policy issues. Again, the squared issue distances are on the x-axis; the dark line gives the curve for the distance between Reagan and the voter, while the light line expresses the effects of the distance between Mondale and the voter on the probability of supporting Mondale.

The effects of issue distances depicted in the curves in figure 7.6 are virtually identical for both candidates, as noted above in the discussion of the empirical results. They show that policy issues did matter in this election. For both candidates, across the total range of squared issue distances, there is an almost .40 change in the probability of supporting Mondale. Therefore, the conclusion is that issues did matter in this election, in spite of the best efforts of the candidates to ignore them in 1984.

So the 1984 election is somewhat of a puzzle. This election could have been one in which policy issues were a central concern, since there were clear

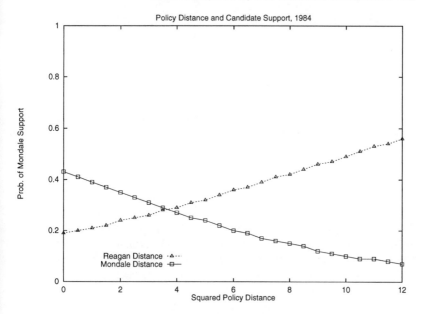

Fig. 7.6. **Effects of policy issues, 1984.**

differences between Mondale and Reagan that were perceived by the electorate. And with clear differences, the effect of uncertainty about their positions might have been reduced. But the candidates chose not to emphasize issues or ideology heavily, which might have had the effect of making it more difficult for voters to determine the positions of the candidates on the issues and to vote accordingly. Thus the empirical results: both the voter's uncertainty about the positions of the candidates and the distance between the voter and the candidates on these policy issues appear to have had some, but not substantial influence in 1984.

Going Negative in 1988

In 1988, neither candidate was an incumbent. However, Bush had some advantages similar to presidential incumbency after serving as Reagan's vice president for the previous eight years. Additionally, the economic recovery which had begun in the early stages of the 1984 campaign was still roaring along, with unemployment in July 1988 reaching its lowest level since the early 1970s. So in a number of ways, Bush was in a good position once the general election campaign began, since he was associated closely with the popular Ronald Rea gan and could plausibly claim some credit for the robustness of the economy.

Despite these strengths, Bush had a number of weaknesses. The most apparent of these was a common perception of Bush's character—the so-called wimp factor—and the surprisingly negative evaluations of Bush by many voters. Yet Dukakis proved unable to capitalize on either of these potential weaknesses.

The inability of Dukakis to hold his early lead over Bush has been widely attributed to disarray in his campaign organization (Germond and Witcover 1989; Morrison et al. 1988). There is no doubt that indecisiveness and heavy-handedness in the Dukakis campaign was partly to blame. However, this explanation overlooks a number of important facts about Dukakis and his campaign strategy. One of these facts is that Dukakis, even though he was the governor of a major state, was not very well known nationally. He had not run a national campaign before 1988, and consequently many voters did not know very much about Dukakis even after the Democratic primaries were concluded. Additionally, Dukakis deliberately chose to follow what might be called a Massachusetts Garden strategy—stay at the governor's helm as much as possible, and campaign on competence and managerial abilities. Therefore, much of the 17 percent Dukakis lead in July 1988 was probably very "soft," and could be eroded once the electorate became familiar with both of the candidates.

It is clear that, with the help of the attack team surrounding Bush, the electorate became familiar with the candidates and their differences. While Dukakis made his pitch about his competence and managerial abilities, the Republicans set out to probe the soft spots in Dukakis's support:

> The Republicans devised a strategy for victory. They would launch an attack campaign against Dukakis, painting him as a liberal who was out of step with the values of the American people. The second aspect of this strategy was that Bush would launch much of the attack himself. In this way Bush would fill in the blanks for the voters about Dukakis, boosting his opponent's negatives, while at the same time reducing his own negatives by creating a new strong and positive image . . . Bush intended at least to give them something to vote against. (Abramson et al. 1989, 44)

Thus, the 1988 election is likely to be one in which both policy issues and policy uncertainty have important effects on voter evaluations of the candidates. Policy issues are likely to be important, since the Bush strategy was to paint Dukakis as a liberal and to point out how out of step with the American electorate his positions on issues as diverse as defense spending, crime, and the Pledge of Allegiance were, while only hinting about Bush's own positions. While focusing on many different issues, the Bush attack was not intended to

TABLE 7.4.   Two-Stage Voting Models, 1988 Election

Independent Variables	2SCML Estimates	2SPLS Estimates
Constant	2.22**	1.88**
	.85	.83
Bush issue distance	.18**	.20**
	.04	.04
Dukakis issue distance	−.15**	−.16**
	.04	.04
Bush uncertainty	.98	.75
	.79	.76
Dukakis uncertainty	−.93*	−.71
	.71	.69
Bush traits	−.15*	−.17**
	.09	.10
Dukakis traits	.09	.12
	.11	.11
Party identification	−.27**	−.28**
	.09	.09
Education	−.09	−.04
	.11	.10
Gender	.37*	.30*
	.23	.22
Bush error	.80	
	.71	
Dukakis error	−.84	
	.78	
% Correct	93.1	92.0
χ^2	1350.5	1330.1
Number of cases	691	691

Note: Entries are maximum-likelihood estimates, and their associated asymptotic standard errors.
* indicates a $p = .10$ level of statistical significance, one-tailed tests.
** indicates a $p = .05$ level of statistical significance, one-tailed tests.

be very specific, and hence uncertainty should also have had a large effect on voter support for the candidates.

The results of the two-stage models for 1988 are in table 7.4. Descriptions of the variables and the reduced-form models are in appendix D. This table is identical to the preceding tables, with the variable labels in the first column, the 2SCML estimates in the second column, and the 2SPLS estimates in the third column. As is seen in the summary statistics for each model, they both fit the data quite well, with highly significant χ^2 statistics, and with prediction success rates above 92 percent. Additionally, all of the coefficients are correctly signed, and most are statistically significant.

Surprisingly, the uncertainty terms do vary depending upon which model was employed, but appear roughly similar for both Bush and Dukakis uncertainty. In the 2SCML model, the Dukakis uncertainty estimate is statistically significant at the $p = .10$ level, and the Bush uncertainty estimate falls just below that minimal standard. However, in the 2SPLS model, the coefficients fall in magnitude, while the standard errors remain roughly constant. This change is likely to be the consequence of the substitution of instrumental variables for the uncertainty terms, which might account for the diminished estimates. And if the instrumental variables are introducing inconsistency in the 2SPLS estimates, it is also the case that the reduced-form error estimates (taken from the same equation) are probably introducing inefficiency in the uncertainty estimates in the 2SCML model. This explanation would account for the large standard errors associated with the candidate uncertainty estimates in both models.[6]

Furthermore, the evidence does indicate that endogeneity is present in this data. Both of the estimates for the reduced form errors are larger than their standard errors, but they are not statistically significant. Yet the likelihood-ratio test produces a χ^2 of 17.5, which is significant at a $p = .05$ level. Thus, in each of the presidential elections examined so far in this chapter, there is empirical support for the argument that candidate uncertainty and evaluations are jointly related.

Also as expected, the issue distance estimates are statistically significant and in the correct directions. Voters who were closer to Dukakis on the issues were more likely to support him, while voters closer to Bush on the issues were more likely to support Bush. There is only a small difference, moreover, in the apparent impact of issues between the two candidates.

However, there is a moderate difference in the apparent impact of candidate traits in these results. The estimates on the trait variables have relatively large standard errors, which accounts for the inability of the Dukakis estimate to reach a minimal level of statistical significance. But the difference here is interesting. Both candidates campaigned on character issues—Bush in an attempt to get away from the wimp factor, and Dukakis in an attempt to persuade voters that he was more competent to run the government. These results

---

6. These differences could also be caused by a substantial degree of correlation between the error terms of the uncertainty and evaluation equations. One of the findings of my Monte Carlo analysis in Alvarez (1995) is that substantial differences exist between 2SPLS and 2SCML only when the errors across equations show high correlation. Of the models discussed in this chapter, only here has such a major difference between the two-stage conditional maximum-likelihood and probit least squares estimation procedures been observed.

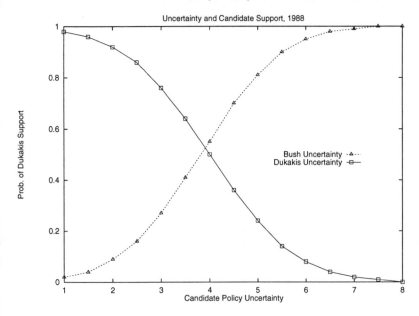

Fig. 7.7.   Effects of uncertainty, 1988.

indicate that Bush's trait factors had a greater effect on candidate support in 1988 than did Dukakis's traits. Judged by the distributions of these trait variables, in which Bush's trait evaluations were somewhat greater in the aggregate than Dukakis's, it appears that Bush might have been successful in convincing many voters about his own character and perhaps casting some doubt about Dukakis's (see appendix D for information on the distributions of these variables).

Turning now to the magnitude of the effects of candidate uncertainty and issue distances in 1988, I present figure 7.7 which gives the graphs of candidate uncertainty and the probability of Dukakis support and figure 7.8 which gives the effects of issue distances on Dukakis support. As was true for the earlier graphs, the y-axis gives the probability of Democratic candidate support, and the x-axis gives the range of the independent variable under examination.

In figure 7.7, the dark line gives the effect of Bush uncertainty on the probability of Dukakis support, and the light line gives the effect of Dukakis uncertainty on the probability of Dukakis support. Despite the relatively large standard errors on the uncertainty estimates in table 7.4, the magnitude of the effects of candidate uncertainty in the 1988 election is apparent in this figure. Additionally, as was apparent in the relative similarity of the estimates, the

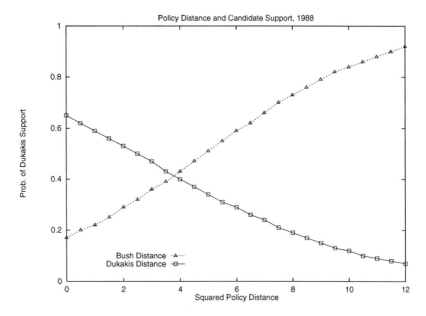

Fig. 7.8.   Effects of policy issues, 1988.

strengths of the effect of uncertainty about each candidate on Dukakis support were virtually identical.

The large effect of uncertainty in 1988 can be seen by using the graphs in figure 7.7 to determine the differences in candidate support for the two average voters. The voter certain of Bush's position would be .79 less likely to support Dukakis than the average voter who is relatively uncertain of Bush's positions on the issues. Likewise, the average voter who is certain of Dukakis's positions on the issues would be .74 more likely to support Dukakis than the voter who was relatively uncertain of where Dukakis stood on the issues. Thus, in spite of the apparent inefficiencies in the model estimates, voter uncertainty of both candidates had relatively large influences on candidate evaluations in 1988. Again, this is confirmation of the hypothesis advanced in chapter 3.

It is apparent in figure 7.8, moreover, that policy issues did figure strongly in voter preferences in this election. Here, the *x*-axis gives the squared distance between the voter and the respective candidate on the issues; the dark line plots the effect of Bush issue distances, and the light line the effect of Dukakis issue distances, on the probability that an average voter would support Dukakis.

Notice that across the range of issue distances for Bush, the probability of Dukakis support drops by .75 as one moves from very near to Bush to very distant from Bush; a voter close to Bush is unlikely to vote for Dukakis while a voter far from Bush is quite likely to vote for Dukakis. The effect of Dukakis's distance from our average voter was somewhat less. This average voter's probability of supporting Dukakis drops by .58 across the entire range of squared issue distances. Both of these curves, then, demonstrate that in the 1988 election, policy issues played a strong role in how voters evaluated both Bush and Dukakis.

1992 and Perot

The 1992 election, which candidate Bush called "this crazy election year," showed some parallels with prior campaigns, yet had many unique features. As in 1988, Bush was a candidate, but this time as an incumbent with his own presidential record to defend. This record was not particularly strong, since Bush had broken a well-publicized promise not to raise taxes and he also had not been able to break the economy out of a lingering weak period, despite the successful Persian Gulf War effort. Second, the Democratic nominee was again a relatively unknown state governor from a small southern state (like Carter in 1976). Third, like the 1980 election, there was a strong independent candidate who repeatedly challenged the major party candidates in the polls.

Even with these similarities, there were features unique to the 1992 campaign. Unlike many of the previous elections, the 1992 race was one which may have focused more on questions of ideology and issue positions, than candidate character. On the Republican side, while the early campaign strategy may have been aimed at attacking Clinton's record and background as governor of Arkansas, after the Republican convention, a cluster of social issues commonly called "family values" rose to prominence from the Republican right. And to further accentuate the issue-content of the campaign, Clinton's emphasis was on his identity as a "New Democrat," a phrase which tried to encapsulate a platform of positions from his days at the helm of the Democratic Leadership Council. Last, during his on-again, off-again campaign, independent candidate Perot raised concerns about the federal budget deficit and the growth of the government bureaucracy.

The Democratic strategy in 1992 differed significantly from previous elections. Clinton and his advisors strongly believed that one cause of recent Democratic presidential losses was their inability to take the offensive against Republican attacks. So, the Democratic team went on the offensive early in the race:

> To avoid being on the defensive, the Democrats sought to present positions on a wide variety of domestic concerns. The campaign's earliest ads

touted Clinton's economic plans, particularly the proposal to raise taxes on the wealthy. Another promised to revamp the welfare system, and in speeches Clinton discussed details of his plan to reform the health care system and proposed to revitalize the economy of rural America. Television ads also contended that Clinton and Gore were "a new generation of Democrats" who "don't think the way the old Democratic party did" because they held differing views on welfare reform, the death penalty, and government spending. (Abramson et al. 1995, 54)

Clearly, Clinton was not against speaking out on his policy ideas and positions during the 1992 campaign.

Then, once Perot decided to reenter the campaign on October 1, 1992, the race intensified. Perot immediately aired another of his infomercials on the state of the national economy and a set of commercials on the federal budget deficit. This was right before a series of candidate debates that were vastly different than debates in previous elections. The first debate between the three candidates was just 10 days after Perot's reentry, and it was in traditional format (candidates being questioned by reporters); little of substance was discussed other than Clinton's draft record (Germond and Witcover 1993, 474). The next two meetings of the candidates, though, used different formats. The second debate employed Clinton's favorite town hall style, and was widely considered an informative debate: "Whatever the reasons, the rest of the (second) debate did concentrate on issues. To many observers, the debate did a good job of demonstrating contrasts between the candidates on those issues. This was especially true on the economy . . . [and] on international trade, school choice, and health care" (Abramson, Aldrich, and Rohde 1995, 60). The last debate saw Bush hammer home his own themes, focusing his attention on Clinton's record. Taken together, these three debates seemed quite informative and attracted a great deal of public attention.[7]

But Perot was quite distinct as an independent candidate, especially when contrasted to Anderson. Perot did not accept federal campaign funding for his campaign, preferring to foot the bill of his candidacy from his own wallet. And showing a disdain for traditional campaign appearances, Perot bought considerable amounts of television time, and used "infomercials" like no previous presidential candidate.[8] Just before the election, it is estimated that Perot had

---

7. Germond and Witcover note: "Contrary to the usual pattern of declining interest in debates, the audience grew over the three debates . . . The first one attracted more than 80 million viewers despite the competition of a major-league baseball playoff game on CBS; the second more than 84 million and the third 88 million—and those numbers did not include the millions watching CNN and C-SPAN on cable systems or PBS" (1993, 480).

8. In the previous chapter, I demonstrated that Perot's use of infomercials may have suc-

spent more than 40 million dollars of his own money on network television. Perot clearly had more direct access to the electorate than Anderson could have dreamed possible just twelve years earlier.

Thus, the 1992 campaign may have been more issue-oriented than any of the elections previously discussed. If the common wisdom about the issue-content of the campaign and the impact of the three debates is correct, then the effect of issues ought to be relatively great and that of uncertainty relatively low on voters in 1992. These two hypotheses can be tested in the multinomial probit results presented in table 7.5.

First, the general fit of the 1992 multinomial probit model is quite good. It correctly classifies 73.3 percent of the voters in the 1992 sample. As for correctly predicting the choices made by voters for specific candidates, the model correctly predicts 88.4 percent of the Clinton votes, 75.6 percent of the Bush votes, and 36.6 percent of the Perot voters. This multinomial probit model fits the data better than the 1980 model, since it does a much better job at predicting the votes for the independent candidate than did the 1980 model. Also, notice that the two estimated error correlations are statistically significant, which implies that the IIA assumption is violated in this data.

Looking at the coefficient estimates, all are correctly signed and most are statistically significant. Partisanship consistently has the predicted effect, with Republicans preferring Bush to Perot and Clinton. Notice as well that just as in 1980, partisanship seems to have a stronger effect on the relative choices between the major-party candidates than on the choice between the independent and incumbent candidates. Also, the trait measures have strong and statistically significant estimated effects, with Perot and Clinton character traits playing a seemingly stronger role on candidate support than Bush traits.

The two sets of coefficients important for the themes of this chapter—ideological distance and uncertainty—deserve extended discussion. To reiterate, the 1992 multinomial probit model has a different operationalization of both distance and uncertainty measures than the previous models; here both are derived simply from placements of the three candidates (and the voter for the distance measure) on ideological scales. This is due to the lack of issue placement questions about Perot in the 1992 NES survey used here.

But ideological distance has a negative and statistically significant impact. As in all of the other models in this chapter, it is apparent that issues or ideology have mattered in recent presidential elections, controlling for other effects. So in 1992 as in the past four presidential races, the closer a voter is to one of the candidates on issues or ideology, the more likely she is to support that candidate.

---

ceeded in providing information about his ideological position; the more Perot commercials a voter could recall seeing, the lower was her uncertainty about Perot's ideological stance.

TABLE 7.5. Two-Stage Voting Models, 1992 Election

Independent Variables	Probability of Voting For:	
	Perot/ Bush	Clinton/ Bush
Ideological Distance		$-.11^{**}$
		.02
Constant	.62*	1.6**
	.40	.40
Bush uncertainty	.04	.17*
	.08	.13
Perot uncertainty	$-.04$	
	.09	
Clinton uncertainty		$-.26^{**}$
		.15
Bush traits	$-.17^{**}$	$-.16^{**}$
	.07	.08
Perot traits	.26**	
	.09	
Clinton traits		.34**
		.07
Party identification	$-.15^{**}$	$-.59^{**}$
	.07	.09
Education	$-.06$	.12*
	.06	.08
Gender	$-.28^{**}$	.08
	.11	.14
σ_{PB}	.60**	
	.19	
σ_{CB}	.33*	
	.21	
% Correct	73.3%	
Number of cases	937	

Note: Entries are maximum-likelihood estimates, and their associated asymptotic standard errors.
* indicates a $p = .10$ level of statistical significance, one-tailed tests.
** indicates a $p = .05$ level of statistical significance, one-tailed tests.

The uncertainty measures are correctly signed in the 1992 multinomial probit models as well. That is, the greater the voter's uncertainty about the candidate, the less likely she is to support that candidate, all things held constant. But neither the Bush nor Perot uncertainty terms in the Bush-Perot coefficient vector are statistically significant; they are at least five times smaller than the uncertainty estimates in the Clinton-Bush coefficient vector. And the latter uncertainty estimates, those examining the role of uncertainty in the choice

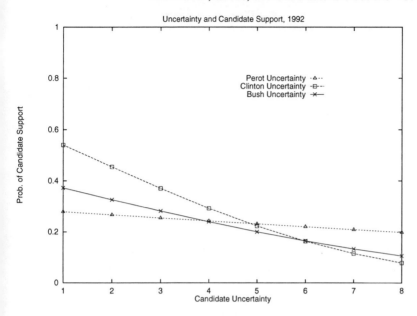

Fig. 7.9.   Effects of uncertainty, 1992.

between Clinton and Bush, are statistically significant at the $p = .10$ level or better.

But, to better see the effects of uncertainty and ideological distance in the 1992 results, I use the same graphical techniques as I did for the previous elections. The results for the effect of candidate ideological uncertainty for the "average" 1992 voter on candidate support are given in figure 7.9. Each line traces the influence of one candidate's uncertainty on the voter's support for the candidate, across the range of the uncertainty variable.

In figure 7.9 it is clear that once again, I can verify the key prediction of the spatial model in chapter 3—the slope of each line is negative. This means that voters in the 1992 election held their uncertainty about the candidate's ideological stance against the candidate. The more uncertain the voter in 1992, the less likely she was to vote for the particular candidate.

For the average voter, ideological uncertainty had the greatest influence on voting for Clinton. There was approximately a .40 point change in the probability of Clinton support over this range of the uncertainty variable for this representative voter. This contrasts to a .20 change for Bush uncertainty, and a small .10 change for Perot uncertainty. Thus, ideological uncertainty had exactly the effect predicted in this election, but it mattered the most in Clinton

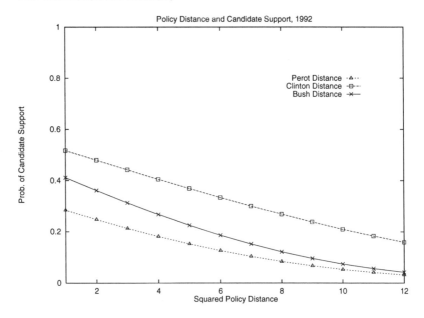

Fig. 7.10.   Effects of policy issues, 1992.

evaluations.

Probably the easiest way to explain these results is to argue that, as found in the past chapter, Perot's positions on the issues he discussed in his campaign were relatively clear; he stood for cutting the budget deficit and government in general. The incumbent had a record to campaign on, and as seen in a number of past elections, voters seem to be clearer about incumbent positions than they are about challengers. Clinton, as the challenger, seems to be the most susceptible to voter uncertainty about his ideological positions. This could be the result of attacks made by Bush on Clinton's record and positions, or it could be the result of Clinton's willingness to discuss many different issues, often presenting in public his deliberations about a particular issue.

The effects of ideological positions on candidate choice in 1992 are given in figure 7.10. Again, ideological positions mattered in this election, as evidenced by the negative slopes of each line. Surprisingly, ideological distance influenced the evaluation of each candidate by this representative voter almost equally. Moving each candidate across this range of ideological distance produces a .35 point reduction in the probability of Clinton support, a .33 reduction in the probability of Bush support, and a .31 loss in the likelihood of Perot support. So, ideological positioning was important in the 1992 election, and it factored strongly into voter decisions (Alvarez and Nagler 1995).

Conclusions

This chapter plays a central role in my analysis. On substantive grounds, the empirical results in this chapter have demonstrated quite clearly that *voter uncertainty of the policy positions of the presidential candidates directly influences voter preferences, or voter evaluations, of the candidates.* This is direct confirmation of the the first hypothesis advanced in chapter 3, where the spatial analysis predicted that the more uncertain a voter was of the positions of a candidate on policy issues, the lower their utility for the candidate. Throughout this chapter, the coefficients on the candidate uncertainty variables were correctly signed, and most were statistically significant.

Additionally, these models have shown that *policy issues mattered in each of the elections under consideration.* This is not a trivial result. The models estimated in this chapter have shown that policy issues have consistent and substantial effects on voter evaluations, controlling for the uncertainty the voters have about the candidates and for other nonpolicy aspects of their evaluations.

Third, to set the stage for the discussion about the influence of the campaign on voter decision making, two things are apparent. The strategies chosen by the candidates competing in each of these elections appear to influence how voters evaluate candidates. Also, there is a lot of variation across these elections in how strongly voter uncertainty, both about the positions of the candidates and the positions of the candidates relative to voters, influences candidate support. This will be taken up in later chapters of the book.

Methodologically, there have been a number of interesting results in the models presented in this chapter. First, there was clear evidence in the major party candidate evaluation models for the endogeneity of evaluations and uncertainty. In chapter 6 this was also apparent, where I presented the results of the uncertainty models. These results have clear implications for research on voting. On one hand, voters appear to engage in selective information processing—they perceive the positions of preferred candidates more precisely. On the other hand, voters prefer the candidate whose positions they perceive with greater certainty. Thus, empirical models of voter preferences or of voter knowledge of candidate policy positions which do not take this endogeneity into account are probably misspecified.

Next, in the results from the 1976 and 1984 major party candidate models, the 2SCML results were virtually identical to the 2SPLS estimates. Neither the estimates, the standard errors, nor the overall model fit varied between estimation procedures. But the 1988 models were substantially different, especially regarding the primary parameter of interest in these models—the effects of candidate uncertainty. There, the estimated effect of candidate policy uncertainty was reduced dramatically, to the point where the estimates were actually smaller than their standard errors. As I noted in the 1988 section, though, this would be expected if there were a high correlation in the 1988 data between the error terms of these two equations.

When faced with a simultaneous model involving dichotomous and continuous variables, then, it would be appropriate to estimate and present the results from both the 2SPLS and 2SCML models. To the extent the results are very similar, our confidence in the results should be greater than had only one or the other estimation procedures been employed. However, when the results disagree, careful consideration of the source of this disagreement is in order. If the disagreement is explicable, as the differences in the 1988 models appear to be, then the researcher can make an informed decision as to which modeling approach might be more appropriate given the data at hand.

Last, I used another relatively new econometric technique, multinomial probit, to examine the three-candidate elections of 1980 and 1992. The multinomial probit results were quite consistent with those for the other three elections and helped to verify the two key hypotheses being examined in this chapter. The multinomial probit models also provide some insight into how voters may have seen the groupings of their choices in these two elections, which I related to the strategies of candidates in the 1980 and 1992 elections. In the coming chapters, I will turn to a closer examination of campaigns, both cross-sectionally and temporally.

CHAPTER 8

Information and Voting Decisions

I think—I think my opinion as the—as the divorce—I mean as the abor-tions have gone up—my, my opposition to abortion has increased. And so I—yes, I think my—I think it's clearer to me now, and I'm not, I'm not going to change my position.

—George Bush, Interview with Barbara Walters on ABC, June 24, 1992

Hear me now, I am not pro-abortion. I am pro-choice, firmly.

—Bill Clinton, Democratic Nomination acceptance speech, July 16, 1992

Sometimes presidential candidates clearly enunciate their positions on impor-tant policy issues. But often they do not. In chapter 7 I demonstrated that voters in the five presidential elections from 1976–92 behaved as would risk-averse individuals, by shunning the candidates they are more uncertain of, and by embracing the candidates they are more certain of. This relationship was shown to hold in the face of the other elements of voter choice—issues, par-ties, and candidate traits—and after statistically accounting for the endogeneity between uncertainty and preferences.

But this presents a dilemma. If voters are risk-adverse, and if they vote for the devil they know more about, then why are presidential candidates ever ambiguous? That is, if voters penalize candidates for policy ambiguity, then why do candidates not *always* devote their campaign to unambiguous elabora-tions of their positions on the important policy issues? A fully specified model of candidate strategies is well beyond the scope of this book. But I am going to suggest that when it comes to developing a campaign strategy about their policy positions, presidential candidates pursue what could be called a "mixed strategy"—sometimes absolutely clear, sometimes quite ambiguous.

This strategic mix involves clear statements of their positions on some issues, and ambiguous statements of their positions on other issues. For a presidential candidate will clearly enunciate a policy position when such a

143

statement has some electoral payoff. On other issues, therefore, they will be ambiguous either to focus attention away from their stance, or to give voters the chance to "fill in the blanks." To put it more directly, if a candidate decides that he will obtain no support from a particular issue or that his position might actually alienate support, then his strategy will be to evade any clear statement of his position. In that way, the candidate can effectively remove a particular issue, which does not help their electoral efforts, from the decision-making processes of the voters—if their opponent and the mass media do not attempt to impede this strategic ambiguity.

Thus, candidates walk a fine line. On one hand, clear statements of their positions on policy issues, while avoiding the loss of voter support due to policy uncertainty, would certainly alienate voters with stands on the issues other than the candidate's. So consistent clarity in their policy positions is probably not a dominant strategy for a presidential candidate. However, total ambiguity, while keeping voters with stands differing from the candidates from deserting due to certain policy stands, certainly risks losses in support. The strategic choice for the candidate falls between these two alternatives—a mix of clarity and ambiguity.

This argument is not easy to test directly with the measure of voter uncertainty regarding candidate policy stands, since the measurement strategy employed in most research examines general voter uncertainty, across a number of issues important in the particular campaign. However, in this chapter I examine the interaction between voter uncertainty about the positions of the candidates and their ability to employ their issue preferences in their evaluations of the candidates. The second hypothesis discussed in chapter 3 stated that voters who are more uncertain of the policy positions of a candidate will have more difficulty evaluating the candidate on the basis of issues. Additionally, voters who are more certain of the candidate's positions will be better able to judge the candidates on the basis of these policy positions.

Furthermore, in this chapter I test the third hypothesis advanced in chapter 3. That hypothesis asserted that voters who are more uncertain of the policy positions of the candidates will have more difficulty evaluating the candidates on the basis of their policy positions, and so they will rely more upon other information. Those voters who are more certain of the candidates, then, will be less likely to employ non-issue information in their decision making.

Both these hypotheses will be examined through the use of the interactive models discussed in the final section of chapter 5. There I discussed the limitations of relying on the functional form of the probit (or any other nonlinear model involving a probabilistic transformation) solely to examine interactions between variables. Instead, two other methodologies are preferred: introducing interactive terms to the models, or estimating the models on subsamples of the data stratified by the variables believed to be causing the interactions (Nagler 1991). I test the interaction between policy uncertainty and voter decision making using the latter approach in three of the elections (1976, 1984, and 1988). The data from each these three elections was divided first into two subsamples of roughly equal size, with voters being grouped according to their policy uncertainty of the Democratic candidate, either above or below the mean level of uncertainty in the larger sample. The voting models were then estimated separately for each sample (without only the Democratic candidate's uncertainty variable). This procedure was then replicated after placing the voters into one of two different groups, this time based on their uncertainty of the Republican candidate's positions on the issues. The models estimated for each election year are presented in appendix E. For the remaining two elections, where the presence of a significant independent or third-party candidate complicated the decision process for voters, I employ the first strategy and add an additional variable to the multinomial probit models which directly operationalizes the hypothesis about the interaction between uncertainty about candidate positions and the distance between the voter and the candidate on the same issues.

The first section of this chapter tests the hypotheses involving the interaction between policy uncertainty and issue voting graphically, by examining the effect of the squared distance between the voter and the candidate on the probability of supporting a presidential candidate, first for voters who were relatively certain of the position of the candidate and then for voters relatively uncertain of the candidate. Empirical support for the hypothesis will be found if the effect of these squared issue distance terms upon candidate support is greater for the more certain voters than the less certain voters.

The second section tests the third hypothesis. Again, graphical methods are used. However, here I examine the interaction between candidate uncertainty and the use of partisan cues by the voters in their decisions in three of the elections (1976, 1984, and 1988). If there is one bit of information virtually all voters would possess about both of the candidates, it is their partisan affiliation. It is commonly asserted that voters rely upon partisan cues as informational shortcuts (Campbell et al. 1960; Conover 1981; Conover and Feldman 1986; Flanigan, Rahn, and Zinagle 1989; Hamill, Blake and Lodge 1986; Rahn 1989, 1990; Shively 1979). Here empirical support for this hypothesis will be found if more uncertain voters appear to use these partisan cues—in the guise of their own partisan identification—in their voting decisions to a greater extent than the more certain voters. That is, the hypothesis will be tested by comparing the relative effects of certain voters' and uncertain voters' partisan identification on candidate support. The relative effects of party identification should be greater for the uncertain voters.

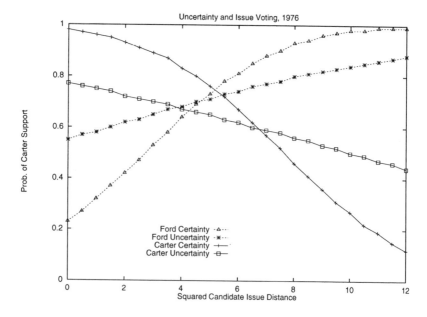

Fig. 8.1. Uncertainty and issue voting interaction, 1976.

Uncertainty and Issue Voting

The graphical presentation of the interaction results for the 1976–92 presidential elections is similar to that in chapter 7. Using the same "average" voter, I present two panels in each figure for each two-candidate election. The top panel gives the results of the interactions between Republican candidate uncertainty and Republican candidate squared issue distances; the bottom panel gives identical results, but for the Democratic candidate in that election. In all of these figures, the x-axis gives the squared distance between the candidate and the voter, while the y-axis gives the probability that these average voters would support the Democratic candidate. In each panel, one line gives the effect of these issue distances on candidate support for certain voters, while the other line gives the effect of these issue distances for uncertain voters.

The results for the two major party candidates in these four elections are given in figures 8.1 through 8.5. Before turning to the specific elections, though, I want to note that *the second hypothesis is supported in each of these figures*. That is, across all of these elections, the evidence supports the hypothesis that more certain voters are better able to judge the candidates on the basis of their policy positions than more uncertain voters.

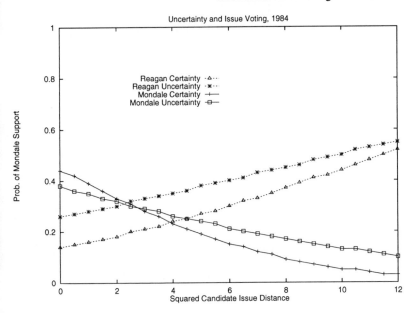

Fig. 8.2. Uncertainty and issue voting interaction, 1984.

In the 1976 election (fig. 8.1), the effects of information on issue voting are especially apparent. What is notable about this figure is the relative slope of lines for certain and uncertain voters for both Ford and Carter issue voting. The lines for the more certain voters have a much greater slope than the lines for the more uncertain voters, indicating that the average voter is better able to employ their policy preferences in their decision making when they are certain of the candidate's position. And the difference between the effects apparent in each panel is particularly large. For an average voter who was certain about Ford, the change in probability of Carter support is .77 across the range of distance between Ford and the voter on the issues. This value is over twice the change in probability for an average voter uncertain of Ford's positions (.33). The difference in effects across certain and uncertain voters is even greater for Carter: the change in Carter support across the range of issue distances is .86 for certain voters, well over twice the change in probability of Carter support for the uncertain voters (.33). Therefore, the results of the interactive models from the 1976 election are strongly supportive of this hypothesis.

In figure 8.2 which describes the 1984 election it is apparent that again the hypothesis receives support, but not to the magnitude seen in the 1976 results. Here, in the top panel (Reagan uncertainty), there is a .38 change in

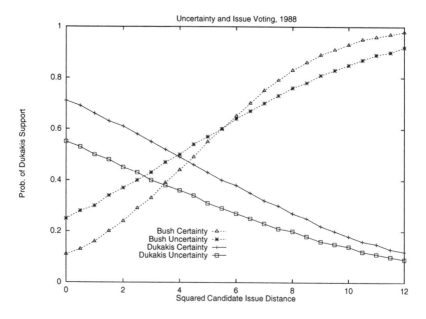

Fig. 8.3.   Uncertainty and issue voting interaction, 1988.

the probability of Mondale support for the certain voters, and a .29 change for the uncertain voters, across the entire range of squared issue distances. The magnitude of the effects of uncertainty on issue voting, though, was greater for Mondale. The average but certain voter would have been .45 likely to support Mondale (very close to Mondale on the issues) and .03 likely to support Mondale (as far as possible from Mondale on the issues), which is a change in probability of .42. The average but uncertain voter would change in likelihood of Mondale support by .27, about half of the change in probability seen for the certain voters. The 1984 election therefore also supports this hypothesis.

Last, figure 8.3 shows the results for the 1988 race. Again the lines in each panel demonstrate the effects of uncertainty on issue voting in this election. In the top panel, voters certain about Bush's positions have a total change in probability of Dukakis support of 87.3, across the range of issue distances, which compares to 66.9 for the average uncertain voters. And in the bottom panel, voters uncertain of Dukakis's positions on policy issues change in their support for Dukakis by 46.1, which is less than the 60.0 change seen for the certain voters. Therefore, the results from these elections support the hypothesis that more certain voters are better able to judge the candidates on the basis of their issue positions than less certain voters.

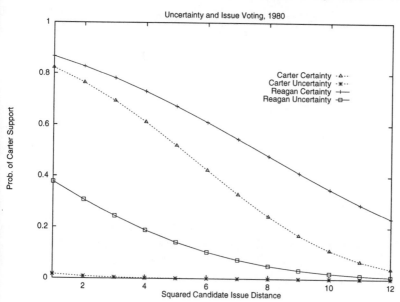

Fig. 8.4.   Uncertainty and issue voting, 1980: Carter and Reagan.

Does this conclusion hold as well for third-party candidates, in particular for the candidacies of Anderson in 1980 and Perot in 1992? To examine whether the hypothesis is supported in the three-candidate races, I estimated interactive models by adding an interaction term to the multinomial probit models discussed in the previous chapter. The results of the multinomial probit models with the interaction terms are presented in appendix E. For ease of interpretation, I present similar graphs in figures 8.4 (major-party candidates in 1980), 8.5 (major-party candidates in 1992), and 8.6 (third-party or independent candidates).

For the major-party candidates in 1980, there is a strong interactive effect between uncertainty and issue information. In the top panel of figure 8.4, notice that for this representative voter, if she were uncertain of Carter's position, *Carter's issue positions would have had almost no effect on her decision.* On the other hand, if she were certain of Carter's positions, the effect of issues is quite strong, with her probability of voting for Carter changing by .80 over this range of the issue distance term. Yet the effect is not so dramatic for Reagan, in the bottom panel of figure 8.4. If the voter is certain of Reagan's positions, the effect of changing Reagan's distance from her over this range of the issue distance variable is a .60 reduction in the probability of supporting Reagan;

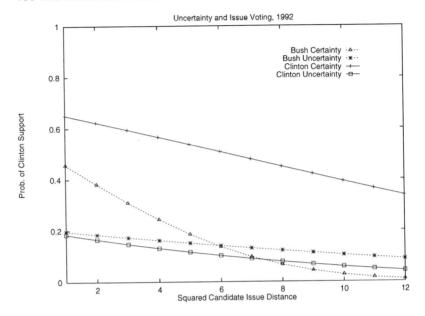

Fig. 8.5.   Uncertainty and issue voting, 1992: Clinton and Bush.

were she uncertain, the same change is about .30.

In the 1992 election, the interaction between uncertainty and issue voting is not as strong. In the top panel of figure 8.5, changing Clinton's distance from this representative voter reduces her probability of voting for Clinton by .30 if she were certain of Clinton's positions. But if she were uncertain, moving Clinton's position relative to the voter the same distance reduces her probability of voting for Clinton by approximately .20. The interaction effect for Bush is somewhat stronger, though, since the bottom panel of figure 8.5 shows almost a .50 reduction in probability of Bush voting for a certain voter relative to a .10 reduction for the uncertain voter.

Next, the two third-party or independent candidates show somewhat different interactive effects (fig. 8.6). For Anderson, in the top panel, the uncertainty and issue-distance interaction is strong. The effect on the probability of voting for Anderson of moving his position close to far from the voter is over .60 points for the certain voter, but .20 points for the uncertain voter. Yet for Perot (bottom panel), the interactive effect is smaller, with almost a .40 point change for the certain voter relative to a .10 point change for the uncertain voter. Thus, the interaction effect between uncertainty and issue voting was slightly stronger in 1980 than in 1992, for the non–major party candidates.

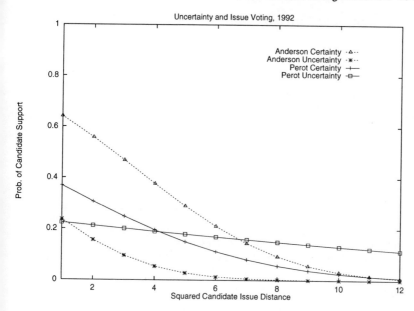

Fig. 8.6. **Uncertainty and issue voting, Anderson (1980) and Perot (1992).**

To conclude, the interactive models presented here strongly support my second hypothesis. Thus, the conclusion is apparent: voters who are relatively certain of a candidate's positions on the policy issues are better able to employ their policy preferences in their decision making. Voters, though, who are relatively uncertain of the candidate's positions are less able to employ issues in their decision-making process. So upon what basis do relatively uncertain voters make their decisions, if not upon issues? I earlier hypothesized that voters who are relatively uncertain of the positions of the candidates should employ nonpolicy information in their decisions. The next section tests this hypothesis.

Uncertainty and Partisan Voting

Here I again use graphical presentation of the interaction results which are virtually identical to those in the previous section.[1] Two panels in each figure for each election are presented for an average voter. In the top panels are the results of the interactions between Republican candidate uncertainty and the voter's partisan identification, and in the bottom identical graphs are presented for the Democratic candidate. In these figures, the x-axis gives the voter's partisan affiliation on the seven-point party identification scale, where 1 represents strong Democratic identification, 4 represents independence, and 7 represents strong Republican affiliation.[2] As in the previous section, the y-axis gives the probability that these average voters would support the Democratic candidate. Last, as in the previous section, one line gives the effect of the voter's partisanship on candidate support for certain voters, while the other line gives the effect of partisanship for uncertain voters.

In figures 8.7 through 8.9 I present the results for the two major-party candidates (the results for Anderson voting will be discussed below). Here, though, what is most striking is *mixed support for the third hypothesis.* Although the results are mixed, it generally appears that contrary to my expectations, voters who are less certain of the policy positions of the candidates do not appear to turn to partisan cues in their voting decision to a greater extent than relatively certain voters. In fact, the changes observed in the likelihood of candidate support shown here are typically greater for the certain voters than for the uncertain voters.

In figure 8.7 are the graphs for the 1976 election. Here the data do not support the hypothesis. For, in both panels of the figure, the change in probability of candidate support is greater for the certain voters (approximately .80 across the range of partisanship) than for an average uncertain voter (about .50 change in probability of Carter support). The differences in the observed changes in probabilities is quite large, around .30, which underscores the extent to which these results run counter to my expectations.

The results for the 1984 election are again mixed (fig. 8.8). Here, in the top panel, the interaction between Reagan policy uncertainty and the voter's use of their partisanship in their decision making runs counter to my hypothesis. For those certain of Reagan's positions, there is a .66 change in probability of Carter support, compared to a .48 change for those uncertain of Reagan's

---

1. Here I do not examine the 1980 and 1992 elections. It is not clear how partisan cues could be used in those elections with the presence of third-party or independent candidates.

2. The 1–7 scale was used for the 1980–88 models, but a 0–6 scale was used in the 1976 models. In the figures for the 1976 election, I have scaled the x-axis 1–7 to ease comparisons between the elections.

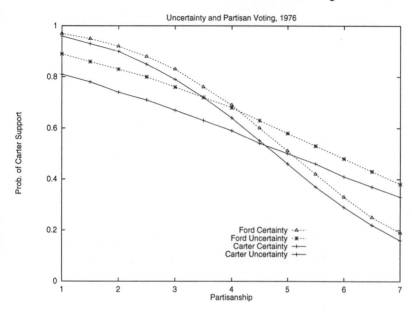

Fig. 8.7.   Uncertainty and partisan voting, 1976.

positions, moving from strongly Democratic to strongly Republican affiliations. But in the bottom panel, the Mondale results support the hypothesis.
Like the results for Carter in 1980, voters uncertain of Mondale's positions—
but who were strongly Democratic—would be more likely to support Mondale
than certain voters (.18 more likely). And voters uncertain of Mondale's positions would be slightly less likely to support Mondale were they strong Republicans. The relevant changes in probabilities of support across the range of
partisanship in the bottom panel are a .51 change for the certain voters and a
.66 change for the uncertain voters. These results provide mixed support for
my third hypothesis.

However, the 1988 results (fig. 8.9) do not conform to my expectations.
Here in both panels, the effects of partisanship on candidate support are greater
for the voters more certain of the positions of the particular candidate. In fact,
the changes in probabilities of candidate support across the range of partisanship are approximately .20 greater for the more certain average voters than for
the less certain average voters. These results are not supportive of the third
hypothesis.

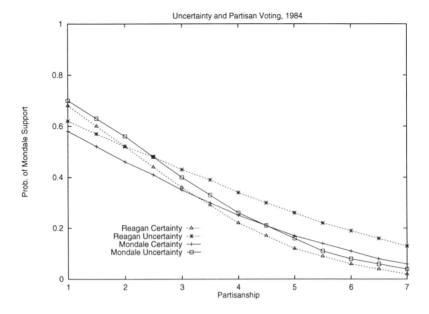

Fig. 8.8.   Uncertainty and partisan voting, 1984.

Information and the Decision-Making Process

This chapter has examined the effects of voter uncertainty of candidate policy positions on the information they use in their decisions. The first hypothesis I advanced was that voters who are relatively certain of a candidate's positions should be able to employ this information in their decisions, while relatively uncertain voters would have considerable difficulty making a decision based on the issue positions of the candidates. This hypothesis received strong and consistent support in the interactive models just presented.

Yet, the other hypothesis tested in this chapter did not fare as well. That hypothesis stated that voters who are uncertain of the candidates' positions would turn to other nonpolicy sources of information to make their decisions, and that voters who are relatively certain of the candidate's positions would tend not to turn to nonpolicy information in their decision making. Very mixed support for this hypothesis was seen in the interactive models, at least concerning the interactive effect of policy uncertainty on partisan voting. This is a surprising result, since partisanship is widely considered to be an accessible and simple decision-making cue for voters.

It is possible that voters who are uncertain of a candidate's policy positions

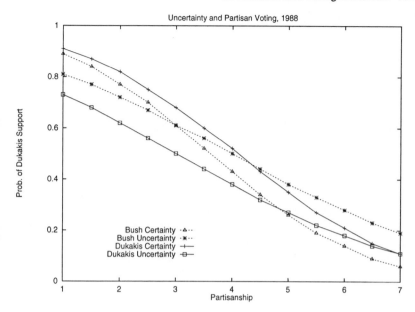

Fig. 8.9.   Uncertainty and partisan voting, 1988.

might turn to other information sources than partisanship. One such alternative decision-making criterion is candidate traits—could it be that voters who are more uncertain of the policy positions of candidates turn not to their partisanship for cues but to candidate traits and personalities (Kelley and Mirer 1974)?

Unfortunately, close examination of the results of the interaction models for 1976, 1984, and 1988, which are presented in appendix E, show little support for this explanation. In fact, all of these models imply exactly the opposite process: more certain voters employed candidate trait information to a greater extent than did less certain voters.

How might these two conclusions be rectified? That is, what could possibly account for the fact that voters who are more certain of the policy positions of a candidate clearly are better prepared to employ policy issue information in their decision making, *but they also seem better able to use other party and candidate information in their decision* than less certain voters?

The literature on voting behavior and public opinion has long argued over the effects of political sophistication, expertise, or information (Converse 1964; Fiske, Lau, and Smith 1990; Hamill and Lodge 1986; Iyengar and Kinder 1987; Krosnick 1990; Luskin 1987; Neuman 1986; Smith 1989; Zaller 1986,

1990). Central to these arguments have been concerns over how to differentiate voters into more or less sophisticated, expert, or informed groups, as well as debates over what effects sophistication or information might have on decision making.

My discrimination of voters into more and less certain groups certainly seems to parallel some of the measurement strategies in these debates in the literature, especially the approaches based on political information (Zaller 1986, 1990). And, not surprisingly, the results I have just presented mesh quite consistently with both survey- and experiment-based findings in this literature.

Indeed, some have argued that better-educated voters are much more attendant to all types of candidate-related information (Glass 1985; Graber 1988; Lau 1986; Miller, Wattenberg and Malanchuk 1986). Or from the experimental literature, that experts are more likely to employ on-line processing of information about candidates (McGraw, Lodge, and Stroh 1990; Rahn 1990). But this might be a function not only of the voter's expertise or store of information, but might be also related to their motivation to obtain information and their interest in politics (Converse 1964; Rahn 1990; Zaller 1990).

Thus, the more certain voters are of a candidate's policy position, the more they appear to be able to use all sorts of candidate-related information in their decision making. This is partly due to the amount of information they possess about the candidates, but is also due to their exposure to information (see chapter 6). So, voters who are more certain of the policy positions of the candidates appear be better informed about the nonpolicy characteristics of the candidates as well, and better able to use this information in their decision making.

Last, the results presented above indirectly help to resolve the dilemma I identified at the beginning of the chapter. While greater uncertainty of the candidate leads voters to be less likely to support the candidate, this uncertainty might alleviate some of this diminution in support. Simply, to the extent that voters with policy positions that conflict with the candidate's are less able to evaluate the candidate *predominantly on the basis of these policy positions*, these voters may be more likely to support the candidate than if they knew the candidate's positions with more certainty. Therefore, a risk-averse voter may prefer the devil they know more about; but this loss of support might be mitigated if the voter is uncertain of positions taken by the candidate that conflict sharply with their own. Further, a candidate whose positions are perceived with uncertainty by the electorate might even come out ahead, if the opponent has taken a clear, but controversial stand. The ambiguous candidate risks alienating risk-averse voters. However, the unambiguous candidate risks alienating voters with differing positions on the issues. Ambiguity might then be a winning strategy for the candidate, if the losses due to risk-aversion are balanced by the gains from voters alienated by their opponent's positions.

CHAPTER 9

Campaigns and Uncertainty

Political campaigns are designedly made into emotional orgies which endeavor to distract attention from the real issues involved.

—James Harvey Robinson, *The Human Comedy*, 1937

The politician is . . . trained in the art of inexactitude. His words tend to be blunt or rounded, because if they have a cutting edge they may later return to wound him.

Edward R. Murrow, London, October 19, 1959

The focus of analysis so far in this book has been on the individual voter. Examining microlevel decision making has yielded a number of insights into how information influences voter choice. I have presented a considerable amount of evidence which documents the variation across the voting public in their uncertainty about the policy positions of presidential candidates, and how differences in relative uncertainty affect voter preferences and the criteria upon which they base their choices.

However, as noted in chapter 3, perceptual uncertainty is rooted in both the voters' own disincentives to gather and process costly information *and in the candidates' incentives to disseminate ambiguous information about their policy positions.* I concentrated in the previous chapters on variables related to voter information costs. Here, in the last two chapters of the book, I turn my attention to uncertainty which is induced in voter perceptions by the campaign (which I termed exogenous uncertainty in chapter 3).

Analysis of candidate-induced uncertainty, then, implies a macrolevel focus on the campaigns conducted by the candidates. This is a difficult task, since the period of analysis covered by this study only contains four elections and nine different campaigns.[1] Methodologically, there are many campaign-level

---

1. In this chapter I do not consider the 1992 election. The operationalization of the uncer-

157

variables which could account for variations in candidate-induced uncertainty, and modeling the independent effects of so many variables is not possible. Although the discussion in this chapter is more qualitative than quantitative, the evidence is compelling.

This chapter begins by recounting briefly the main findings thus far in the study of voter uncertainty. Then, I present data on the aggregate distribution of voter uncertainty across the four elections. The chapter turns to a discussion of the patterns apparent in these aggregate distributions, and I first present evidence of some of the campaign-specific factors that do not account for the apparent patterns. I then argue that the distributions of voter uncertainty across the four elections are actually part of a general process of learning about political candidates.

Explaining Aggregate Uncertainty

In chapters 7 and 8, I presented tests of three hypotheses. Two of the hypotheses received strong and consistent empirical support: that the greater the voter's uncertainty about a presidential candidate, the lower their evaluations of that candidate, and the greater this policy uncertainty, the lesser the voter's ability to employ their issue preferences in their decision making. The third hypothesis, which asserted that voters uncertain of the policy positions of the presidential candidates would be more likely to utilize nonpolicy (partisan) information in their decisions, received only mixed support.

However, there was considerable variation across the four elections in the apparent magnitude of these effects of policy uncertainty on voter choice. Here, I recount this variation and argue that the patterns shown in these previous results are related to the aggregate levels of uncertainty in these campaigns. First, regarding the direct effects of voter uncertainty on candidate preference, I demonstrated that these effects were the greatest in the 1976 and 1988 elections, followed by the 1980 election. The 1984 election showed the least influence of voter uncertainty on candidate preferences.

Next, I presented evidence about the extent of issue voting in each of these elections. The effect of policy issues was greatest in the 1980 and 1988 elections, closely followed by the 1976 race. Policy issues were shown to have had the least effect in the 1984 election.

Thirdly, regarding the effects of uncertainty on issue voting, the interactive models of chapter 7 demonstrated the largest effects of uncertainty in the 1976 and 1980 elections. The 1988 election followed, while in the 1984 election uncertainty had the least interactive effect. Also, the interactive models pro-

---

tainty variable is different enough for the 1992 election (since it is based only on ideology) to make it difficult to compare directly to the other elections.

vided support for the hypothesis regarding uncertainty and the use of nonpolicy information in the voter's decision-making process in only the 1984 election.

Therefore, the results of the two-stage statistical models lead to the conclusion that policy uncertainty had the greatest effects, both direct and interactive, in the 1976 and 1988 elections. The 1980 election follows closely, while the 1984 election appears to have witnessed the least effect of uncertainty among this set of recent elections. Yet in spite of the strong effect of policy uncertainty in the 1988 and 1976 races, policy issues were shown to have had a relatively strong influence on voter preferences, which was also true of the 1980 election. The 1984 election, as mentioned in chapter 7, is something of a puzzle, since policy uncertainty had a small effect, as did policy issues.

These patterns in the individual-level results become more understandable by considering the aggregate distributions of uncertainty across these four elections. In table 9.1 I give summary statistics for the mean level of uncertainty for each candidate in each election, followed by the standard deviation, then the skewness and kurtosis of the distributions. The first two statistics in the columns simply give the central tendency and the square root of the variance of the uncertainty for each candidate across the sample of respondents, often termed the first- and second-order moments of the distribution.[2] The third- and fourth-order moments of the distribution are termed the skewness and the kurtosis, respectively. Skewness (third column of the table) is a measure of the asymmetry of the uncertainty distributions, and it takes an increasingly positive value as the distribution has an increasingly long tail in the positive direction. Kurtosis (fourth column of the table) measures the "thickness" of the tails of the uncertainty distributions, and it takes a larger value when the distribution's tails are thicker. Thus, with these four statistics, a complete description of the uncertainty distributions is possible.[3]

---

2. These statistics are for all respondents for whom it is possible to calculate the uncertainty measure for each candidate. However, similar summary statistics from the set of voters in the models in the previous chapters do not differ greatly from those reported in the table.

3. The definitions of each statistic make the distinctions between the four moments of the distribution clear. The mean of the distribution is the expected value, or the average of the values the variable (X) can take weighed by the relative probabilities: $E(X) = \sum_i p_i x_i$ where $i = 1, 2, \ldots, n$. The variance is the expected value of X^2 minus the square of the mean: $\sigma^2 = \sum_i p_i (x_i - EX_i)^2$, $\sigma^2 = \sum_i p_i x_i^2 - (EX)^2$, $\sigma^2 = E(X^2) - (EX)^2$. The skewness is given by

$$\frac{\mu_3}{\sigma^3} = \frac{E[(X-\mu)^3]}{(\sigma^2)^{3/2}} \tag{9.1}$$

while the kurtosis is given as

$$\frac{\mu_4}{\sigma^4} = \frac{E[(X-\mu)^4]}{(\sigma^2)^4} \tag{9.2}$$

TABLE 9.1.   Uncertainty Distributions

Election	Candidate	Mean	Standard Deviation	Skewness	Kurtosis
1976					
	Carter	4.37	3.32	1.09	3.44
	Ford	4.39	3.38	1.20	3.76
1980					
	Carter	2.56	2.58	1.71	6.01
	Reagan	3.61	3.65	1.48	4.65
	Anderson	5.02	3.70	0.04	1.37
1984					
	Mondale	2.96	2.92	2.05	7.31
	Reagan	2.53	2.36	2.62	12.9
1988					
	Dukakis	4.56	3.94	1.15	3.39
	Bush	3.78	3.49	1.43	4.37

Note: Statistics reported in the table were calculated from samples in each election of respondents for whom an uncertainty measure was available for the particular candidate in that election.

In table 9.1, not surprisingly, the candidate with the highest mean level of uncertainty was John Anderson. This indicates that in the aggregate there was a much greater level of uncertainty concerning John Anderson's policy positions. However, Anderson uncertainty was much less skewed than the other distributions, which indicates that the aggregate distribution of Anderson uncertainty was not nearly as skewed in a positive direction relative to the other candidates. Additionally the kurtosis of this distribution was smaller, implying that the tails of aggregate Anderson uncertainty were relatively "thinner" than those for the other candidates. All of this evidence demonstrates that most of the respondents had a relatively high level of uncertainty about Anderson, with fewer respondents being either very certain or very uncertain about Anderson's policy positions.

Among the major party candidates, Dukakis in 1988, followed by Carter and Ford in 1976, had the next highest mean levels of uncertainty. Also note that these distributions had similar amounts of both skewness and kurtosis. These latter statistics indicate that the distributions of uncertainty for these three candidates did have a longer positive tail, with more respondents in the tails, than did the distribution for Anderson. Therefore, while the mean levels of uncertainty were lower for Dukakis, Carter (1976), and Ford, there were still

---

For an excellent summary of these statistics, see Theil, chapter 2 (1971). These statistics were calculated in SST, version 2.0.

many respondents who were relatively uncertain about the positions of these candidates.

The next two candidates, ranked in terms of mean uncertainty levels, are Bush and Reagan in 1980. While the mean levels of uncertainty are lower for Bush and Reagan (1980) relative to Dukakis, Carter (1980), and Ford, the skewness and kurtosis of the distributions of Bush and Reagan (1980) uncertainty are greater. Again, the central tendency of the uncertainty distributions for these candidates are moving to the left, toward zero, implying that in the aggregate that more respondents had more certainty concerning where these candidates stood on the issues; but the skewness and kurtosis show that a number of respondents still were relatively uncertain of the positions of both Bush and Reagan (1980).

But three candidates had the lowest aggregate uncertainty: Mondale, Carter (1980), and Reagan (1984). And accordingly, while these distributions have shifted even closer to zero, there are still many respondents who had a great deal of uncertainty about these candidates, as seen in the skewness and kurtosis of these distributions.[4]

These trends in uncertainty across these four elections relate directly to the findings in the previous chapters. In the elections where the level of policy uncertainty about the candidates was the greatest—the 1976 Carter-Ford and the 1988 Dukakis-Bush races—I showed that uncertainty had the greatest influences at the individual voter level. When the aggregate levels of voter uncertainty were the lowest in 1984, uncertainty had the least influence on individual voter decision making. And in the 1980 election, where aggregate uncertainty was slightly greater than in 1984, uncertainty had a stronger effect on the individual level. Therefore, the aggregate distributions of uncertainty across these four elections merge in an understandable manner with the results of the individual voter models.

---

4. These distribution statistics are influenced by the inclusion in the uncertainty measures of respondents who claimed not to know the position of the candidate on any particular issue. In chapter 3, I argued that there are strong theoretical reasons to include these respondents in the measurement of uncertainty since *they are the very respondents we would expect to be the most uncertain.* Excluding them from the analysis would induce selection bias into the models, which would attenuate the effects of uncertainty in the statistical models. As you might expect, the distributions are all shifted to the left, toward relatively less uncertainty, and the skewness and kurtosis statistics change slightly, if all the respondents who did not place the candidates on one issue or more are excluded from the analysis. *However, the relative ordering of the major party candidates remains identical.* The only major deviation from the results in the table is Anderson, since only half of the respondents placed Anderson on all of the scales. Removing those who did not place Anderson on all of the issue scales from the calculation of the uncertainty measure seriously biases the analysis since only a small number (338) of respondents, all relatively well-informed and highly educated, placed Anderson on each issue scale in the 1980 cross-section. Accordingly, the mean of the distribution falls.

The only apparent anomaly yielded by the comparison of the findings from the individual voter results and these aggregate distributions concerns the magnitude of issue voting. The election with the lowest level of voter uncertainty about the policy positions of the two candidates was 1984, which was the election in which the magnitude of estimated issue voting was the lowest. And in the elections where the magnitude of issue voting was argued to be the greatest, the highest aggregate levels of uncertainty are seen (1976 and 1988). The answer to this puzzle seems to be the nature of the 1984 campaign. Neither Mondale nor Reagan in 1984 campaigned deliberately on either policy issues or ideology (see chapter 7). Thus, even though they were distinct on most policy issues, voters appear to have responded reasonably to the campaigns, even though the levels of uncertainty were the lowest in this election.

Uncertainty by Elections and Candidates

In this section, I examine a number of possible explanations for the variation in aggregate levels of uncertainty seen in table 9.1. First, I identify the broad patterns in the distributions of uncertainty across these four elections and nine candidates. This develops into my account of the patterns discussed in the previous section. Then I discount other sources of variation across these elections.

To facilitate this discussion, I begin by showing the differences in uncertainty levels graphically. In figure 9.1 I present a bar chart with the mean levels of uncertainty on the y-axis, and the election years arrayed on the x-axis. The dark bar for each election year gives the mean uncertainty level for the Republican candidate, while the open bar gives the uncertainty mean for the Democrat. To show the trend across the elections, I averaged the two candidates' uncertainty means—the line in the figure depicts the changes in this average over the four elections.

The figure gives a different presentation of the statistical data in table 9.1. Again, Carter and Ford in 1976, and Dukakis in 1988, had the highest mean levels of uncertainty; Reagan (1980) and Bush in 1988 followed with somewhat lower mean uncertainty scores; last was Carter (1980) and Reagan (1984). The data in figure 9.1 shows that the average uncertainty was highest in 1976 and 1988, and the lowest in 1984, with the 1980 election showing a slightly greater level of uncertainty than 1984.

The first apparent pattern in the distributions of uncertainty is that the third-party candidate, John Anderson, had a greater mean level of voter policy uncertainty than any other candidate in these four elections. While not graphed in figure 9.1, the mean level of uncertainty for Anderson stands heads above the others (5.02). Clearly, this first observation underscores the common wisdom about third party candidates—that they are handicapped in most instances by

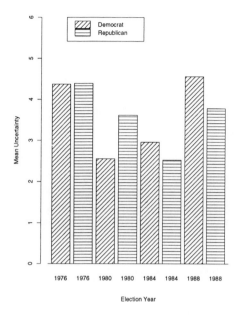

Fig. 9.1.   Mean uncertainty levels across the four elections.

the fact that many voters know little about their candidacies, and, in this case, their policy positions.

The second observation to make about these mean levels of uncertainty is that with only one exception, *the candidate from the party challenging an incumbent always has greater uncertainty associated with their policy stands.* Again, this fits with the common wisdom about the uphill task facing challenging candidates, especially in both congressional elections and in presidential primaries (Jacobson 1992; Bartels 1988). However, most researchers often assume that there is little difference in the relative knowledge of challengers and incumbents in presidential races. This is certainly an incorrect assumption, as shown in figure 9.1. Here Carter's candidacy in 1976 is the exception, since he and Ford had almost identical mean levels of uncertainty. But Reagan in 1980 and Mondale in 1984 both had levels of uncertainty greater than their opponents.

Next, consider the uncertainty levels of the two sitting incumbent presidents. Both Carter in 1980, and Reagan in 1984, had lower levels of uncertainty than their challengers. It is more interesting to note that the mean uncertainty levels of each of these candidates dropped greatly from their first election, when they themselves were challengers to sitting incumbent presidents.

Moreover, notice that the mean uncertainty levels of both Ford in 1976 and Bush in 1988 are higher than the levels of uncertainty associated with the policy positions of the two "true" incumbents (Carter in 1976 and Reagan in 1984). Ford was not an incumbent president in the sense that he had never stood in a national election, having succeeded Nixon. It is no surprise that the uncertainty levels associated with his positions are relatively high compared to the other candidates shown in figure 9.1, and that he alone of the "incumbents" was not better known (in terms of his policy positions) than his opponent.

Bush, on the other hand, is associated with a lower mean level of policy uncertainty than his opponent and a somewhat lower uncertainty than Ford in 1976. It certainly is true that Bush was more prominent among the national electorate in 1988 than Ford was in 1976, since Bush had stood for election (as a vice presidential candidate) in the two previous elections. Contrary to the claims of some, in this case it appears that being vice president for eight years might be worth more than "a warm bucket of spit."

This observation about the electoral value of holding the vice presidency appears to hold for Mondale in 1984. The mean level of policy uncertainty shown in figure 9.1 for Mondale is the lowest of any nonincumbent party presidential candidate, even lower than George Bush. And this is true, even though Mondale had served a single vice presidential term and had actually sat out of office for the three and a half years preceding the 1984 election.

By now it should be apparent that these patterns in the aggregate levels of uncertainty seem very reasonable. The basic observation is that the more exposure a candidate has had to the national audience, the lower the electorate's uncertainty about their policy stands. Thus, in 1976 comparison of a nonelected incumbent president who had been virtually invisible as the House Minority Leader before his appointment by Nixon to the White House to an admitted Washington outsider from rural Georgia led to high levels of uncertainty associated with the positions of both candidates. In 1988 a similar situation existed, since Dukakis had not been a national political figure until after he emerged on the national scene in the spring primaries. But his opponent, having had the exposure of eight years as vice president, did have an edge over Dukakis in terms of voter certainty of Bush's policy positions.

But the 1980 and 1984 elections witnessed a much lower level of policy uncertainty about the positions of the candidates. In part, this is due to the presence of elected incumbent presidents in office. But it is also due to the prominence of their challengers. Both Reagan and Mondale clearly had established records as leaders within their parties before they stood for election, and both had run national campaigns in the past.

Therefore, these reasonable patterns fit quite well with the model of learning I advanced in chapter 4. Consider first the changes in aggregate voter uncertainty seen for Carter between 1976 and 1980, and for Reagan between 1980 and 1984. Carter's uncertainty drops quite substantially, while Reagan's drops somewhat. This is clear evidence that the electorate became more certain about where both these presidents stood on the policy issues. Of course the voters had a considerable amount of time to familiarize themselves with the positions of the two presidents, since by the time both Carter and Reagan stood for reelection they had conducted at least two primary and general election campaigns, and had served in the White House for four years. Therefore, the conclusion is clear: *voters do learn about the policy positions of incumbent presidents.*

Additionally, the electorate also appears to learn about the positions of prominent political figures, especially vice presidents and former presidential candidates. Mondale in 1984 is a clear case in point, since aggregate voter uncertainty about his positions was the lowest for any of the challenging candidates. However, both Reagan in 1980 and Bush in 1988 had lower levels of aggregate uncertainty than did Ford, which is important to note. Reagan and Bush certainly were more prominent national political figures than Ford, since both had been heavily involved in previous national campaigns. In contrast, Ford had only run in his Michigan House district.

Thus, to conclude, three factors account for the patterns in both table 9.1 and figure 9.1: incumbency, previous electoral experience, and national prominence. Each of these factors, either independently or interactively, provides explanations for the levels of aggregate uncertainty in these elections. Additionally, I find this to be support for the hypotheses that voters do learn about the positions of presidential candidates and that this learning is reflected directly in their relative certainty of the policy stands of these candidates.

To refine this explanation, I present next a handful of variables which *do not* account for the variation across these elections in the patterns of uncertainty. These additional variables measure different aspects of the information flow and the intensity of the campaigns, and I show quite clearly that they do not account for the *variation across elections in policy uncertainty.*

The first of these variables deals with the flow of information across these four campaigns, as it is transmitted through the media coverage of the campaigns of each candidate. One hypothesis regarding media coverage would be that fluctuations over duration of the campaigns in the type of stories upon which the news media chose to focus could influence the information voters were exposed to and hence their relative uncertainty about the policy positions of the candidates. If the media focused relatively more on policy issues in the 1980 and 1984 elections than in 1976 and 1988, this could account for the variations in aggregate uncertainty levels. I undertook an extensive content analysis of the coverage of the *New York Times* during October of each election year. Following the approach of Graber (1983), I used stories only with a clear reference to at least one of the candidates, as they were summarized in the *New York Times Index*. Each index story was then categorized into the seven story types used by Patterson (1980). Following the methodology of Graber and the coding scheme of Patterson insures continuity with their studies.[5]

The results of this content analysis are given in table 9.2. This table is organized so that the columns give the percentages of index stories which fall into each of the categories listed in the left-hand column. The last two rows, however, give the sum of the number of stories falling into Patterson's "campaign" (stories about winning, strategy, or hoopla) or "substance" (stories about issues, traits, or endorsements) in each election year.

First, the amazing observation regarding the figures in table 9.2 is the stability of coverage over time. Consider the bottom two rows first. The relative percentage of stories in the *New York Times* during the last month of the general election are predominantly about the campaign (two-thirds) while one-third concern more substantive matters. By scanning the rows for each reference category, it is apparent that the aggregations in the last two rows are not masking dramatic changes in campaign coverage.

It almost appears as if the *New York Times* coverage of the general election campaign every four years follows a rigid formula. While surprising, these figures in Table 9.2, are consistent with the media content analysis of Patterson (1980) for the 1976 election, and by Graber (1983) for the 1976 and 1980

---

5. Patterson's categories are winning and losing, strategy and logistics, appearances and crowds, issues and policies, traits and records, endorsements, and a residual category. The scheme used to define stories as falling into one of these categories is in Patterson (1980, chap. 3, 186), and in the documentation to his media content analysis of the 1976 election. Here is a typical entry from the 1976 election: "Ford vows to make another Fed income tax reduction (a priority) in next Ford Adm, Cleveland speech; views econ policy as fundamental issue of contest between Carter and him; suggests that Carter's precipitious decline in opinion surveys was consequence of Carter's reliance on discredited old formula of more promises, more programs, and more spending . . . Cheney, White House chief of staff, says Pres Ford Com surveys show Ford and Carter even in NY, Ford slightly ahead in Texas and Carter slipping badly in 5 Southern states (M), O 29, 1,1:1." This was coded as a reference to issues and policies (taxes, economic policy), to appearances and crowds (the Cleveland speech), and to winning and losing (the survey evidence). To eliminate the possibility of including an indexed story more than once in my sample, I examined only stories from the index subheadings for presidential election of the election year for the two major party candidates and the general election campaign. In all, 718 entries were coded for the 1976 election, 903 for the 1980 election, 655 in 1984, and 600 for 1988.

TABLE 9.2.   Media Coverage, 1976–1988

	Election Year			
	1976	1980	1984	1988
Winning	14.9	12.5	16.7	13.5
Strategy	19.8	16.5	16.9	22.8
Hoopla	32	39.6	32.7	30.2
Issues	14.2	13.1	13.6	15.3
Traits	6.7	6.9	9.5	6.7
Endorsements	5.3	7.1	2.3	4.3
Other	7.1	4.3	8.4	7.2
Total campaign	66.5	66.3	68.6	66.7
Total substance	33.5	33.7	31.4	33.3

Note: Entries are percentages of total stories coded from the *New York Times Index* from each election year (years in columns). The last two rows represent the sum of the stories referring to the campaigns (winning, strategy, hoopla) or to substance (issues, traits, endorsements).

elections.[6] But since the media coverage of the campaign, especially in the focus on substantive affairs or political issues, does not vary across the four elections, information as presented by the media *cannot account for the variations observed across these four elections in voter uncertainty about the policy positions of the candidates.*

Another possible explanation which can be rejected is that campaign intensity has varied across these campaigns. It could be argued that with more intense campaigns, voters would have more information and exposure to the candidates and hence be more certain of their positions on policy issues. One indication of campaign intensity is the amount of competition faced by the candidates in their primary struggles. A candidate who faces intense competition in the primary election might therefore begin the general election with voters being more aware of their policy positions.

But the evidence does not support this hypothesis, either. In 1976, there were a total of 15 viable candidates competing in the primaries, 13 on the Democratic side and 2 on the Republican side (Aldrich 1980). Contrast this to 1980, when there were 2 in the Democratic primaries and 7 in the Republican (Bartels 1988). This indicates that neither having many opponents in a primary (Carter in 1976, Reagan in 1980) nor having only one very competitive opponent (Ford in 1976, Carter in 1980) could account for the variations in voter policy uncertainty. Thus, primary competitiveness can be eliminated as

6. Both find that between 50 and 60 percent of coverage was devoted to the campaign, and that roughly 30 percent was devoted to substantive issues, with the remainder fitting into no other categories.

an explanation.

Another indicator of campaign intensity, though, could be campaign spending. Of course, presidential campaign finance is heavily regulated, if the candidate chooses to take public funding: in the nomination period they face both total expenditure and state-by-state spending ceilings, while in the general election they have only caps on their total expenditures. However, while candidates usually spend to the limit in the general election, they do not do so in the nomination contests (Sorauf 1988). The relationship between campaign spending and voter uncertainty should be direct: the more a candidate spends, the lower should be the electorate's uncertainty. Also, the more that is spent by both candidates, the lower should be the electorate's aggregate uncertainty in that election.

From the Federal Election Commission I obtained the election year "Candidate Index of Supporting Documents," which is better known as the "short E-index," for each major party candidate. This lists the receipts and expenditures of the principal campaign committees and other authorized committees for each candidate. I summed the primary and general election expenditures made by the principal (committee authorized for the general election) and the major authorized committee (authorized to spend public funds in the primary) and adjusted the figures for inflation into 1985 dollars.[7] The results are in table 9.3.

Here one fact is clear—the amount of money spent in presidential elections since 1976 rose steeply until 1984. But there was a smaller increase in expenditures in 1988 than in previous years. However, the trends in the data here are inconsistent with the variations in voter uncertainty about the policy positions of the candidates. To the extent that campaign expenditures indicate campaign intensity and "getting the message out," I expected to see that expenditures adjusted for inflation should have been the highest in 1980 and 1984. That is certainly not the case in table 9.3, since the general trend across the four elections is that campaign expenditures in general and primary elections have increased.

There is one last possible explanation, and that is the nature of the cam-

---

7. I would like to thank Warren Miller, Office of Public Records, Federal Election Commission for his assistance in obtaining these figures and in their interpretation. Note that the expenditures reported here are the net disbursements reported by the campaigns, and they do include expenditures not subject to the expenditure limits. Typically these expenditures above the limits are fundraising costs, and I have included them in these calculations since fundraising is clearly exposure for the candidate and often the candidate appears at the fundraising event or makes a speech. In many cases these appearances are covered by the local and national news media. But these expenditures above the limit do not include legal and accounting costs, since all of the candidates had distinct committees (usually called compliance committees) that made disbursements for these purposes.

TABLE 9.3.   Campaign Expenditures, 1976–88 (millions 1985 dollars)

Election Year	Democrat Primary	General	Total	Republican Primary	General	Total	Election Total
1976	8.16	14.1	22.3	8.15	13.1	21.2	43.5
1980	15.8	22.6	38.4	20.7	24.5	45.1	83.6
1984	36.2	43.3	79.5	27.1	42.6	69.7	149.2
1988	32.8	59.2	92.0	36.2	56.4	92.6	184.6

Note: Entries are taken from data made available by the Federal Election Commission in the "Candidate Index of Supporting Documents" forms. Each entry includes expenditures made by principal and major authorized committees and has been adjusted for inflation into 1985 dollars.

paigns conducted by the candidates in these elections. In chapter 6 I briefly discussed the consensus in the journalistic and academic literatures concerning these campaigns. There I noted that the 1976 campaign was focused largely on questions about the character and leadership abilities of the candidates, but that policy issues were discussed somewhat by the candidates; that the 1980 campaign again concerned character issues, but split in its focus on both retrospective and prospective issues; that the 1984 race saw Reagan employ the Rose Garden strategy while Mondale simply consolidated coalitions; and that the 1988 election, while faulted for the attention played to symbols, saw a Bush strategy devoted almost entirely to explicitly presenting the differences between himself and Dukakis.

Again, these differences fail to explain the variations in voter uncertainty about the positions of the candidates across these elections. Based on these campaigns, my expectation is that the 1984 election should have produced the greatest aggregate uncertainty about the positions of the candidates, since policy concerns were often absent from the campaign rhetoric. This is certainly not the case, since 1984 witnessed the lowest aggregate levels of uncertainty among these elections. Another case in point is the 1988 election, since the Bush campaign deliberately attempted to point out the differences between the candidates, which should reduce voter uncertainty relative to the other elections. However, the level of policy uncertainty in 1988 was relatively great.

Conclusion

In this chapter I moved from the individual-level models of voting to a discussion of voter uncertainty at the aggregate level. I first demonstrated that the results from the individual-level statistical models made a great deal of sense when compared to the aggregate distributions of voter uncertainty across these elections. Then I discussed the variation in aggregate uncertainty in more detail and argued that the patterns observed in both table 9.1 and figure 9.1 made a great deal of sense.

In particular, I noted that three variables appeared to account for the variation in voter uncertainty over these elections and candidates: incumbency, previous electoral experience, and national prominence. These three factors also mesh with the model of voter learning advanced in chapter 2, since voters seem to learn about the positions of candidates to whom they are regularly exposed. And this learning is seen, in this case, in reductions in uncertainty about the policy stands of the candidates. For example, in the two cases of incumbent presidents standing for reelection, the mean uncertainty levels associated with their positions was lower than their challengers, and, more importantly, substantially lower than the level of uncertainty associated with their positions in the previous election.

Then I refuted a number of competing explanations concerning variations in media coverage of these campaigns, changes in campaign intensity, and differences in the themes of the campaigns. While more descriptive than quantitative, these arguments demonstrated that none of these factors could account for the patterns observed in the aggregate distributions of uncertainty.

This does not mean that these campaigns did not influence how certain the voters were of the policy positions of the different candidates, nor that voters did not learn about the candidates during these elections. Rather, these campaign-related factors simply seem not to account for the differences in aggregate uncertainty levels *across these campaigns*. The aggregate of data on uncertainty I presented in this chapter is only a snapshot of voter knowledge of the candidates late in the general election. Thus, it is still likely as the learning model predicted that during a presidential campaign, voters can reduce their uncertainty about the positions of the candidates considerably if presented with information about the candidates. In the next chapter, I show that across two of these campaigns, the 1976 and 1980 races, voters did learn about the positions of the candidates on the issues and that this learning occurred in response to the information made available during these campaigns.

CHAPTER 10

The Dynamics of Uncertainty

We have undertaken to teach the voters, as free, independent citizens, intelligent enough to see their rights, interested enough to insist on being treated justly, and patriotic enough to desire their country's welfare. Thus this campaign is one of information and organization. Every citizen should be regarded as a thoughtful, responsible voter, and he should be furnished the means of examining the issues involved in the pending canvass for himself.

—Grover Cleveland, Letter to Chauncey E. Black, September 14, 1888

The amount of information voters possess about the policy positions of presidential candidates varies in an understandable fashion examined in the previous chapter. There I demonstrated that voters do seem to learn about the positions of the candidates, especially if the focus covers more than just one general election period. It was particularly apparent in the previous chapter that voters retain information about candidates from previous elections, and from that base they can develop relatively precise understandings of candidate positions. Also, voters appear to learn about the positions of incumbent presidents. But do the campaigns themselves provide information to voters about the positions of the candidates? And do voters learn about these positions during the campaign? These will be the central questions of this chapter.

Here I focus solely on the 1976 and 1980 elections. Using data from Thomas Patterson's panel study and media content analysis from the 1976 election and the 1980 NES Major Panel Study and media content data I have collected, I test the hypotheses derived from the Bayesian learning model of chapter 3. This chapter begins by discussing the information provided to the electorate in 1976, as reflected by mass media coverage of the candidates. In this first section I show, contrary to other claims, that the media provided a great deal of coverage of the positions of both Ford and Carter in the 1976 election and that the dynamics of this coverage correspond to campaign events. Then I turn to the individual-level 1976 survey data and show that there are

171

substantial reductions in voter uncertainty of the positions of the candidates during the campaign that are directly related to the flow of information. These reductions in uncertainty, moreover, occurred for the *least educated, informed, and politically-exposed* respondents. Then I examine the 1980 election in the same fashion, showing dramatically different results. In 1980, the flow of information was quite different than 1976 and was not as informative. Consequently, the dynamics of voter learning in 1980 differ from the dynamics in 1976 since there is little, if any, learning occurring during the 1980 election. But again, what learning there was in 1980 did occur among voters with the highest information costs. I close with a discussion of these important results.

Information Dynamics in the 1976 Campaign

For learning about the positions of the candidates to occur, a baseline level of information is necessary. That even minimal levels of information about the positions of the candidates in 1976 was made available by the mass media is in dispute. Thomas Patterson, analyzing the same data I use in this section, concluded that "the press concentrates on the strategic game played by the candidates in their pursuit of the presidency, thereby deemphasizing questions of national policy and leadership" (Patterson 1980, 21). As shown in the last chapter and in Patterson's analysis, the media does appear to focus on the strategic aspects of the presidential contest more than on substantive matters.

So in order to discuss the effect of the campaign on voter perceptions of candidate issue positions, I must first present evidence on the information dynamics of the 1976 presidential campaign. A precondition for voter learning is that the electorate must be presented with information during the campaign. But to show that learning occurred regarding the uncertainty of the electorate about the positions of Ford and Carter in 1976, I need to demonstrate that information about their positions was in fact transmitted during this election and that voter perceptions responded to this information. The Bayesian model developed in chapter 3 posited that when presented with new information, voter uncertainty should fall. The central task of this chapter is to demonstrate that by increasing the amounts of substantive, issue-related information presented to the electorate during the 1976 campaign, aggregate voter uncertainty fell accordingly.

As I show in this section, coverage of the two major candidates was quite substantial—more information about the major candidates was made available to the electorate as the campaign progressed. But more importantly, the relative proportions of substantive information (including information about the positions of the candidates) to strategic information changed dramatically across the campaign. Moreover, during the general election period, substantive in-

TABLE 10.1. Campaign Events, 1976

Iowa caucuses	January 19
New Hampshire primary	February 25
Arkansas primary (last)	June 26
Democratic convention	July 12–17
Republican convention	August 17–20
Domestic policy debate	September 23
Foreign policy debate	October 6
Third debate	October 22
Election day	November 2

formation actually exceeded strategic information. And last, the dynamics of information during the election are related to campaign events.

To simplify discussion of the 1976 campaign, I present in table 10.1 a breakdown of the major events during the ten-month period from January to October 1976. This table gives the beginning and ending events of the primary season, which stretched from January until the end of June. The party conventions were held in mid-July (Democrats) and in mid-August (Republicans). After the conventions, the general election campaign proceeded and was structured around three major debates. The first debate (September 23) was focused on domestic and economic issues, and Ford was eventually declared the winner. With Ford's support increasing after the debate, Carter began to attack Ford more directly (Kessel 1984, 157). The second debate (October 6) was held in San Francisco and covered foreign policy. It was during this debate that Ford, responding to a question about relations with the Soviets, remarked, "There is no Soviet domination of Eastern Europe, and there never will be under a Ford Administration" (*New York Times*, October 7, 1976, 1:6). Ford eventually recanted and in the aftermath was forced to campaign very heavily both personally and through paid advertising, while the Carter campaign engaged in an increasingly negative campaign against Ford. Perhaps in response to a tighter race, during the third debate both candidates were very cautious. Then, with just over a week remaining, both candidates began the final phase of their campaigns with a flurry of advertisements and appearances. On November 2, Carter barely won by sweeping the South and taking enough Northern states to give him a slim electoral college victory.

So, did the media coverage of the campaign correspond to these campaign events? To examine the information dynamics of the campaign I used Patterson's media content data. Patterson randomly selected over 6,500 politically related news stories concerning the 1976 election from nine mass media outlets, including newspapers, magazines, and television networks. These stories

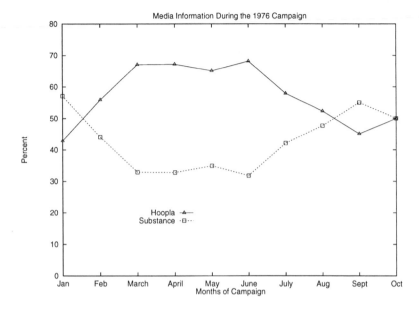

Fig. 10.1.   Hoopla and substance, 1976.

were analyzed in great detail, and from the content codes I extracted 8,834 "candidate mentions," in which Patterson coded a reference for a specific candidate relating to a specific topic.[1]

Using these data, I first aggregated the reference topics during each month of the campaign following Patterson's guidelines: stories relating to evaluations of the candidate, strategies, tactics, logistics, support, campaign style, horse race, appearances, and chances for victory were grouped under the label "hoopla," while stories about the issue stands, ideologies, records, traits, and endorsements, of the candidate were categorized as "substance."[2] The results of this analysis are presented in figure 10.1.

Here the percentage of stories falling into either category is given on the

---

1. Patterson's media content analysis actually is contained in two data sets. The first is the content analysis of more than 6,500 stories. The second is a subset of the first data set, into which Patterson placed all candidate-specific media references. For each story, up to eight specific candidate "mentions" were coded and placed in the second data set. My data were drawn from this second set. Each observation in this data set is a story, with source and date information. Each candidate mention is indexed by candidate, the subject of the reference, and a number of evaluation codes. Here I employ only the date, candidate, and subject codes.

2. See Patterson 1980, 186, note 5.

y-axis, and the *x*-axis presents the month of the campaign. The dark line gives the percentage of substantive stories, while the light line gives the percentage of stories focused on the campaign (hoopla). Recall that in my analysis of the media coverage of the 1976–88 campaigns obtained from the *New York Times Index*, I found using a similar coding scheme that two-thirds of the general election media coverage focused on the campaigns, and only one-third on substance. That result paralleled the findings of both Patterson (1980) and Graber (1983).

Here, notice that there is a great deal of temporal fluctuation in the proportions of coverage relating to each topic. Not surprisingly, the primary election period, from January to June, is overwhelmingly devoted to the campaign and hoopla. That is, during the 1976 primary election season, the information transmitted to the electorate about the campaign by the mass media primarily concerned stories about the candidates' positions in the horse race, their strategies and tactics, and other nonsubstantive information.

However, during the general election period, this trend changes dramatically. In July and August, during both party conventions, coverage of substance rose greatly. Thus, in 1976 it is apparent that during the late stages of the nomination process and in the early stages of the general election, the information dynamic of the campaign shifted heavily away from *primarily hoopla to a more balanced coverage of substance and the campaign.* In September, coverage of substance actually was greater than that of the campaign, and in October the levels of hoopla versus substantive coverage were virtually identical.

Therefore, figure 10.1 provides evidence of an important informational dynamic in the 1976 campaign. The coverage relating specifically to the candidates was largely devoted to the campaign throughout the primary election. However, a dramatic shift was initiated during the transition from primary to general elections (during the conventions), until there were roughly equivalent amounts of both types of candidate references in the general election. Since the amount of substantive coverage concerning the candidates increased during the general election, one precondition for voter learning about the positions of the candidates exists.

Yet, was the coverage of the two major party candidates also evenly balanced, or did one candidate receive more coverage during the campaign? Or did candidate coverage fluctuate over the election year? To probe into these questions, I present in figure 10.2 the percentages of references each month to Ford (dark line) and Carter (light line). Again, the *y*-axis gives the percentage of stories for each candidate, while the *x*-axis gives the month of the election. Note, however, that the percentages are calculated here as the number of coded references to the particular candidate out of the total number of references to

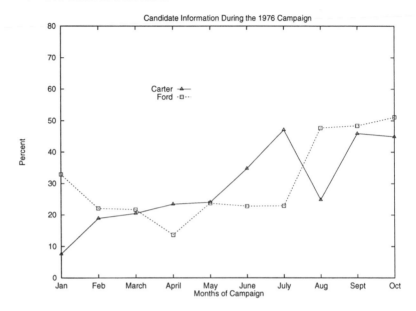

Fig. 10.2.   References to Carter and Ford.

all candidates in that period.[3]

The trends in information during the election about the two major party nominees parallel the events in the campaign. In figure 10.2 note that in the early days of the primary season, Ford received a great deal of coverage while Carter received little: in January, Ford received over one-third of all references to candidates in the sampled news media, while Carter was mentioned in less than ten percent of references. While Ford's coverage remained relatively constant throughout the primary election period, the upward trend in Carter references is striking and closely parallels his success in the Democratic primaries.

Then, Carter's references peak during July—the month of the Democratic convention. Ford's mentions, after remaining at about 20 percent, climb to almost half of all candidate references in August—the month of the Republican convention. In September and October, the general election period, both Carter and Ford received similar levels of references. However, Carter had slightly less coverage in the last two months of the election year, which gives another indication of the difficulties of challenging even a nonelected incum-

---

3. That is why the percentages, especially in the primary season, do not sum to one hundred.

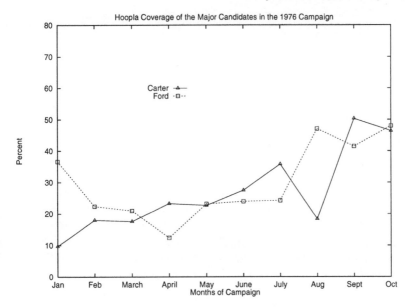

Fig. 10.3.   Hoopla coverage, 1976.

bent president.[4]

Next, I examined the trends in hoopla versus substantive references to both Ford and Carter. These are presented in figures 10.3 and 10.4. Figure 10.3 gives the percent of hoopla references in each month for both candates on the *y*-axis, and the month of the campaign on the *x*-axis. Figure 10.4 is identical, except that the percentages of substantive stories for the two candidates are graphed. In each figure, the dark line gives the percentages for Ford over the election year, and the light line for Carter.

Starting with figure 10.3, notice that the trends in hoopla coverage for each candidate roughly parallel those for total candidate coverage just discussed. Carter received very few campaign-related references early in the primary season, but the percentage of mentions concerning Carter's campaigning steadily climbed to peak at 35.8 percent in July, the month of the Democratic convention. Campaign references for Carter dropped sharply during August, the month of the Republican convention, but jumped quickly back upward during the last two months of the election. Ford received a great deal of hoopla refer-

---

4. In September and October Carter received 45.9 and 44.9 percent of the references, respectively, while Ford picked up 48.4 percent in September and 51.1 percent in November.

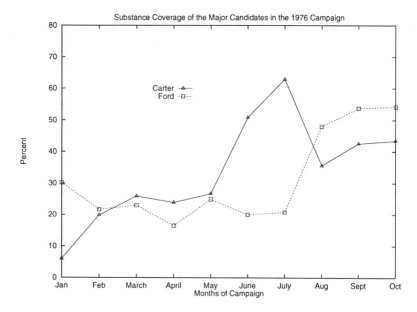

Fig. 10.4.   Substance coverage, 1976.

ences in the first month of the election, with almost 37 percent of the references in January. Again, this dropped immediately to just over 20 percent, where his campaign-related references hovered until August. During the month of his party's convention, the campaign-related mentions for Ford jumped to almost 50 percent of all such references. During September and October, Ford's hoopla references in the mass media were very similar to Carter's.

But a different dynamic is clear in figure 10.4. Here, Carter begins the election with almost no substantive coverage (only 6 percent). This is not surprising, given that he was competing for substantive coverage with so many other, better-known primary candidates from both parties. But with early successes, Carter's substantive coverage climbed to almost 30 percent of all references in March through May. During June and July, though, the percentage of substantive mentions of Carter skyrocketed: 50.8 percent in June (the last months of the Democratic primary) and 62.9 percent in July. The substantive references to Carter did drop during August, and leveled off at just over 40 percent during the general election months of September and October.

Ford, on the other hand, began with the lion's share of substantive coverage in January (30 percent). He received approximately one-fifth of substantive

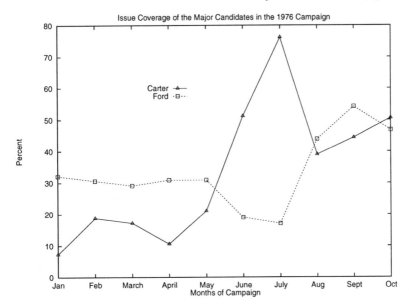

Fig. 10.5.   Issue coverage, 1976.

coverage from February until July, during the entire primary and early convention season. But during August, and the Republican convention, substantive coverage of Ford jumped considerably, to 48 percent. And Ford received over half of the substantive mentions in September and October, at least 10 percent more than Carter obtained.

Thus, I have established that dramatic changes occurred in the media coverage of the 1976 election, especially as it pertained to references to Carter and Ford. And it is clear that the informational dynamics in figures 10.1– 10.4 coincide closely with the major events of the campaign. This evidence alone shows that in 1976 the preconditions for substantial voter learning about the positions of both Carter and Ford existed. That is, during the campaign, considerable information about the candidates was available in the mass media, and the coverage of both major candidates, especially their substantive coverage, did increase dramatically in the post primary period of the election year.

Yet substantive coverage is not solely due to references to the issue positions of the two candidates. To more precisely understand the dynamics of issue coverage, I graphed only those references to Carter and Ford that dealt with their positions on domestic or foreign policy issues.[5] These are given in figure 10.5, where the y-axis now gives the percentage of issue-specific mentions for Ford (dark line) and Carter (light line) during each month of the campaign.

The trends in figure 10.5 are even more intriguing than those shown for the broader category of substantive references. Here, Carter once again begins with exceptionally low levels of issue references (less than 10 percent in January), which is quite understandable given that he was the unknown outsider candidate in the early Democratic primaries. Befitting his success in the early primaries, though, Carter does pick up a reasonable level of references to his issue stands from February to May.

But in June, and then in July, mentions of Carter's positions on issues rose to 52 percent (June) and 76.2 percent (July), as the campaign progressed from the late primary stage to the Democratic convention. In particular, that Carter's issue positions received almost eight out of ten references relative to all candidates in July is amazing. The tremendous coverage of Carter's positions dropped to 40 percent in August, climbing to just over 50 percent by October.

Ford received a constant 30 percent of the issue-specific coverage during most of the primary period, from January to May. When it became clear that Carter would be the Democratic nominee and attention shifted to Carter's positions, references to Ford's positions fell to approximately 20 percent of all candidate issue mentions in June and July. Yet with the advent of the Republican convention in August, Ford's positions received a great deal of coverage by the mass media. And again, the coverage devoted to Ford's issue stands during the general election was almost identical to that given to Carter.

These five figures demonstrate three points about the 1976 election. The first point is that there was a substantial amount of information available about the two major party candidates in this election. The entire sample from which these percentages were calculated had over 8,000 candidate-specific references and were drawn from a random sample of 6,500 political news stories. Thus, a great deal of information was available about the candidates in 1976.

---

5. Patterson coded as issue references those mentions that concerned the economy, unemployment, government employment, inflation, tax reforms, abortion, working with Congress, crime, social welfare, government spending, government efficiency, social security and medicare, minority rights, women's rights, federalism, health care, the environment, consumer protection, gun control, education, drugs, energy, cities, and busing, as domestic issues; military spending, foreign involvement, détente, foreign aid, the Middle East, OPEC, U.S. world prestige, general foreign policy, Panama Canal, nuclear weapons, and other miscellaneous foreign and defense topics, as foreign issues. There were a total of 482 domestic issue references (152 for Carter, 219 for Ford, 111 for other candidates) and 1,003 foreign issue references (385 for Carter, 350 for Ford, and 268 for the other candidates).

Second the flow of information during this campaign had clear and understandable dynamics. Each of the five figures demonstrates that the information available about the two party candidates varied over the election year. Hoopla coverage exceeded substantive coverage—but only in the primary campaign. Substantive coverage rose dramatically during the period of the party conventions and actually was greater than campaign coverage during the two general election months (fig. 10.1). Total references to Carter were few in the early primary months, but they rose greatly in June and July of the election year; references to Ford were relatively constant through the entire campaign period, only rising after July (fig. 10.2). Hoopla and substantive coverage specifically devoted to Carter and Ford followed similar dynamics (figs. 10.3 and 10.4).

And third, both the broader substantive references and the narrow issue-specific references to these two candidates show dramatic increases during the convention and general election periods (figs. 10.4 and 10.5). Therefore, information about the positions of both Ford and Carter, while relatively sparse before June of the election year, became relatively abundant thereafter. This implies that the informational environment in 1976 could have been conducive to voter learning about the policy positions of both Ford and Carter, since a great deal of information was clearly transmitted via the mass media during the later stages of this presidential campaign. Note last that the trends in information are especially strong for Carter, who as the outsider began with a considerable deficit in media coverage of his campaign. That substantive and particularly issue-specific coverage of Carter skyrocketed in the early stages of the general election campaign provided an excellent opportunity for voters to learn about his policy positions. These findings perhaps explain why he ended up as well known as the (unelected) incumbent.

Voter Learning in 1976

Yet it remains to show that voters did learn from this information flow in 1976. To demonstrate that voter learning did occur, I return to the Bayesian learning model derived in chapter 2. It is possible to test the hypotheses that were deduced from the theoretical analysis by exploiting the panel data collected by Patterson in 1976. The first hypothesis from the Bayesian model stated that with increasing information, voter uncertainty should change. I have shown in the previous section that increasing information about the candidates *and about their policy positions* was made available as the campaign progressed. To substantiate this first hypothesis, I must show that voter uncertainty of the positions of the candidates was reduced accordingly.

First, I calculated the uncertainty measure for Carter and Ford for each of the five waves of the 1976 Patterson panel survey (February, April, June,

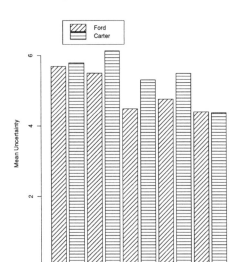

Fig. 10.6.   Mean uncertainty levels across the 1976 election.

August, and October). The uncertainty measure called the fifth survey wave uncertainty measure is the same measure as used in previous chapters for the 1976 election. Unfortunately, the three issue scales used to calculate the fifth wave uncertainty measures were not available in the first two survey waves and are not included in the calculation of the uncertainty measure for these two waves.[6] These uncertainty measures for the two candidates across the five panel waves are the basis for the rest of the analysis in this section.

A simple test is to examine the aggregate levels of uncertainty across the five panel waves. Thus, I calculated the uncertainty means for each candidate in each survey wave. These means are given graphically in figure 10.6. There, the mean uncertainty level in a particular survey wave is given by the y-axis, and the consecutive survey waves are given along the x-axis.[7] One bar indicates the mean uncertainty level for Ford, and the other bar the mean

6. The three issues not in the first two waves were foreign involvement, crime, and wage and price control scales.

7. The five survey waves were February, April, June, August, and October.

uncertainty for Carter, in the particular survey wave.

Figure 10.6 affirms that aggregate uncertainty levels did drop substantially between February and October. The mean level of voter uncertainty about Ford's positions dropped from 5.69 in February to 4.40 in October, a change of 1.3 points. Most of this drop occurred between the second and third waves of the panel survey, between the April and June interview periods. Mean uncertainty about Carter's positions dropped virtually the same amount, as shown in the figure. Most of the reduction in Carter policy uncertainty, though, occurred between August (fourth wave) and October (fifth wave), just after the massive flow of substantive and issue-specific information about Jimmy Carter (figs. 10.4 and 10.5). Interestingly, however, these reductions in Carter uncertainty may be heavily understated. While most respondents in the first wave of the panel study recognized Ford and were able to place him on most of the policy scales, only 20 percent of these same respondents recognized Carter or were able to place him on the seven-point policy scales.[8] Those who could recognize Carter and place him on the scales in February were better educated, more informed about politics, and more exposed to political information—and hence they were probably much more certain of Carter's positions on the issues. This no doubt explains the increase in Carter mean uncertainty which is seen between the first two survey waves.

Thus, these observed reductions in voter uncertainty about the policy positions of both candidates in 1976 across the campaign are evidence that voter learning occurred during the campaign. This supports the hypothesis taken from the Bayesian learning model, that as more information about the positions of the candidates is made available to the electorate, reductions in uncertainty should occur.

But what of the patterns at the individual level? It is possible that the reductions in voter uncertainty at the aggregate level are masking more dramatic changes in the uncertainty voters had of the two candidates in the 1976 election. So I now turn to an analysis of the changes in the individual-level survey data.

My measure of individual-level changes in uncertainty about the presidential candidates is simply the difference between the voter's uncertainty about the policy stands of each candidate at two different points in time. I examined the changes in uncertainty between the second and third (April and June) and the fourth and fifth (August and October) survey waves. These two different time periods were chosen deliberately, since the change in voter uncertainty between April and June occurred late in the primary season, while the change

---

8. There were 898 respondents for whom it was possible to calculate the uncertainty measure for Ford in the February panel. But only 184 respondents are included in the identical calculation for Carter in the first panel wave.

between the August and October waves fell during the general election contest. Examining the changes in uncertainty between the primary and general election contexts should provide insight into the possible effects each of these electoral institutions had on voter awareness of the policy positions of the candidates.

Rather than study the simple differences between each voter's uncertainty for the candidates at two points in time, I have analyzed only the reductions in voter uncertainty which were substantial. To determine substantial changes in voter uncertainty, I calculated the two uncertainty differences and their standard errors. Changes between the two uncertainty measures at the individual level were deemed substantial if they were greater or less than one standard deviation from zero. That is, positive changes greater than one standard deviation from zero were termed substantial *increases* in uncertainty, while negative changes grater than one standard deviation from zero were called substantial *reductions* in voter uncertainty.

Table 10.2 shows the percentages between the April and June, and the August and October, uncertainty measures. The first observation to make about the percentages in table 10.2 is that most changes in uncertainty were within a standard deviation of zero. Since the standard deviations of the differences in candidate uncertainty presented here all were approximately three, this means that most of the observed changes in voter uncertainty between these survey waves were plus or minus three points from zero. This is clearly a conservative

TABLE 10.2.   Changes in Voter Uncertainty, 1976

Candidate Periods	Change in Voter Uncertainty		
	Substantial Reduction	No Change	Substantial Increase
Carter			
April–June	22.4	70.0	7.6
August–October	23.4	72.8	3.8
Ford			
April–June	22.0	71.2	6.8
August–October	15.7	77.1	7.2

Note: Entries in the three right columns are the percentages of respondents for whom the difference in their uncertainty for each candidate was more than a standard deviation less than zero (substantial reduction), within a standard deviation of zero (no change), or a standard deviation greater than zero (substantial increase).

measure of the individual-level change in uncertainty.

Secondly, note that in the primary period, approximately 20 percent of respondents had substantial *reductions* in their uncertainty of both candidates. The percentages with substantial reductions in their uncertainty increased by one percent for Carter, but fell by almost seven percent for Ford. According to this measure of change in uncertainty, around one-fifth of the respondents became *more certain of the positions of the candidates in either survey period.*

Third, note that the percentages of respondents deemed to have had substantial *increases* in their uncertainty of the candidates during this election were generally small. The percentage of respondents who appear to have become more uncertain of the positions of Ford and Carter is never much over seven percent of the sample.

Again, the results reported in table 10.2 provide support for the hypothesis that learning occurred during the 1976 campaign. Approximately one-fifth of the respondents in either the primary period or the general election period became more certain of the positions of Ford and Carter. Given that my approach to categorizing respondents as becoming more certain of the positions of the candidates is quite conservative, this is an important finding.

Yet the question remains—which respondents appear to have learned about the positions of the candidates in either the primary or general election period? Do voters with high information costs, or low exposure to political information, learn about the campaign? Or is learning confined only to voters with greater access to information and lower costs of processing that information?

To answer these questions, I examined the mean education, political information, and media exposure levels for those respondents who had a substantial reduction in uncertainty in the primary and general election periods relative to the means of the same three variables for those who had no substantial changes in uncertainty.[9] To ascertain the magnitude of the differences, I performed difference-of-means tests to check that the observed difference between the means implies a significant difference between population means.[10]

The results of this analysis are given in tables 10.3 (differences in education), 10.4 (differences in political information), and 10.5 (differences in media exposure). Each table gives the mean level of the particular variable for the respondents who became substantially less uncertain about the candidate across the survey periods, the mean level for those with no substantial change in un-

---

9. These three independent variables were operationalized from the 1976 survey data as described in the appendix to chapter 5.

10. The simple *t*-test for differences between means was implemented in SAS, using the GLM procedure. This test is subject to Type I error, in which one falsely rejects a null hypothesis, since the probability of incorrectly rejecting a null of no difference in population means increases as the number of *t*-tests increases.

TABLE 10.3.   Education and Changes in Voter Uncertainty, 1976

Candidate Periods	Education Mean Substantial Reduction	Education Mean No Change	Education Differences		
			Difference In Means	Lower Bound	Upper Bound
Carter					
April–June	5.06	5.13	−0.07	−0.42	0.28
August–October	4.74	5.14	−0.41*	−0.74	−0.08
Ford					
April–June	4.56	5.10	−0.54*	−0.86	−0.22
August–October	4.33	5.08	−0.75*	−1.11	−0.39

Note: Entries give the education means and differences in these means, for respondents who substantially reduced their uncertainty of the particular candidate versus those who had no substantial change across the two survey waves. The two right columns give the 95 percent confidence interval bounds.
* denotes that the difference in means is statistically significant at the $p = 0.05$ level.

TABLE 10.4.   Political Information and Changes in Voter Uncertainty, 1976

Candidate Periods	Information Mean Substantial Reduction	Information Mean No Change	Information Differences		
			Difference In Means	Lower Bound	Upper Bound
Carter					
April–June	5.33	5.60	−0.27	−1.11	0.56
August–October	5.00	6.72	−1.72*	−2.42	−1.02
Ford					
April–June	4.39	5.18	−0.79*	−1.53	−0.04
August–October	4.25	6.37	−2.11*	−2.88	−1.34

Note: Entries give the political information means and differences in these means, for respondents who substantially reduced their uncertainty of the particular candidate versus those who had no substantial change across the two survey waves. The two right columns give the 95 percent confidence interval bounds.
* denotes that the difference in means is statistically significant at the $p = 0.05$ level.

TABLE 10.5.   Media Exposure and Changes in Voter Uncertainty, 1976

			Media Exposure Differences		
Candidate Periods	Exposure Mean Substantial Reduction	Exposure Mean No Change	Difference In Means	Lower Bound	Upper Bound
Carter					
April–June	8.90	9.04	−0.14	−0.85	0.55
August–October	9.34	10.1	−0.71*	−1.18	−0.25
Ford					
April–June	8.75	8.75	−0.00	−0.63	0.62
August–October	9.02	9.90	−0.87*	−1.39	−0.39

Note: Entries give the political exposure means and differences in these means, for respondents who substantially reduced their uncertainty of the particular candidate versus those who had no substantial change across the two survey waves. The two right columns give the 95 percent confidence interval bounds.
* denotes that the difference in means is statistically significant at the $p = 0.05$ level.

certainty, the difference in the two means, and the lower and upper bounds for the 95 percent confidence interval. The tables are arranged so that a positive difference between the means indicates that those with substantial reductions in candidate policy position uncertainty would be better educated, politically informed, and media exposed than those with no substantial change in uncertainty; a negative difference indicates that those respondents with substantial reductions in uncertainty are less educated, informed, and exposed to the mass media.

Notice first that in each table, *the differences between the means are always negative.* Thus, respondents in the 1976 survey who became less uncertain of the positions of the candidates between the April and June survey waves, or the August and October waves, were less educated, less politically informed, and less exposed to the media than those who had no substantial change in their uncertainty. Secondly, most of these differences in means are statistically significant, meaning that for the differences in means that are starred, the null hypothesis that there is no difference in the population between the mean values of these three variables can be rejected with confidence. The only exceptions to this second observation are the differences in means for changes in Carter uncertainty between the April and June survey waves, and the differences in mean media exposure levels for Ford uncertainty reductions in the primary period.

These results are fascinating. As I demonstrated in chapter 6, respondents who are better educated, informed, and exposed to the mass media coverage of the campaign are more certain of the candidates' positions at the end of the general election. The implication of these results is that in general these same voters do not become more certain of the positions of the candidates during the campaign, either in the primary or general election period. Thus, the voters who do reduce their uncertainty of the positions of the candidates by learning from the campaign are less educated, informed, and exposed to the media coverage of the campaign.

Information Dynamics in the 1980 Campaign

The 1980 campaign was quite different than the 1976 race. Most of the major campaign events in the 1980 race are given in table 10.6. The primary campaign schedule is similar to 1976, with the early primaries taking place at about the same time in the election cycle. Before the close of the primary season, though, Anderson realized that he was not going to obtain the Republican presidential nomination, and on April 24 he announced his independent bid for president.

The general election campaign in 1980 saw Carter and Reagan begin with virtually even support in the polls and with Anderson a distant third (Abramson et al. 1982). The first debate of the 1980 campaign occurred on September 21 in Baltimore. This debate is remembered mainly for to the absence of Carter, who reasoned that his presence on the stage with Anderson would only shift his supporters to the independent candidate. Otherwise, both Anderson and Reagan did well in the debate.

Within the next two weeks, the Carter campaign opened fire personally on Reagan and also on the media coverage of the race. As a result, the campaign became increasingly negative, and this dynamic seemed to favor Carter (Harwood 1980). To stop the attacks and the changes in the polls, Reagan announced he would debate Carter, one-on-one. The candidates met on October 28 in Cleveland. The questions ranged across foreign and domestic issues, and by most accounts, the candidates were relatively forthcoming with their positions on these issues. In the end, though, the polls gave Reagan a slight victory, which gave him the momentum to carry him to a victory over Carter on November 4.

But were these campaign events reflected in media coverage of the 1980 race? More generally, what were the dynamics of media coverage across the 1980 campaign? To answer these questions, I undertook a content analysis of one major national newspaper—the Los Angeles Times—during the entire

TABLE 10.6.   Campaign Events, 1980

Iowa caucuses	January 21
New Hampshire primary	February 26
Anderson announces independent candidacy	April 24
Republican convention	July 14–17
Democratic convention	August 14–17
Reagan-Anderson debate	September 21
Carter-Reagan debate	October 28
Election day	November 4

election year (January 1 through November 4). I attempted to replicate the story selection and content coding procedures outlined by Patterson (1980) as closely as possible. This produced 5523 specific "candidate mentions"—the relationship of a candidate to a specific topic—across the election year.[11]

As in the 1976 media data analysis, I begin by aggregating the stories into two categories, hoopla and substance (the same coding guidelines as used earlier in this chapter apply). I present these data by month in figure 10.7. In 1980, substantive coverage of the candidates has a slight edge over hoopla in January, which is lost during the rest of the primary season as the media concentrates on who will win each party's primary. Then, beginning in June and lasting through the end of the election (with a slight dip in July), substantive coverage of the candidates slightly dominates hoopla coverage.

This is similar to the 1976 election. In both races, hoopla information—coverage of who's ahead, poll results, and campaign events—predominated during the primary campaign period. However, as the general election begins, substantive coverage (coverage of issues and candidates) becomes the major form of newspaper coverage. The only differences between the two races were that the gap between hoopla and substantive coverage was wider during the primary season in 1976 and that substantive coverage predominated longer in the fall campaign (June through September) in 1980.

What about coverage specifically regarding the three major candidates in the race? Was candidate coverage balanced? Did the incumbent president receive more newspaper coverage? And what about the independent candidate, John Anderson? In figure 10.8 I give the total newspaper coverage for each of the major candidates as a percentage of all references to all candidates during

---

11. Specifically, all stories with direct mention of one of the 1980 candidates, or the election, were included in the sample if they were from Section A and the Opinion pages of the *Los Angeles Times*. Each distinct statement relating to a candidate was coded, following Patterson's guidelines. I did not include stories about Jerry Brown's state duties in the sample to avoid a bias toward a "favorite son."

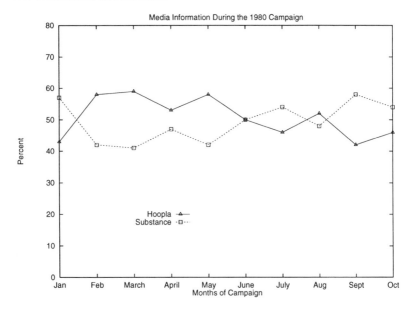

Fig. 10.7.   Hoopla and substance, 1980.

that month.

In figure 10.8 a number of patterns emerge. In general Carter, as the incumbent president, did receive at least as much or more coverage relative to the other candidates through the end of the primary season. Of course, this edge in candidate references reflects the fact that Carter was the incumbent president, and as such obtained more coverage due to presidential actions (recall that the Iranian hostage crisis occurred during this period, as well as the aftermath of the Soviet invasion of Afghanistan). Also, while he did face a serious primary challenge from Kennedy, Carter was the undisputed front-runner in the Democratic primary, which must have generated some of this newspaper coverage.

Second, notice the impact of two important campaign events on candidate coverage—the party conventions. Carter's general election coverage dominates the other candidates only in August (the time of the Democratic convention), while Reagan sees one peak of coverage in July, during the Republican convention. That this same pattern occurred in the 1976 election is obviously no coincidence since candidates count on the coverage generated by their party conventions, which they hope to translate into a surge in postconvention popu-

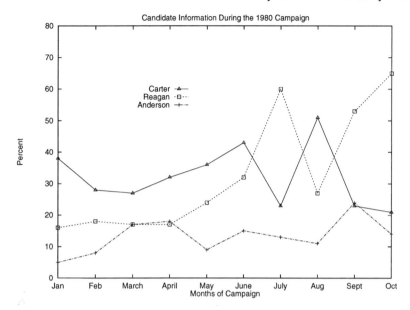

Fig. 10.8.   Candidate references.

lar support. Thus, major campaign events like party conventions do influence media coverage of presidential campaigns.

The third important aspect of figure 10.8 is the coverage of Anderson. Early in the Republican primaries, Anderson receives virtually no coverage. However, when Anderson did relatively well in a handful of Republican primaries (Massachusetts, Vermont, Illinois, Wisconsin, and Connecticut were his best primaries), note that his newspaper coverage increases, averaging almost 20 percent of candidate coverage in March, April, and June. Unfortunately for his independent bid, his lack of headway in the polls led to less press coverage relative to Carter and Reagan until late in the general election season, when he receives slightly more coverage than Carter.

Relative to the 1976 race, the dynamics of candidate coverage in 1980 are somewhat different. In 1980, Reagan's coverage shows an enormous increase, from less than 20 percent of candidate stories in January to almost 65 percent in October and early November. Carter has relatively constant coverage through July, but despite increased August coverage, the general trend in the fall campaign for Carter's coverage is down. And last, Anderson sees some increase throughout the race, but only in the last month does he outstrip Carter,

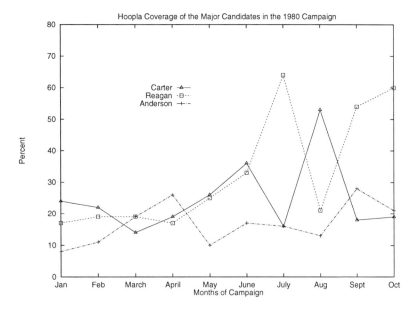

Fig. 10.9.   Hoopla coverage, 1980.

and then by only 5 percent. In comparison the 1976 election (fig. 10.2) showed sharper increases for both candidates across the election year, with Carter going from less than 10 percent to 45 percent across the year as a challenger, and Ford going from over 30 percent to over 50 percent during the election year as the incumbent. While the 1980 challenger fared about as well as the 1976 challenger in media coverage of their candidacy, the story for the incumbents in these two elections is vastly different.

The major questions, though, about candidate coverage relate to its content. Next, I broke the candidate coverage data into hoopla and substantive coverage by candidate, which are in figures 10.9 and 10.10, respectively. The hoopla coverage during the primary period shows Anderson outstripping Carter and Reagan when he did better than expected in a handful of primaries. After that, hoopla coverage of Reagan begins to increase, peaking in July during the Republican convention. Carter receives the bulk of hoopla coverage the following month, as expected. During the last two months of the general election, Reagan receives vastly more hoopla coverage than Carter or Anderson— an indication of his increasing momentum after his debate with Carter.

The substantive coverage of the candidates, given in figure 10.10, shows a

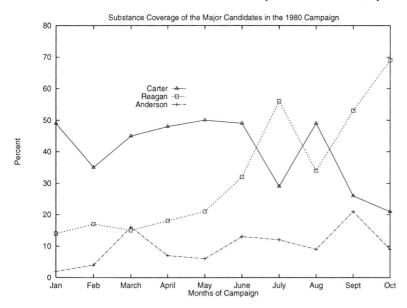

Fig. 10.10. Substance coverage, 1980.

different dynamic. First, Carter receives almost a sheer majority of substantive coverage during the primary season—he gets approximately 50 percent of the substantive coverage through June, except for slightly less in February. Again, as president and as the front-runner in his party's primary, Carter clearly benefited from tremendous substantive coverage in the newspapers.

Reagan, though, begins with little substantive coverage through May. From May until July his substantive coverage skyrockets, and after a dip during the Democratic convention in August, it shoots to 70 percent of candidate-related substantive coverage in October and early November. On the other hand, Anderson receives a small bit of substantive coverage, which peaks in March (during his primary run) and September (when he debates Reagan).

Virtually identical trends are shown for the three candidates' issue-specific coverage in figure 10.11. Again, Carter receives the bulk of the primary issue coverage, although this falls considerably (from 50 percent in June to 20 percent in October and early November) during the general election. Reagan's issue coverage picks up dramatically in the general election; Anderson's shows only a very slight increase.

Yet the substantive and issue coverage of the candidates in 1980 is very

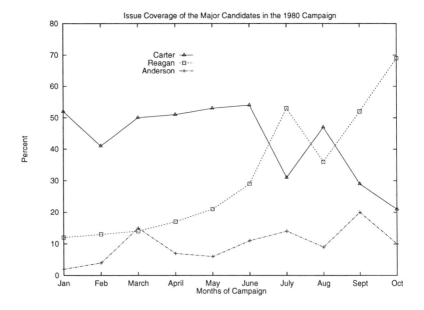

Fig. 10.11. Issue coverage, 1980.

different from that seen in the 1976 data. In the newspaper coverage in 1980, the incumbent candidate receives enormous coverage of his candidacy and is-sue positions through the primary election period; his Republican challenger picks up substantive and issue coverage in the general election *at Carter's ex-pense*. But in 1976 (figs. 10.4 and 10.5) the substantive and issue coverage of *both* candidates *increased significantly* throughout the 1976 campaign.

This comparison between the 1976 and 1980 campaigns, then, leads to an important test of the Bayesian learning model presented in chapter 3. For learning to occur, information must be presented to the electorate. In 1976, increasing amounts of substantive and issue information were provided to the electorate in the print media; and as I demonstrated in the previous section, that information led to substantial reductions in voter uncertainty about the two candidates. But the 1980 election begins with enormous amounts of substan-tive and issue coverage of the incumbent, which drop considerably during the general election campaign. Also, there was little change over the entire elec-tion year in the substantive and issue coverage of the independent candidacy of Anderson. Thus the information environment is not one in which I expect substantial learning about Carter and Anderson to occur *during the election campaign.* Yet Reagan's issue and substantive coverage increases during the 1980 campaign, which may produce more voter learning.

Voter Learning in 1980

While the dynamics of information in the 1980 campaign provide an important test of whether voters learn about candidate issue positions during a presidential election campaign, the available survey data are not as extensive as for the 1976 election. In 1980, the NES mounted a panel survey of national voters, with interviews taken in late January, June (immediately after the last primary), September, and a postelection interview in November. Unfortunately, issue placement questions were asked for Carter and Reagan in only the January, June, and September waves, which provide little opportunity to evaluate whether the large changes in coverage of Reagan's issue positions in the last two months of the campaign influenced voter uncertainty of Reagan. Also, issue placements were asked for Anderson only in the June and September waves of the 1980 NES Major Panel Survey.[12]

Using the available 1980 NES data, I constructed uncertainty scales for the candidates in the first three waves of the panel data. The sample uncertainty mean values for each candidate are given in figure 10.12. The trends in the aggregated uncertainty measures are in line with the dynamics in newspaper coverage presented in the previous section. Carter, who had been in office for the previous four years, begins the campaign with voters generally very certain of his positions on the issues. Compare how certain voters were of his positions at the beginning of this campaign (mean uncertainty of 2.81) relative to how uncertain they were of Carter's positions at the beginning of the 1976 campaign (mean uncertainty of 5.79 in the February wave of the 1976 data, fig. 10.6). Clearly, one aspect of the incumbent advantage for presidential candidates is their ability to convey their issue positions during four years of service. Since Carter begins the 1976 election with voters being so certain of his positions, there is then very little change over the next three waves in mean uncertainty of Carter's positions. It does drop slightly in June and September,

---

12. There were also significant differences in the issue placement questions across the first three waves of the 1980 Panel Study. In the January panel, issue placements were asked for defense spending, government spending, Russian relations, and the government's anti-inflation policies; respondents were asked to place both Carter and Reagan on these scales. In the June panel, issue questions for defense spending, government aid to minorities, government spending, Russian relations, and the government's anti-inflation plan were asked for Carter, Reagan, and Anderson. By the September panel, the issue questions were on defense spending, whether or not the government should insure a good standard of living, Russian relations, or whether the government should fight inflation or unemployment. In the construction of the uncertainty scales in each wave, all of these questions were used.

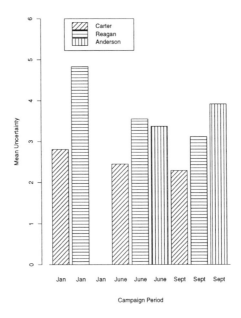

Fig. 10.12.   Mean uncertainty levels across the 1980 election.

but by very small amounts.

Reagan, however, begins the election year with voters being very uncertain of his positions on the issues. From a mean uncertainty of 4.83 in January, the electorate's uncertainty of Reagan's positions falls to 3.55 in June, and to 3.14 in September. Thus it appears that in the aggregate the electorate did obtain information about Reagan's positions from the increased newspaper coverage of Reagan's positions, especially in the later months of the general election campaign.

Last, John Anderson seems to be the loser in terms of voter learning about his positions. While Anderson's "National Unity" campaign was supposed to inform the electorate about Anderson's differences from Carter and Reagan, in the previous section it was apparent that the newspaper coverage of Anderson was relatively insignificant over the entire campaign. While voters are about as uncertain about Anderson's positions as they were about Reagan's in the June wave of the panel survey, by September the electorate seems to have become more uncertain about Anderson and more certain about Reagan.

Thus, the aggregate changes in voter uncertainty of the candidate's positions in 1980 do match the trends in the information made available in the newspapers. Carter, the incumbent, begins the election year with a tremendous amount of substantive and issue coverage of his candidacy; voters are correspondingly very certain of his issue positions. Since the electorate begins the election with relative certainty about Carter's positions, there is little room for additional learning—so the mean uncertainty levels for Carter are basically constant during the entire election year. Reagan, who receives increasing amounts of coverage toward the end of the general election campaign, is benefited by this coverage with increasing voter certainty of his positions. And last, Anderson receives little coverage, and voters learn little about his issue positions.

Are these aggregate changes also seen in the individual-level data? In table 10.7 I present the percentages of voters with substantial reductions, substantial increases, or no change in their uncertainty of each candidate across the waves of the 1980 Panel Study. Again, I use a conservative estimate of voter learning by classifying a voter as having a substantial reduction in uncertainty when between the later and the earlier time periods the difference between candidate uncertainty in each period is more than one standard deviation below zero.

In table 10.7 there is evidence of voter learning in the 1980 campaign. For Carter, between January and June, 13.9 percent of the voters in this sample experienced substantial reductions in uncertainty, while 14.6 percent also had substantial reductions in uncertainty between June and September. Most of the voters in this sample, though, did not have a substantial change in their uncertainty of Carter. And few (about 10 percent between each period) had substantial increases in their uncertainty of Carter's issue positions.

For Reagan, though, there is slightly more evidence of voter learning. In the January–June primary period, 19 percent of the voters had a substantial reduction in their uncertainty of Reagan's positions. This dropped slightly to 14.7 percent in the June–September general election period. But 25.8 percent of the voters in this sample had a substantial reduction in their uncertainty of Reagan's positions across the entire election year. Thus, over one-quarter of the voters had a significant reduction in their uncertainty of Reagan's positions, despite the fact that I am measuring uncertainty only through September and not in the last months of the 1980 election when issue information about Reagan continued to increase.

The results for Anderson continue to demonstrate the inability of his campaign to get information across to the electorate. During the early part of the general election campaign (June–September) only 10.1 percent of the voters had substantial reductions in their uncertainty of Anderson's positions. Yet

15.6 percent had substantial increases in their uncertainty of Anderson, the highest rate in any period in both the 1976 and 1980 elections. Again, the independent candidacy of John Anderson failed to get information about Anderson's issue positions to the electorate—information which might have brought him more votes.

So learning did occur in the 1980 election, and it seems to have happened in response to the information which was provided to the voters by the mass media. In the primary and early general election periods in 1980, between 15 and 20 percent of the voters in my sample had substantial reductions in their uncertainty of Carter and Reagan. This supports the learning model developed in chapter 3, despite the fact that I am using a very conservative measure of learning and that the 1980 Panel Study does not allow me to examine issue uncertainty in the last months of the campaign.

Next, which voters experienced substantial reductions in their uncertainty in the 1980 campaign? To determine whether education, media exposure, or political information influenced the amount of learning in the 1980 campaign, I undertook the same analysis as for the 1976 election. I looked at the mean

TABLE 10.7.   Changes in Voter Uncertainty, 1980

Candidate Periods	Change in Voter Uncertainty		
	Substantial Reduction	No Change	Substantial Increase
Carter			
January–June	13.9	74.4	11.7
June–September	14.6	75.7	9.6
January–September	17.8	73.1	9.1
Reagan			
January–June	19.0	75.3	5.8
June–September	14.7	78.3	7.0
January–September	25.8	70.1	4.2
Anderson			
June–September	10.1	74.3	15.6

Note: Entries in the three right columns are the percentages of respondents for whom the difference in their uncertainty for the each candidate was more than a standard deviation less than zero (substantial reduction), within a standard deviation of zero (no change), or a standard deviation greater than zero (substantial increase).

TABLE 10.8. Education and Changes in Voter Uncertainty, 1980

			Education Differences		
Candidate Periods	Education Mean Substantial Reduction	Education Mean No Change	Difference In Means	Lower Bound	Upper Bound
Carter					
January–June	2.30	3.00	−.70*	−1.02	−.39
June–September	2.44	2.99	−.55*	−.87	−.22
January–September	2.53	3.06	−.53*	−.83	−.23
Reagan					
January–June	2.77	2.97	−.21	−.49	.08
June–September	2.48	3.00	−.53*	−.85	−.21
January–September	2.90	3.02	−.12	−.39	.14
Anderson					
June–September	3.11	3.19	−.08	−.50	.35

Note: Entries give the education means and differences in these means, for respondents who substantially reduced their uncertainty of the particular candidate versus those who had no substantial change across the two survey waves. The two right columns give the 95 percent confidence interval bounds.
* denotes that the difference in means is statistically significant at the $p = 0.05$ level.

levels of education, media exposure, and political information for voters who had a substantial reduction in uncertainty relative to the mean values of these same three variables for voters who had no change in their uncertainty.[13] In tables 10.8, 10.9, and 10.10 I give the means for the different groups, the differences between the means, and the $p = .05$ confidence interval.

Notice that the differences in means for education and political information are *all negative*. This means that voters with substantial reductions in uncertainty are less educated and less politically informed than those with no

13. Education, political information, and media exposure are coded to closely follow their usage in previous chapters. Education is a four-category variable, measuring whether a voter had less than a high school diploma (1), a high school diploma (2), education short of a college degree (3), or a college degree (4). Political information was measured by whether the respondent could place the two parties on the correct ends of four issue scales in the September wave of the survey; the measure of political information ranges from 0 to 4. Media exposure is an additive scale using whether a voter read a daily newspaper and how many days a week they watched national network news on the television.

TABLE 10.9. Information and Changes in Voter Uncertainty, 1980

			Information Differences		
Candidate Periods	Information Mean Substantial Reduction	Information Mean No Change	Difference In Means	Lower Bound	Upper Bound
Carter					
January–June	1.28	1.90	−.37	−.83	.08
June–September	2.24	2.37	−.13	−.58	.32
January–September	2.31	2.35	−.05	−.46	.37
Reagan					
January–June	2.07	2.15	−.07	−.48	.33
June–September	1.51	2.34	−.61*	−1.04	−.18
January–September	2.37	2.49	−.11	−.48	.25
Anderson					
June–September	2.44	2.61	−.17	−.80	.47

Note: Entries give the education means and differences in these means, for respondents who substantially reduced their uncertainty of the particular candidate versus those who had no substantial change across the two survey waves. The two right columns give the 95 percent confidence interval bounds.
  * denotes that the difference in means is statistically significant at the $p = 0.05$ level.

change in their uncertainty. However, in table 10.8 (education) the strongest effects are seen, since four of the seven differences in means are statistically significant. In table 10.9 (political information) only one of the seven differences in means is statistically significant (Reagan from June to September) while one other (Carter from January to June) approaches statistical significance. Unfortunately, none of the media exposure differences in means are statistically significant.

While the evidence is much weaker in the 1980 data than was true for the 1976 results, the general conclusions are similar. Those voters who learned the most from the 1980 presidential campaign—those voters with substantial reductions in their uncertainty about the issue positions of the candidates—tended to be less educated and less politically informed than those who have no changes in their uncertainty. This indicates that presidential campaigns are providing information to those voters who need it the most.

TABLE 10.10.   Media Exposure and Changes in Voter Uncertainty, 1980

Candidate Periods	Media Mean Substantial Reduction	Media Mean No Change	Media Exposure Differences		
			Difference In Means	Lower Bound	Upper Bound
Carter					
January–June	2.56	2.54	.01	−.31	0.33
June–September	2.71	2.54	.17	−.15	.49
January–September	2.61	2.59	.02	−.28	.32
Reagan					
January–June	2.53	2.56	−.03	−.32	.26
June–September	2.45	2.58	−.13	−.46	.19
January–September	2.51	2.64	−.13	−.39	.14
Anderson					
June–September	2.35	2.64	−.29	−.72	.15

Note: Entries give the education means and differences in these means, for respondents who substantially reduced their uncertainty of the particular candidate versus those who had no substantial change across the two survey waves. The two right columns give the 95 percent confidence interval bounds.
* denotes that the difference in means is statistically significant at the $p = 0.05$ level.

Conclusion

In this chapter I provided evidence that during the 1976 and 1980 campaigns voters did learn about the policy positions of both candidates. First, I argued that during these campaigns the preconditions existed for voter learning to occur, since as the campaigns progressed, the information flow increasingly concentrated on the substantive aspects and policy positions of the candidates. This was primarily true for both Carter and Ford in 1976 and for Reagan in 1980. Then, I showed with both aggregate and individual-level evidence that reductions in voter uncertainty occurred across both election years; I interpreted these findings as confirmation of the prediction from the learning model in chapter 3. Lastly, I demonstrated that these reductions in voter uncertainty did not occur randomly across voters, but rather were concentrated among the less educated and informed individuals who were exposed to the mass media. These results confirm the prediction of the Bayesian learning model, since these are the voters with the least well-formed prior perceptions of candidate positions. New information made available by the campaign is incorporated into voter perceptions of the candidates, especially in their uncertainty of candidate policy positions.

This implies that presidential campaigns are important sources of information for voters. Additionally, campaigns provide information for those less informed, providing them the vehicle that enables them to be more certain of where the candidates stand on the issues. By becoming more certain of the positions of the candidates, these same voters become better able by the end of the general election to make their decision on the basis of policy issues.

Unfortunately, demonstrating that substantial changes in voter uncertainty led to changes in preferences is not possible with the either the 1976 or 1980 survey data. The learning model predicted that as voters became dramatically more certain of a candidate's policy positions, they would also become more likely to vote for that candidate. There simply are too few respondents in the survey sample who had what I defined as substantial reductions in their uncertainty, and who changed their candidate preferences in the general election, to test this hypothesis. Yet given that the voters who appear to learn the most during the campaign may be the most likely to have malleable preferences, it is likely that their preferences do change in response to the information they obtain from the campaign (Converse 1964; Zaller 1989).

CHAPTER 11

Information and Elections

A dependence on the people is, no doubt, the primary control on the government.

—James Madison, *Federalist 51*, 1788 (1961)

Information is an essential element of representative democracy. The linkage between the governed and the governors is a two-way flow of information, with those who are governed expressing their preferences, and those who are the governors explaining their activities. Elections are a very important component of representation, a period in which this reciprocal information flow is at the greatest. Elections are a time of accountability, and a time of virtually mandatory contact between the candidate and the voter.

This is perhaps more true now than at most points in American history. In the past, the political parties served as the primary intermediary between voter and candidate. Parties provided the organizational basis for candidates seeking office, and they helped structure the process of governing in the periods between elections. They structured the flow of information to the electorate, by presenting their platforms and candidates in partisan terms. Parties also provided a means for voters to organize their political decision making by giving an informational filter to reduce information costs and by providing cues in the actual making of decisions.

Yet the parties have lost their monopoly. Now candidates, especially at the presidential level, can compete for office more independently, using their own organizations and those of supporting interests. The mass media has risen as a primary source of political information for both candidates and voters. And increasingly, voters themselves are turning away from the parties (Wattenber 1990).

Thus, while campaigns have always been a primary vehicle of communication for candidates and voters, the shift from party- to candidate-based elections has made the task of both candidate and voter more difficult. Neither can rely upon the party to provide information nor cues, or can the parties be trusted any longer to structure consistently the flow of information.

The research in this book focused directly on only one aspect of this information transmission process, the information held by voters about the policy positions of presidential candidates. I began this work by arguing that the literature on campaigns and voting behavior has only slowly returned to a focus on the role of information in American presidential elections (e.g., Popkin 1991). While some have addressed the importance of information in elections, few have incorporated information directly into their theoretical or empirical models of voting and elections.

I asserted that a theory of voter preferences and perceptions must be based on the assumption of imperfect information. It should come as absolutely no surprise that most voters cannot recite minute details about government actions or candidate policy positions, since neither candidates nor government officials have the incentive to disseminate this information unambiguously and since voters do not have the incentive to gather this costly information. Thus, voter preferences and perceptions must be assumed to be imperfect and to be known to the voter with some degree of uncertainty.

My conceptualization of voter perceptions about the positions of candidates is that these perceptions can be understood as probability distributions. In this model, the perception has a central tendency and a variance, with the latter representing the voter's uncertainty about their perception. After making certain assumptions about voters, I demonstrated that uncertainty has a number of significant ramifications for voter decision making. Also, it is through changes in uncertainty that a campaign can have a strong impact on voting behavior, since an important component of learning involves changes in perceptual uncertainty.

These hypotheses generated by the theoretical models of voting and learning under imperfect information were supported by the empirical tests in the book. I demonstrated:

- That voter uncertainty directly influences candidate preferences; the more uncertain a voter is about a candidate's issue positions, the less likely she is to vote for the candidate.
- That uncertainty influences the decision-making process by altering the information a voter uses in making her choices; uncertain voters are less likely to use issue information in their decisions.
- That uncertainty varies across candidates as a function of incumbency, previous political experience, and national prominence.
- That uncertainty generally diminishes across the course of a presidential campaign in response to issue and substantive information.

These results were obtained across a span of recent elections, which demonstrates their generality. Thus, I believe that this research shows that *imperfect information must be incorporated directly into theoretical and empirical models of voter behavior.*

Political science is slowly beginning to incorporate imperfect information into theoretical models, largely under the influence of psychological and economic models. However this trend in our theoretical literature is only beginning to seep into our empirical literature. This is partly due to a divergence in the theoretical and empirical literatures on elections. But most of the inability of empirical models to incorporate information is driven by the lack of empirical measures of information.

Thus it is essential that progress be made in the development of measures of information. The recent work of Zaller (1989) is a case in point, as is my work with Franklin (1994). Strategies to measure information in our existing data, and the development of new approaches to measuring information are increasingly imperative.

I discussed two measurement strategies in chapter 4. Both have promise, but both certainly have drawbacks. In particular, adding indicators of voter information or uncertainty levels to surveys is necessary. The addition of some general information indicators into the 1988 National Election Study, following the work of Zaller, is commendable. Also, the studies I have done with Franklin on direct indicators of candidate uncertainty have shown considerable promise. Yet placing more and more questions in academic surveys, at a time of increasing survey nonresponse, is clearly costly.

Thus using existing survey data to operationalize measures of information and uncertainty is critical. The indicator of uncertainty I developed and analyzed in this book performed quite well, as *a general indicator of uncertainty*. The primary drawback to this measurement approach is that it does not measure voter uncertainty on specific policy issues. This is certainly the next direction of research.

The work in this book must also be extended to other aspects of candidate evaluation and public opinion. Throughout this work I have assumed that voters perceive candidate policy positions with uncertainty, but that they are certain of other attributes of the candidates, namely their leadership skills, their competence, and their personal traits. Direct survey measures of voter certainty about these other components of candidate evaluation should provide additional insights into how imperfect information influences how voters make decisions.

Surprisingly, public opinion researchers who focus on trends in public perceptions during and between elections typically assume that survey respondents are certain of the stated responses they give in public opinion polls. I have demonstrated here that as far as policy issues are concerned this is clearly a false assumption, since, as shown in chapter 4, survey respondents are often very willing to admit they are uncertain about the positions of even the president on the simple liberal–conservative dimension.

That people may be uncertain about public affairs may not concern scholars, since this could just mean that there is some error or "noise" in the public opinion polling data many use in their research. But I showed in chapters 4 and 6 that uncertainty about policy issues *varies systematically across respondents;* this implies that there is not random error in the data many use to study public opinion, but systematic noise. So, to the extent that people are uncertain about political affairs, this could substantially bias current public opinion data.

Additionally, the inability to measure imperfect information is impeding progress toward an understanding of two important questions. One, which I have addressed in the research above, concerns the factors which influence information levels across voters and campaigns in American presidential elections. Few would argue that a desirable goal would be to increase the certainty of voter perceptions of candidate policy positions. Reaching that goal, however, is impossible without understanding the factors which influence voter uncertainty.

To reiterate, three basic factors influence voter uncertainty: the costs to voters of gathering, processing, and utilizing information; the attachment of the voters to the political system and their exposure to information; and the flow of information during a campaign. There are some factors which are difficult to change—like the amount of education possessed by the electorate. But the last factor, the flow of information during the campaign, could be a major focus of efforts to make voters more informed about their choices.

The other important question concerns how different electoral institutions influence this two-way transmission of information during an election. My focus in this book has been on general elections at the presidential level, so discussion of institutional effects on information has not been considered in this research. However, I did discuss some of the ways in which the primary process might differ from the general election process in terms of information transmission. Clearly this comparison needs to be understood, as well as how other electoral institutions, both here and abroad, influence the transmission of information in an election.

In this book I have compared only presidential elections over a very brief time. One of the problems I encountered in my analysis of the contextual factors which influence uncertainty between elections was that I did not have enough cases (five) to account for the many factors which may account for the cross-election variation in uncertainty. But there are other neglected laboratories that can be used to understand in greater detail the contextual factors which influence uncertainty. For example, Senate and gubernatorial elections, when they occur simultaneously, provide a vehicle to better understand the institutional and contextual influences of uncertainty. They involve well-known and well-heeled candidates, who typically run intense campaigns. These, and other subpresidential elections, deserve further examination.

Appendixes

Data and Models for Chapter 4

Operationalizations of Independent Variables

Most of the data used in this chapter were taken from the 1993 Pilot Study component of the National Election Studies' "The 1992–1993 Panel Study on Securing Electoral Success/The 1993 Pilot Study" (ICPSR 6264). Some of the independent variables (demographic variables, primarily) were taken from the 1992 component of this study, which are described extensively in the documentation for the 1992 American National Election Study (ICPSR 6067). The development of the various measures of uncertainty was discussed in the text of the chapter. The independent variables used in this chapter were coded:

1. Media attention: constructed as an additive index of the average of the number of days the respondent reported reading a newspaper each week and watching television news (both items from the 1992 study).
2. Age: the age in years of the respondent (from the 1992 study).
3. Education: the education level of the respondent (from the 1992 study).
4. Gender: the gender of the respondent [females coded 1] (from the 1992 study).
5. Minorities: the race of the respondents [African-Americans coded 1, all others 0] (from the 1992 study).
6. Political information: an additive index of six information items, recoded to a 0–1 scale (from the 1993 study).
7. Feeling thermometers: 0–100 point thermometer ratings for the candidates and parties (from the 1993 study).
8. Party identification dummy variables [Independents as the excluded comparison category] (from the 1993 study).
9. Ideological extremity: the absolute value of the difference between the midpoint of the seven-point ideological scale (4) and the respondent's position (from the 1993 study).

TABLE A.1. Estimates of Bartels Uncertainty Measures

Independent Variables	Clinton	Perot	House
Constant	.10	−1.6**	−.15
	.34	.41	.32
Education	−.11**	−.01	−.08**
	.05	.05	.04
Media attention	−.10	−.35*	−.43**
	.22	.27	.22
Political information	−1.8**	−.01	−.31
	.37	.43	.34
Age	.01**	.02**	.01**
	.004	.005	.004
Minorities	−.03	.31*	.11
	.20	.23	.21
Gender	−.09	.28**	.06
	.13	.17	.13
Ideological extremity	−.41**	−.19**	−.11*
	.08	.09	.07
Strong Democrat	.06	−.35	−1.2**
	.27	.29	.27
Weak Democrat	.17	−.28	−.94**
	.26	.27	.24
Leaning Democrat	.28	−.60**	−.57**
	.26	.30	.23
Leaning Republican	−.23	−.47*	−.23
	.29	.33	.24
Weak Republican	.04	−.39*	−.76*
	.27	.30	.25
Strong Republican	.12	−.48*	−.68*
	.30	.34	.27
% Correct	81.7	73.8	72.0
Model χ^2	134.9#	37.4#	57.6#
Sample n	679	679	679

Note: Entries are maximum-likelihood probit estimates, with their standard errors below.
* indicates statistically significant estimates significant at the $p = .10$ level, one-tailed tests.
** indicate statistically significant estimates at the $p = .05$ level, one-tailed tests.
# indicates a significant model χ^2, with 13 degrees of freedom.

Derivations for Chapter 5

Estimation of Two-Stage Models

The procedure for estimating the two-stage models is simple to implement. First, I estimate reduced-form models for the uncertainty and vote choice equations. Note that the reduced-form models are merely regression or probit models with all of the exogenous variables from both the uncertainty and vote choice models. From the reduced-form probit models, I generate a linear predictor for the vote choice, which can be thought of as an instrumental variable for the voter's utility for one of the candidates. From the reduced-form regressions, I generate an instrumental variable for each candidate uncertainty term. From the reduced-form regressional I also generate the regression residual.

Next, I estimate the probit vote choice equations in three different ways. First, I estimate the vote choice model without the candidate uncertainty instruments. Second, I estimate the Rivers-Vuong 2SCML model by adding the uncertainty reduced-form regression residuals. Third, I estimate the 2SPLS model by substituting the predicted candidate uncertainty values, from the reduced-form regressions, for the actual uncertainty variables.

In chapter 7 I present the two-stage results for the second and third estimations, for 1976, 1984, and 1988. The first probit model produces estimates of the restricted model, from which I construct the likelihood-ratio test statistic for exogeneity.

After estimating the two-stage probit models, I use the linear predictors from the reduced-form probit models as instruments for candidate preference in the uncertainty regressions. I then calculate the standard error weights discussed in the text and weight the standard errors from the second-stage regression accordingly. The results are presented in chapter 6.

This same procedure was followed for the three-candidate multinomial probit models for 1980 and 1992, with one exception. In the multinomial probit model there are a number of different linear predictors which can be estimated for a particular candidate, since there are six different utility differences between candidate-pairs. In 1980, I use the Reagan-Anderson linear

213

predictor in the Reagan uncertainty model, the Carter-Anderson linear predictor in the Carter uncertainty model, and the Anderson-Carter linear predictor in the Anderson uncertainty model. In 1992 I use the Bush-Perot linear predictor in the Bush uncertainty model, the Clinton-Perot linear predictor in the Clinton model, and the Perot-Clinton linear predictor in the Perot uncertainty model. These linear predictors were used so that the predicted coefficient sign was the same in the multinomial probit models as in the binary probit models (negative).

As I discussed in this chapter, these two-stage continuous regression and discrete choice models have not been widely used. Other than the work of Rivers and Vuong, little is known about the properties of these models in finite samples. I explored these issues in Alvarez (1995). There I showed that, given the nonlinearity of the discrete choice model, the consequences of ignoring endogeneity in the discrete choice model are severe. Also, the bias can be substantial in the regression component of the model, especially when the error terms across equations are highly correlated (when endogeneity is the most severe).

With a series of Monte Carlo simulations and an empirical example similar to the analysis of the 1976 election in chapters 6 and 7, I demonstrate that the two-stage models must be used when endogeneity is suspected. Secondly, in finite samples 2SCML is consistent but understates the uncertainty in the estimates. In other words the standard errors estimated by 2SCML need to be evaluated conservatively. Last, both the regression and probit aspects of 2SPLS estimate the coefficients consistently in finite samples, but the standard error estimates are inefficient especially when the error correlations (and hence endogeneity) are great. Clearly these models ought to be used more frequently in political science, and the properties of these models for a wider class of discrete choice models deserves additional examination. In more complicated choice models there obviously can be more complicated across-equation error processes; future work needs to explore the properties of two-stage continuous and discrete choice models across a wide array of choice models.

Details of the Multinomial Probit Model

The Basics of the Model

The multinomial probit model lets me estimate the coefficients of the choice model while assuming the errors are correlated, then estimate these error correlations. Here, I present the details of the multinomial probit model, which follows a framework originally proposed by Hausman and Wise (1978) and utilized in joint work with Nagler (Alvarez and Nagler 1995, 1997); though I deviate from Hausman and Wise in the specification of the covariance matrix of the error terms. First, I discuss the basics of a multinomial probit model for a three-candidate election, then I describe the error covariance model.

Define a random utility function for voter i over each candidate j, where $j = 1, 2, 3$:

$$U_{ij} = \overline{U}(X_{ij}, a_i) + \varepsilon(X_{ij}, a_i) = X_{ij}\beta + a_i\psi_j + \varepsilon_{ij} \tag{B.1}$$

where X_{ij} is a vector of characteristics unique to the candidate choice j relative to voter i, a_i is a vector of characteristics unique to the individual decision maker i, ε is a random variable, and $\overline{U}$ defines the systematic component of the utility function of a voter. $\overline{U}$ is assumed to have the following functional form:

$$\overline{U} = \overline{U}(X_{ij}, a_i) = X_{ij}\beta + a_i\psi_j \tag{B.2}$$

Note that this assumes that $\overline{U}$ is a linear function of both the characteristics specific to the choice (X_{ij}) and the individual (a_i), with respective parameters β for the choice-specific characteristics and ψ_j for the individual-specific characteristics. The latter coefficient is subscripted by j to indicate that the effects of the individual-specific characteristics vary across choices. Note also that ψ_3 is normalized to zero.

I follow my past work (Alvarez and Nagler 1995) and assume that the random elements of the utility functions, ε_{ij}, have a multivariate normal distribution with mean zero and covariance matrix:

$$\Sigma = \begin{bmatrix} \sigma_1^2 & & \\ \sigma_{12} & \sigma_2^2 & \\ \sigma_{13} & \sigma_{23} & \sigma_3^2 \end{bmatrix} \tag{B.3}$$

Following the theory in chapter 3, assume that the voter chooses the candidate who will bring him or her the greatest utility. This gives the following expression for the probability that the voter would choose the first of the three alternatives:

$$P_{i1} = Pr[(U_{i1} > U_{i2})(U_{i1} > U_{i3})]$$
$$P_{i1} = Pr[(\overline{U}_{i1} + \varepsilon_{i1} > \overline{U}_{i2} + \varepsilon_{i2})(\overline{U}_{i1} + \varepsilon_{i1} > \overline{U}_{i3} + \varepsilon_{i3})]$$
$$P_{i1} = Pr[(\varepsilon_{i2} - \varepsilon_{i1} < \overline{U}_{i1} - \overline{U}_{i2})(\varepsilon_{i3} - \varepsilon_{i1} < \overline{U}_{i1} - \overline{U}_{i3})]$$
$$\tag{B.4}$$

Following Hausman and Wise (1978), let

$$\eta_{i,21} = \varepsilon_{i2} - \varepsilon_{i1} \tag{B.5}$$

$$\eta_{i,31} = \varepsilon_{i3} - \varepsilon_{i1} \tag{B.6}$$

The joint distribution for the $\eta_{i,j1}$ is bivariate normal, with covariance matrix:

$$\Omega_1 = \begin{bmatrix} \sigma_1^2 + \sigma_2^2 - 2\sigma_{12} & \\ \sigma_1^2 - \sigma_{13} - \sigma_{12} + \sigma_{23} & \sigma_1^2 + \sigma_3^2 - 2\sigma_{13} \end{bmatrix} \tag{B.7}$$

Then, the probability that voter i will choose candidate 1 as:

$$P_{i1} = \int_{-\infty}^{\frac{\overline{U}_{i1} - \overline{U}_{i2}}{\sqrt{\sigma_1^2 + \sigma_2^2 - 2\sigma_{12}}}} \int_{-\infty}^{\frac{\overline{U}_{i1} - \overline{U}_{i3}}{\sqrt{\sigma_1^2 + \sigma_3^2 - 2\sigma_{13}}}} b_1(\eta_{21}, \eta_{31}; r_1) d\eta_{21} d\eta_{31} \tag{B.8}$$

with b_1 being the standardized bivariate normal distribution and r_1 being the correlation between η_{21} and η_{31}:

$$r_1 = \frac{\sigma_1^2 - \sigma_{13} - \sigma_{12} + \sigma_{23}}{\sqrt{(\sigma_1^2 + \sigma_2^2 - 2\sigma_{12})(\sigma_1^2 + \sigma_3^2 - 2\sigma_{13})}} \tag{B.9}$$

Similar expressions for P_{i2} and P_{i3} can be easily obtained.
Define:

$$\hat{U}_{i,12} = \frac{\overline{U}_{i1} - \overline{U}_{i2}}{\sqrt{\sigma_1^2 + \sigma_2^2 - 2\sigma_{12}}} \tag{B.10}$$

which again produce similar definitions for $\hat{U}_{i,jk}$. This simplifies equation B.8 into:

$$P_{i1} = \int_{-\infty}^{\hat{U}_{i,12}} \int_{-\infty}^{\hat{U}_{i,13}} b_1(\eta_{21}, \eta_{31}; r_1) d\eta_{21} d\eta_{31} \tag{B.11}$$

Parameterization of the Error Variances and Estimation

I estimate the multinomial probit model under the following assumptions about the error process. Using the covariance matrices defined above, I can identify and estimate selected elements of the utility function errors, Σ_i (Bolduc

1992; Bunch 1991; Daganzo 1979; Keane 1992). In the empirical models used in this book, I assume homoskedasticity; in other words, I assume that $\sigma_1^2 = \sigma_2^2 = \sigma_3^2 = 1$ (this is the same assumption used in Alvarez and Nagler [1995, 1997]). Where Hausman and Wise posited the error variances to be functions of independent variables, I directly estimate values for $J - 1$ pairs of the error covariances, σ_{12}, σ_{13}, σ_{23} (presented in Chapter 7 with subscripts indicating the candidate pairs). These estimates can be considered error correlations, due to the normalization of the error variances. However, these error correlations are quite difficult to estimate in small samples, a fact pointed out in Alvarez and Nagler (1996). This does not mean that the MNP model is inappropriate, but rather that with more data, the error process which underlies the choice process in multi-candidate elections can be estimated more accurately.

Data and Models for Chapter 6

Operationalizations of Variables

In the first section of this appendix I present the operationalizations of the variables employed in the uncertainty models. The operationalization of the variables in the evaluation models are in the appendix to the next chapter.

The coding of the 1976 variables from the Patterson panel study is complicated by the fact that in the ICPSR documentation for the study there are no variable numbers. Consequently, I assigned variable numbers to the ICPSR codebook (ICPSR study 7990, first edition, 1982) sequentially (question 1, page 1, "location number" is V1, while the last codebook entry for "weight factor" on page 195 is the last variable, V1664). The variable for education was taken from V9 and was coded 1 for those with a grade school education or less; 2 for those with a high school education; 3 for those with some college or vocational education; 4 for those with college degrees. Political information is a ten-point scale where the respondent was given a point for each time both parties were placed, and the Democratic party was placed to the left of the Republican party on the seven-point issue and ideology scales. Gender and Race are dummy indicators, where Gender is 1 for females and 0 for males (from V21), and race is 1 for minorities and 0 for whites (from V24). Partisan strength is the folded partisan identification scale (V1569). Media exposure was constructed as a factor scale from variables measuring the regularity with which the respondent was exposed to news coverage in newspapers (V1328), news magazines (V1339), television news (V1358), and conversations with others (V1348). The principal components factor analysis yielded one factor, eigenvalue 8.37. The political efficacy variable is an index of external political efficacy from questions concerning big interests and government (V1575), faith and confidence in government (V1577), public officials and people like me (V1579). A principal components factor analysis was used to make a factor scale; the eigenvalue of the only factor extracted from the data was 2.8. The indicators for the first and second debates and for whether the voter saw a candidate's advertisement are dummy indicators, from V1455 and V1456 (for the debates), and V1386 and V1393 (for candidate advertisements). Nine seven-point issue scales are available in this survey: government provision of employment, involvement in the internal affairs of other nations, wage and price controls, defense spending, social welfare spending, tax cuts, legalized abortion, crime, and busing. The uncertainty variable was constructed by subtracting the respondent's placement of the candidate on the issue from the candidate's position, where the latter was measured by the mean position across all respondents placing the candidate on the issue. Respondents who did not place the candidate were assumed to be maximally uncertain about the candidate's position.

The 1980 data was taken from the cross-sectional component of the 1980 pre- and postelection presidential study. The education variable was taken from V436 and was coded 1 for education short of completion of high school, 2 for high school completion, 3 for some post–high school education short of college, and 4 for college and postgraduate education. The political information indicator was constructed as a ten-point scale where the respondents were given a point for each time they placed the two parties, with the Democrats to the left of the Republicans, on the six issue and ideology seven-point scales; they were also given a point for recognition of Howard Baker, Phillip Crane, Robert Dole, and Patrick Lucey. Gender and Race were dummy variables, 1 for females (from V720) and 0 for males, and 1 for racial minorities and 0 for whites (from V721). The partisan strength variable was a folded partisan scale (from V266). The media exposure scale was a simple additive scale of V217 (how often the respondent watched television news per week) and V218 (how much attention they paid to political news). Political efficacy was a factor scale constructed from three external efficacy measures (V401, V404, V405). The principal components factor analysis of these three items had an eigenvalue of 1.59. The uncertainty measure was constructed from the three seven-point scales available in the preelection survey: defense spending, government services, and inflation/unemployment.

The 1984 education measure was derived from V438 and was recoded so that 1 indicated education short of completion of high school, 2 for high school completion, 3 for some post-high school education short of college, and 4 for college and postgraduate education. The political information scale was constructed as an eight-point scale, where the respondent received one point for placing both parties on each issue scale, with the Democratic party to the left of the Republicans. Gender and Race are dummy indicators, from V707 and V708 (1 indicates females, 0 males; 1 racial minorities, 0 whites). The partisan strength variable was the folded partisanship scale (from V318). Media exposure was constructed as a factor scale from V107, V111, V116, and V118— how much the respondent had discussed, watched television news, read in the newspapers, or read in a news magazine, information about the 1984 campaign. The eigenvalue of the principal components factor analysis was 1.96. The efficacy scale was also constructed from a principal components factor analysis of V309, V310, V312, and V313. The eigenvalue of this factor analysis was 1.98. The uncertainty measure was constructed as described in the previous chapter, from seven-point scales for government services, minority aid, involvement in Central America, defense spending, improving the social-economic status of women, cooperation with Russia, and government provision of jobs.

The 1988 education measure was taken from V422, where 1 indicated education short of completion of high school, 2 for high school completion, 3 for some post-high school education short of college, and 4 for college and postgraduate education. The political information scale was an eight-point scale, where the respondent received one point for placing both parties on each issue scale, with the Democratic party to the left of the Republicans. Gender and Race are dummy indicators, from V413 and V412 (1 indicates females, 0 males; 1 racial minorities, 0 whites). The partisan strength variable was the folded partisanship scale (from V274). Media exposure and political efficacy were both derived from principal components factor analyses. Variables V127, V129, V135, V137 were used in the media exposure scale, expressing the respondent's exposure to information about the campaign in the media; the eigenvalue for the factor analysis was 2.0. In the political efficacy scale, V937, V938, V955, V957, and V960 were combined into a factor scale measuring external political efficacy from the results of a principal components analysis with an eigenvalue of 2.29. The uncertainty measure was calculated from the seven-point issue scales: government services, defense spending, government guaranteed provision of jobs, minority aid, cooperation with Russia, and women's rights. The minority aid placements were complicated by the fact that in the 1988 survey, two different minority aid questions were posed to respondents: I simply used the responses to whichever of the two questions the respondent was given.

In 1992, education was taken from V3908 and coded as in the earlier NES studies. Political information is a four-point scale, where each voter got one point for placing both parties on each issue scale, with the Democrats to the left of the Republicans. Gender and Race are again dummy indicators, from V4201 and V4202, respectively, and are coded as in the earlier NES studies. Partisan strength is the folded partisanship scale (V3634). Both media exposure and political efficacy are taken from principal components factor analysis. V3202, V3205, and V3270 were used in the media exposure scale (eigenvalue 1.59); V6102, V6103, V6120, V6122, and V6125 in the political efficacy scale (eigenvalue 1.90). The uncertainty measure is different in these models, given the lack of Perot issue placement questions. It is constructed from the placement of each candidate on the ideological dimension, relative to their average position for the sample. Last, the 1992 NES had a series of campaign advertisement recall questions. I constructed an additive scale from these recall questions, in which each respondent got one point for each advertisement they recalled, up to five.

Reduced Form Equations for the Candidate Preference Instruments

In the next four tables are the reduced form models for each for the candidate preference instruments. The details of the procedure are discussed in chapter 5 and briefly in the text of chapter 6. The dependent variables in the 1976, 1984, and 1988 models are dichotomous; they are coded with the high category (1) as preference for the Democratic candidate and with the low category (0) as preference for the Republican candidate. The dependent variables in the 1980 and 1992 reduced-form models can take three values: in 1980, Anderson is coded 1, Reagan coded 2, and Carter coded 3; in 1992, Perot is coded 1, Clinton coded 2, and Bush coded 3. The models are constructed so that the coefficients involve comparisons of one of the first two candidates with the incumbent president.

TABLE C.1.   Reduced Form Probit Model, 1976 Election

Independent Variables	Carter
Constant	.04
	1.1
Education	−.43
	.16
Partisan strength	.51
	.16
Gender	−.4
	.28
Race	2.4
	2.5
Political information	−.01
	.05
Political efficacy	−.009
	.03
Media exposure	.01
	.06
Ford ad	−.57
	.39
Carter ad	.05
	.39
First debate	−.07
	.19
Second debate	−.14
	.18
Ford issue distance	.29
	.08
Carter issue distance	−.26
	.07
Ford traits	−.46
	.06
Carter traits	.41
	.06
% Correct	95.7
χ^2	697.8

Note: Entries are probit maximum-likelihood estimates and their associated standard errors.

TABLE C.2. Reduced Form Multinomial Probit Models, 1980 Election

Independent Variables	Probability of Candidate Vote Anderson/ Carter		Reagan/ Carter
Issue distance		−.22	
		.05	
Constant	.19		1.2
	1.0		1.1
Education	.21		−.05
	.16		.14
Partisanship	.18		.53
	.12		.06
Gender	.05		−.19
	.19		.23
Race	−.03		−.45
	.29		.42
Political information	.02		−.04
	.04		.05
Political efficacy	−.10		−.31
	.13		.15
Media exposure	−.05		.00
	.06		.07
Reagan traits	.03		.14
	.04		.03
Carter traits	−.11		−.16
	.05		.03
Anderson traits	.00		−.03
	.02		.02
σ_{AR}		.06	
		.93	
σ_{AC}		.76	
		.22	

Note: Entries are multinomial probit maximum-likelihood estimates with their associated standard errors. The column headings indicate the relevant candidate comparisons for each model. The reduced form multinomial probit model correctly predicts 89.4 percent of the Reagan voters, 85.0 percent of the Carter voters, and 2.3 percent of the Anderson voters.

TABLE C.3.   Reduced Form Probit Model, 1984 and 1988 Elections

Independent Variables	Probability of Democratic Vote	
	1984 Election	1988 Election
Constant	1.1	1.4
	.68	.87
Education	−.04	.007
	.09	.09
Partisan strength	−.06	.09
	.09	.1
Partisanship	−.32	−.34
	.05	.05
Gender	.02	.12
	.15	.17
Race	.24	.94
	.27	.35
Political information	−.002	.05
	.03	.04
Political efficacy	−.03	−.05
	.07	.04
Media exposure	−.001	−.01
	.03	.02
Republican issue distance	.08	.19
	.03	.05
Democrat issue distance	−.11	−.16
	.04	.04
Republican traits	−.17	−.27
	.02	.03
Democrat traits	.17	.23
	.02	.04
% Correct	91.6	91.9
χ^2	1504.1	1353.2

Note: Entries are probit maximum-likelihood estimates with their associated standard errors. The second column gives the reduced-form for the 1984 election, and the third column gives the reduced-form for the 1988 election.

TABLE C.4. Reduced Form Multinomial Probit Models, 1992 Election

Independent Variables	Probability of Candidate Vote	
	Perot/ Bush	Clinton/ Bush
Issue distance	−.14	
	.03	
Constant	.46	1.6
	.54	.65
Education	−.07	.11
	.07	.09
Partisan strength	−.11	.07
	.08	.08
Partisanship	−.21	−.60
	.10	.13
Gender	−.34	.06
	.14	.15
Political information	.04	.12
	.07	.07
Political efficacy	.07	−.04
	.03	.03
Media exposure	.06	−.04
	.05	.06
Bush traits	−.20	−.28
	.07	.08
Clinton traits	.16	.48
	.08	.10
Perot traits	.28	−.05
	.09	.08
Bush ad	.06	−.13
	.12	.15
Clinton ad	−.15	−.33
	.15	.18
Perot ad	.36	.83
	.21	.25
σ_{PB}	.33	
	.35	
σ_{CB}	.27	
	.33	

Note: Entries are multinomial probit maximum-likelihood estimates with their associated standard errors. The column headings indicate the relevant candidate comparisons for each model. The reduced form multinomial probit model correctly predicts 75.6 percent of the Bush voters, 88.4 percent of the Clinton voters, and 36.6 percent of the Perot voters.

Data and Models for Chapter 7

Variables Employed in the Models

In the 1976 models, the candidate traits variables were taken from questions in the Patterson study asking respondents to rate the attractiveness of the candidate's personality (V1426, V1427), their leadership abilities (V1431, V1432), their trustworthiness (V1436, V1437), and their ability or competence (V1441, V1442), for Ford and Carter. Factor scales were constructed of these items for each candidate, with eigenvalues of 11.5 (Ford) and 8.28 (Carter). All of the available seven-point issue scales were used to calculate the uncertainty and squared issue-distance terms (with the candidate means employed in the latter variable for the position of the candidates). Party identification came from the standard seven-point scale (V1569). The dichotomous candidate preference variable came from the postelection interview question as to whom the respondent had voted for (V1614). The descriptive statistics for the variables in these models are in table D.1.

In the 1980 models, candidate traits variables were taken from the pre-post NES cross-section for each of the three candidates. These questions asked the respondents to rate each candidate on scales relating to how moral they were, how dishonest, how weak, how knowledgeable, how power hungry, how inspiring, their abilities to solve economic problems and to provide good foreign policy leadership, and their capabilities for strong leadership (V374– V400). Principal components factor analysis was used to make factor scales for each candidate from these items: for Reagan, the eigenvalue of the factor analysis was 5.46; for Carter, 5.54; and for Anderson, 5.47. All of the available seven-point issues were employed, using candidate means as indicators of their actual positions. Party identification was from the seven-point scale (V266), and the vote indicator came from the postelection vote question (V994). The descriptive statistics for the variables in the 1980 models are in Table D.2.

For the 1984 models, the candidate traits variables came from the following questions: how moral they were, how knowledgeable, how inspiring, their capabilities for strong leadership, how hard working, how decent, how compassionate, how intelligent, and whether the candidate cares about people like the respondent (V319–V321, V323–V324, V326–V327, V329–V330, V335–V337; V339–V340, V342–V343, and V345–V347). Principal components factor analyses were used to produce factor scales for each candidate's trait indicator (eigenvalue 5.30 for Reagan, 4.62 for Mondale). All of the available seven-point issue scales were used for both the uncertainty and squared issue distance variables (with candidate means used as measures of their actual positions). Party identification was from the seven-point scale (V318). The voter's candidate preference was taken from the postelection question (V788). The descriptive statistics for the variables are in table D.3.

The 1988 models used candidate trait measures which were factor scales from V277–V292, probing the following qualities for each candidate: intelligence, compassion, morality, inspiration, strong leadership, decency, cares about people like the respondent, knowledgeable, and honest. The principal components factor analysis of these items had eigenvalues 5.20 (Bush) and 5.37 (Dukakis). All of the seven-point issue variables were employed to measure both uncertainty and issue distances (again, the candidate mean placement in the sample was used as a measure of their actual position). However, a single minority group aid variable was constructed from the responses to the Form A and Form B questions (which varied over the two forms, but probed the respondent's attitudes and perceptions about federal government support for minorities). The party identification variable came from the seven-point scale (V274). The respondent's candidate preference was measured using the postelection indicator (V763). The descriptive statistics are in table D.4.

The 1992 models employed some different operationalizations of key variables. The descriptive statistics for these variables are given in table D.5. First, as I have mentioned repeatedly in the past two chapters, the 1992 NES study did not include issue placement questions for Perot; accordingly I use ideological distance between each candidate and the voter as my measure of issue voting, and I use the difference between the voter's placement of each candidate and the "true" position of the candidate as my measure of candidate ideological uncertainty. Partisanship (V3634), gender (V4201), and education (V3908) are coded as in previous election models. The trait measures in 1992 are coded from the candidate likes and dislikes questions. Each candidate trait measure is the difference between the number of likes and the number of dislikes mentioned by the voter. There were no candidate quality questions in the 1992 NES survey for Perot.

TABLE D.1. **Summary Statistics for Variables in 1976 Voting Models**

Independent Variables				
Variable	Mean	S. Dev.	Min.	Max.
Ford issue distance	5.60	2.63	.50	12.7
Carter issue distance	5.21	2.33	.84	12.5
Ford uncertainty	3.96	3.03	.23	13.8
Carter uncertainty	4.08	3.07	.19	13.2
Ford traits	12.0	5.46	3.51	24.6
Carter traits	10.8	4.70	3.38	23.7
Party identification	3.36	2.16	1.0	7.0
Education	2.62	.87	1.0	4.0
Gender	.54	.50	0	1
Ford error	−.18	2.66	−7.45	8.53
Carter error	−.14	2.67	−7.19	8.06

TABLE D.2. **Summary Statistics for Variables in 1980 Voting Models**

Independent Variables				
Variable	Mean	S. Dev.	Min.	Max.
Reagan issue distance	3.05	2.65	.18	14.7
Carter issue distance	3.55	2.63	.06	12.6
Reagan uncertainty	3.47	3.49	.18	14.8
Carter uncertainty	2.53	2.57	.07	12.6
Reagan traits	18.1	8.10	6.98	62.8
Carter traits	18.1	8.08	6.97	62.8
Party identification	2.53	1.99	0	6
Education	2.71	1.01	1	4
Gender	.50	.50	0	1
Reagan error	.00	3.09	−5.73	1.6
Carter error	−.003	2.39	−4.04	1.6

TABLE D.3. Summary Statistics for Variables in 1984 Voting Models

Independent Variables				
Variable	Mean	S. Dev.	Min.	Max.
Reagan issue distance	4.04	3.02	.31	16.2
Mondale issue distance	3.33	2.30	.26	13.1
Reagan uncertainty	2.49	2.30	.07	16.2
Mondale uncertainty	2.88	2.84	.09	13.9
Reagan traits	24.6	6.76	6.9	34.5
Mondale traits	22.9	4.61	6.4	32.2
Party identification	2.87	2.08	0	6
Education	2.80	.94	1	4
Gender	.50	.50	0	1
Reagan error	.001	2.02	−5.10	12.5
Mondale error	.0	2.44	−5.09	11.5

TABLE D.4. Summary Statistics for Variables in 1988 Voting Models

Independent Variables				
Variable	Mean	S. Dev.	Min.	Max.
Bush issue distance	3.81	2.47	.05	13.6
Dukakis issue distance	3.78	2.42	.33	13.6
Bush uncertainty	3.54	3.37	.05	14.0
Dukakis uncertainty	4.29	3.80	.09	14.5
Bush traits	18.2	3.77	6.59	26.4
Dukakis traits	18.0	3.05	6.36	25.5
Party identification	3.08	2.08	0	6
Education	2.67	1.03	1	4
Gender	.50	.50	0	1
Bush error	.00	3.12	−8.60	10.3
Dukakis error	.00	2.78	−6.18	10.6

TABLE D.5. Summary Statistics for Variables in 1992 Voting Models

Independent Variables				
Variable	Mean	S. Dev.	Min.	Max.
Bush ideological distance	2.91	3.78	.002	16.4
Clinton ideological distance	3.04	3.36	.035	14.5
Perot ideological distance	2.13	2.48	.098	11.0
Bush uncertainty	2.20	3.67	.002	16.4
Clinton uncertainty	2.16	3.51	.035	14.5
Perot uncertainty	3.99	4.07	.098	1.9
Bush traits	.196	1.31	−5.0	5.0
Clinton traits	−.266	1.40	−5.0	5.0
Perot traits	−.052	1.11	−4.0	4.0
Party identification	2.91	2.11	.00	6.00
Education	3.04	.900	1.0	4.0
Gender	.475	.500	0	1

Reduced Form Models

The reduced form models for the uncertainty indicators are presented for each election in the following tables. The methodology employed was discussed in chapter 5. The reduced forms for the 1976 election are in table D.6, for the 1980 model in table D.7, for the 1984 election in table D.8, for the 1988 election in table D.9, and for the 1992 election in table D.10.

TABLE D.6.   Reduced Form Models for 1976 Uncertainty Variables

Independent Variables	Candidate Uncertainty	
	Ford	Carter
Constant	5.02	5.34
	.88	.87
Education	−.29	−.32
	.14	.13
Party strength	.008	.02
	.13	.12
Gender	.72	.56
	.22	.22
Political information	−.32	−.33
	.04	.04
Media exposure	−.25	−.17
	.05	.05
Political efficacy	−.02	−.04
	.02	.02
Race	.80	.25
	.44	.44
Candidate advertisements	−.50	−.12
	.29	.31
First debate	−.17	.02
	.16	.15
Second debate	−.14	−.20
	.15	.15
Ford traits	−.01	.02
	.02	.02
Carter traits	−.01	−.08
	.03	.02
Adjusted R^2	.27	.26
Model S.E.	2.77	2.75
Uncertainty Mean	4.17	4.14

TABLE D.7. Reduced Form Models for 1980 Uncertainty Variables

Independent Variables	Candidate Uncertainty		
	Reagan	Carter	Anderson
Constant	5.06	2.95	6.40
	1.00	.78	1.05
Education	−.04	−.07	−.13
	.13	.10	.13
Party strength	−.09	−.05	.30
	.13	.10	.14
Party identification	−.21	.007	−.11
	.07	.05	.07
Gender	1.19	.69	1.20
	.24	.19	.26
Political information	−.42	−.23	−.50
	.05	.04	.06
Media exposure	.02	.02	−.06
	.07	.05	.07
Political efficacy	−.22	−.39	−.27
	.16	.12	.16
Race	.30	.47	−.47
	.39	.30	.41
Reagan traits	−.005	.08	.03
	.03	.02	.03
Carter traits	.05	−.0002	−.008
	.03	.02	.03
Anderson traits	.05	.02	.07
	.02	.01	.02
Adjusted R^2	.22	.13	.23
Model S.E.	3.11	2.40	3.25
Uncertainty Mean	3.50	2.55	4.96

TABLE D.8.   Reduced Form Models for 1984 Uncertainty Variables

Independent Variables	Candidate Uncertainty	
	Reagan	Mondale
Constant	5.19	6.68
	.50	.61
Education	−.24	−.33
	.07	.08
Party strength	.20	.21
	.06	.08
Party identification	−.01	.12
	.04	.05
Gender	.10	.33
	.12	.14
Political information	−.37	−.52
	.03	.03
Media exposure	.03	.03
	.02	.03
Political efficacy	−.06	−.04
	.06	.07
Race	.68	.05
	.20	.25
Reagan traits	−.06	.002
	.01	.01
Mondale traits	.03	−.06
	.01	.02
Adjusted R^2	.22	.26
Model S.E.	2.03	2.45
Uncertainty Mean	2.33	2.67

TABLE D.9.   Reduced Form Models for 1988 Uncertainty Variables

Independent Variables	Candidate Uncertainty	
	Bush	Dukakis
Constant	6.83	7.97
	.78	.87
Education	−.22	−.28
	.10	.11
Party strength	.09	.10
	.09	.11
Party identification	.06	.17
	.05	.06
Gender	.45	.70
	.18	.20
Political information	−.54	−.59
	.04	.04
Media exposure	−.07	−.11
	.03	.03
Political efficacy	−.10	−.12
	.04	.05
Race	.31	.09
	.29	.32
Bush traits	−.05	.08
	.03	.03
Dukakis traits	.06	−.08
	.03	.03
Adjusted R^2	.28	.31
Model S.E.	2.79	3.13
Uncertainty Mean	2.87	3.92

TABLE D.10. Reduced Form Models for 1992 Uncertainty Variables

Independent Variables	Candidate Uncertainty		
	Bush	Clinton	Perot
Constant	4.7	5.0	6.1
	.83	.77	.77
Education	−.42	−.28	−.13
	.14	.13	.13
Party strength	.30	.30	.08
	.13	.12	.12
Gender	.58	.40	.48
	.24	.22	.22
Political information	−1.6	−1.4	−1.5
	.13	.12	.12
Media exposure	.19	.01	.24
	.10	.09	.09
Political efficacy	.09	.05	.01
	.05	.05	.05
Race	1.4	.67	.60
	.37	.34	.34
Bush traits	−.23	.12	.002
	.10	.09	.09
Clinton traits	.31	−.03	.11
	.09	.09	.09
Perot traits	.06	.03	−.30
	.11	.10	.10
Bush ad	.45	−.36	−.30
	.27	.25	.25
Clinton ad	−.28	.13	−.19
	.31	.29	.29
Perot ad	−.10	−.57	−1.0
	.36	.33	.33
Adjusted R^2	.21	.14	.19
Model S.E.	4.23	3.91	3.92
Uncertainty Mean	3.04	2.71	4.66

Data and Models for Chapter 8

In this appendix are the estimates and standard errors for the interactive models discussed in the text of the chapter. All of the variables have been discussed in chapters 6 and 7. The interactive models employed here were discussed in chapter 5 and briefly above. Within each sample, the mean uncertainty values for each candidate were obtained. The samples were stratified first into two groups for the Democratic candidate's uncertainty, and then models identical to the 2SPLS models in chapter 7 were estimated for the two-candidate elections (1976, 1984, and 1988). The only difference was that in this first set of interactive models the variable for the Democratic candidate's uncertainty—the variable used to group the sample—is not included in the estimation procedure. Note also that an instrument was substituted for the variable used to account for the voter's uncertainty of the Republican candidate due to the presence of endogeneity. This procedure was then repeated, after placing all voters into one of two groups depending upon their uncertainty of the Republican candidate.

The procedure for both three candidate races (1980 and 1992) is different. There I created an interaction variable by multiplying the voter's uncertainty about each candidate by their issue or ideological distance from the candidate. This interaction variable was then added to the multinomial probit model; thus the multinomial probit models for these two elections are identical to those in the last chapter, except for the addition of this interaction variable.

The estimates and standard errors for all of these interaction models are presented in tables E.1 through E.5.

TABLE E.1. Uncertainty Interaction Models, 1976 Election

Independent Variables	Probability of Carter Support			
	Carter Certainty	Carter Uncertainty	Ford Certainty	Ford Uncertainty
Constant	2.2*	.94	4.0**	1.3
	1.6	1.4	1.8	1.4
Ford issue distance	.11	.20	.27**	.09
	.14	.10	.14	.10
Carter issue distance	−.27**	−.07	−.30**	−.02
	.16	.09	.14	.09
Ford uncertainty	.19	−.004		
	.20	.13		
Carter uncertainty			.02	−.17
			.18	.16
Ford traits	−.65**	−.35	−.64**	−.38**
	.13	.07	.13	.07
Carter traits	.69**	.32	.77**	.2**
	.16	.07	.18	.07
Party identification	−.46**	−.22	−.46**	−.25**
	.14	.10	.15	.10
Education	−.03	−.46	−.38*	−.50**
	.30	.25	.29	.29
Gender	−.46	−.12	−.21	−.008
	.51	.38	.46	.40
% Correct	97.2	93.6	96.3	95.0

Note: Entries are maximum-likelihood estimates, and their associated standard errors.
* indicates a $p = .10$ level of statistical significance, one-tailed tests.
** indicates a $p = .05$ level of statistical significance, one-tailed tests.
Certain voters are those below the mean uncertainty level of the candidate; uncertain voters are those above the mean. Instrumental variables have been substituted for the RHS uncertainty indicators, and the appropriate reduced-form equations are in the appendix to chapter 7.

TABLE E.2.   Uncertainty Interaction Models, 1980 Election

Independent Variables	Probability of Candidate Support	
	Anderson-Carter	Reagan-Carter
Issue distance	−.22**	
	.07	
Interaction	−.006	
	.02	
Constant	.18	.06
	.83	.94
Reagan uncertainty		−.39
		.31
Carter uncertainty	.38*	.81*
	.29	.51
Anderson uncertainty	−.21*	
	.17	
Reagan traits		.06
		.05
Carter traits	−.13**	−.15**
	.05	.04
Anderson traits	.03*	
	.02	
Party identification	.18**	.46**
	.10	.09
Education	.24*	−.03
	.15	.13
Gender	.07	−.22
	.26	.27
σ_{AR}	.02	
	.63	
σ_{AC}	.67**	
	.29	

Note: Entries are maximum-likelihood multinomial probit estimates, and their associated standard errors.
* indicates a $p = .10$ level of statistical significance, one-tailed tests.
** indicates a $p = .05$ level, level of statistical significance, one-tailed tests.
Instrumental variables have been substituted for the RHS uncertainty indicators, and the appropriate reduced-form equations are in the appendix to chapter 7.

TABLE E.3.   Uncertainty Interaction Models, 1984 Election

Independent Variables	Probability of Mondale Support			
	Mondale Certainty	Mondale Uncertainty	Reagan Certainty	Reagan Uncertainty
Constant	−.73	1.9**	−.11	1.5
	1.1	1.0	1.2	.94
Reagan issue distance	.14**	.05	.09**	.06*
	.05	.04	.05	.04
Mondale issue distance	−.15**	−.08*	−.16**	−.09*
	.07	.05	.07	.06
Reagan uncertainty	.15	−.13		
	.13	.13		
Mondale uncertainty			.16*	−.12*
			.10	.08
Reagan traits	−.21**	−.13**	−.19**	−.16**
	.03	.02	.03	.02
Mondale traits	.24**	.12**	.19**	.16**
	.04	.03	.04	.03
Party identification	−.29**	−.39**	−.41**	−.23**
	.07	.07	.07	.06
Education	.07	−.23*	.20	−.21*
	.16	.14	.16	.14
Gender	−.20	.29*	.13	−.07
	.22	.22	.24	.21
% Correct	91.8	92.1	91.4	92.5

Note: Entries are maximum-likelihood estimates, and their associated standard errors.
* indicates a $p = .10$ level of statistical significance, one-tailed tests.
** indicates a $p = .05$ level, of statistical significance, one-tailed tests.
Certain voters are those below the mean uncertainty level of the candidate; uncertain voters are those above the mean. Instrumental variables have been substituted for the RHS uncertainty indicators, and the appropriate reduced-form equations are in the appendix to chapter 7.

TABLE E.4. Uncertainty Interaction Models, 1988 Dukakis-Bush

Independent Variables	Probability of Dukakis Support			
	Dukakis Certainty	Dukakis Uncertainty	Bush Certainty	Bush Uncertainty
Constant	3.5**	.30	2.3*	2.3**
	1.3	1.0	1.6	1.0
Bush issue distance	.25**	.18**	.27**	.17**
	.08	.05	.09	.05
Dukakis issue distance	−.15**	−.12**	−.18**	−.17**
	.07	.05	.09	.05
Bush uncertainty	.05	−.06		
	.10	.08		
Dukakis uncertainty			.08	−.13**
			.09	.07
Bush traits	−.38**	−.21**	−.42**	−.21**
	.06	.04	.08	.04
Dukakis traits	.24**	.22**	.34**	.16**
	.06	.04	.07	.04
Party identification	−.43**	−.31**	−.46**	−.30**
	.07	.06	.08	.06
Education	−.13	.03	−.17	.04
	.16	.13	.16	.13
Gender	.41*	.12	.31	.04
	.28	.25	.29	.25
% Correct	93.0	92.2	93.9	89.8

Note: Entries are maximum-likelihood estimates, and their associated standard errors.
* indicates a $p = .10$ level of statistical significance, one-tailed tests.
** indicates a $p = .05$ level of statistical significance, one-tailed tests.
Certain voters are those below the mean uncertainty level of the candidate; uncertain voters are those above the mean. Instrumental variables have been substituted for the RHS uncertainty indicators, and the appropriate reduced-form equations are in the appendix to chapter 7.

TABLE E.5.   Uncertainty Interaction Models, 1992 Election

Independent Variables	Probability of Candidate Support	
	Perot-Bush	Clinton-Bush
Ideological distance	−.19**	
	.04	
Interaction	.03**	
	.009	
Constant	.69**	1.7**
	.37	.40
Bush uncertainty	.08	.23**
	.08	.10
Clinton uncertainty		−.32**
		.13
Perot uncertainty	−.08	
	.08	
Bush traits	−.18**	−.18**
	.06	.07
Clinton traits		.34**
		.07
Perot traits	.26**	
	.08	
Party identification	−.15**	−.60**
	.06	.09
Education	−.05	.12*
	.07	.08
Gender	−.29**	.07
	.11	.15
σ_{PB}	.62**	
	.17	
σ_{CB}	.25	
	.21	

Note: Entries are maximum-likelihood multinomial probit estimates, and their associated standard errors.
* indicates a $p = .10$ level of statistical significance, one-tailed tests.
** indicates a $p = .05$ level of statistical significance, one-tailed tests.
Instrumental variables have been substituted for the RHS uncertainty indicators, and the appropriate reduced-form equations are in the appendix to chapter 7.

References

Abramson, P. R., J. H. Aldrich, and D. W. Rohde. *Change and Continuity in the 1988 Elections.* Washington, D.C.: CQ Press, 1989.

Abramson, P. R., J. H. Aldrich, and D. W. Rohde. *Change and Continuity in the 1992 Elections.* Washington, D.C.: CQ Press, 1995.

Achen, C. H. *The Statistical Analysis of Quasi-Experiments.* Berkeley and Los Angeles: University of California Press, 1986.

Achen, C. H. "Breaking the Iron Triangle: Social Psychology, Demographic Variables, and Linear Regression in Voting Research." *Political Behavior* 14 (1992): 195–211.

Aldrich, J. H. *Before the Convention.* Chicago: The University of Chicago Press, 1980.

Aldrich, J. H. *Why Parties?* Chicago: The University of Chicago Press, 1995.

Aldrich, J. H., and R. D. McKelvey. "A Method of Scaling with Applications to the 1968 and 1972 Presidential Elections." *American Political Science Review* 71 (1977): 111–30.

Aldrich, J. H., R. G. Niemi, G. Rabinowitz, and D. W. Rohde. "The Measurement of Public Opinion About Public Policy: A Report on Some New Issue Question Formats." *American Journal of Political Science* 26 (1982): 391–414.

Aldrich, J. H., J. L. Sullivan, and E. Borgida. "Foreign Affairs and Issue Voting: Do Presidential Candidates 'Waltz Before a Blind Audience' "? *American Political Science Review* 83 (1989): 123–42.

Almond, Gabriel A. *The American People and Foreign Policy.* New York: Praeger, 1960.

Alvarez, R. M. *Issues and Information in Presidential Elections.* Ph.D. Dissertation, Duke University, 1992.

Alvarez, R. M. "Two-Stage Estimation of Discrete Choice Models." California Institute of Technology, manuscript, 1995.

Alvarez, R. M., and C. H. Franklin. "Uncertainty and Political Perceptions." *Journal of Politics* 56 (1994): 671–89.

Alvarez, R. M., and P. W. Gronke. "Perception and Misperception: Constituent Knowledge of the Persian Gulf War Vote." *Legislative Studies Quarterly* 21 (1995): 105–28.

Alvarez, R. M., and J. Nagler. "Voter Choice in 1992: Economics, Issues and Anger." *American Journal of Political Science* 39 (1995): 714–44.

Alvarez, R. M., and J. Nagler. "Correlated Disturbances in Discrete Choice Models: A Comparison of Multinomial Probit Models and Logit Models." *Political Analysis*, in press, 1996.

Alvarez, R. M., and J. Nagler. "When Politics and Models Collide: Estimating Models of Multiparty Elections." *American Journal of Political Science*, in press, 1997.

Amemiya, T. "The Estimation of a Simultaneous Equation Generalized Probit Model." *Econometrica* 46 (1978): 1193–1205.

Asher, H. *Polling and the Public*. Washington, D.C.: CQ Press, 1992.

Bartels, L. M. "Issue Voting Under Uncertainty: An Empirical Test." *American Journal of Political Science* 30 (1986): 709–28.

Bartels, L. M. *Presidential Primaries and the Dynamics of Public Choice*. Princeton: Princeton University Press, 1988.

Bartels, L. M. "Messages Received: The Political Impact of Media Exposure." *American Political Science Review*, 87 (1993): 267–85.

Berelson, B. R., P. F. Lazarsfeld, and W. N. McPhee. *Voting*. Chicago: The University of Chicago Press, 1954.

Berger, J. O. *Statistical Decision Theory and Bayesian Analysis*, second edition. New York: Springer-Verlag, 1985.

Berry, F. S., and W. D. Berry. "State Lottery Adoptions as Policy Innovations: An Event History Analysis." *American Political Science Review* 84 (1990): 395–415.

Bishop, G. F., A. J. Tuchfarber, and R. W. Oldendick. "Change in the Structure of American Political Attitudes: The Nagging Question of Question Wording." *American Journal of Political Science* 22 (1978): 250–69.

Bishop, G. F., A. J. Tuchfarber, R. W. Oldendick, and S. E. Bennett. "Pseudo-Opinions on Public Affairs." *Public Opinion Quarterly* 44 (1980): 198–209.

Bishop, G. F., A. J. Tuchfarber, R. W. Oldendick. "Opinions on Fictitious Issues: The Pressure to Answer Survey Questions." *Public Opinion Quarterly* 50 (1986): 240–50.

Black, D. *Theory of Committees and Elections*. Cambridge: Cambridge University Press, 1958.

Bogart, L. "No Opinion, Don't Know, and Maybe No Answer." *Public Opinion Quarterly* 31 (1967): 331–45.

Bolduc, D. "Generalized Autoregressive Errors in the Multinomial Probit Model." *Transportation Research B* 26 (1992): 155–77.

Brady, H. E. "Factor and Ideal Point Analysis for Interpersonally Incomparable Data." *Psychometrika* 54 (1989): 181–202.

Brady, H. E. "Dimensional Analysis of Ranking Data." *American Journal of Political Science* 34 (1989): 1017–48.

Brady, H. E., and P. M. Sniderman. "Attitude Attribution: A Group Basis for Political Reasoning." *American Political Science Review* 79 (1985): 1061–78.

Brady, H. E., and S. Ansolabehere, "The Nature of Utility Functions in Mass Publics." *American Political Science Review* 83 (1989): 143–63.

Brehm, John. *The Phantom Respondents.* Ann Arbor, Michigan: The University of Michigan Press, 1993.

Bunch, D. S. "Estimability in the Multinomial Probit Model." *Transportation Research B* 25 (1991): 1–12.

Calvert, R. L. "On the Role of Imperfect Information in Electoral Politics." Ph.D. Dissertation, California Institute of Technology, 1980.

Calvert, R. L., and M. MacKuen. "Bayesian Learning and the Dynamics of Public Opinion." Paper presented at the Annual Meetings of the Midwest Political Science Association, Chicago, Illinois, 1985.

Campbell, J. E. "Ambiguity in the Issue Positions of Presidential Candidates: A Causal Analysis." *American Journal of Political Science* 27 (1983): 284–93.

Campbell, A., P. E. Converse, W. E. Miller, and D. E. Stokes. *The American Voter,* unabridged edition. Chicago: The University of Chicago Press, 1980.

Carmines, E. G., and J. A. Stimson. "The Two Faces of Issue Voting." *American Political Science Review* 74 (1980): 78–91.

Cavanagh, T. E., and J. L. Sundquist. "The New Two-Party System." In J. E. Chubb and P. E. Peterson, *The New Direction in American Politics.* Washington, D.C.: The Brookings Institution, 1985.

Ceaser, J. W. *Presidential Selection.* Princeton: Princeton University Press, 1979.

Cook, T. D., and D. T. Campbell. *Quasi-Experimentation.* Boston: Houghton Mifflin Company, 1979.

Coombs, C. H., and L. C. Coombs. "'Don't Know': Item Ambiguity or Respondent Uncertainty?" *Public Opinion Quarterly* 40 (1976): 497–514.

Conover, P. J. "Political Cues and the Perception of Political Candidates." *American Politics Quarterly* 9 (1981): 427–48.

Conover, P. J., and S. Feldman. "Candidate Perception in an Ambiguous World: Campaigns, Cues, and Inference Processes." *American Journal of Political Science* 33 (1989): 912–39.

Converse, J. M. "Predicting No Opinion in the Polls." *Public Opinion Quarterly* 40 (1976): 515–30.

Converse, P. E. "Information Flow and the Stability of Partisan Attitudes." In A. Campbell et al., *Elections and the Political Order.* New York: John Wiley, 1962.

Converse, P. E. "The Nature of Belief Systems in Mass Publics." In D. E. Apter, *Ideology and Discontent.* New York: Free Press, 1964.

Daganzo, C. *Multinomial Probit.* New York: Academic Press, 1979.

Davis, O. A., and M. J. Hinich. "A Model of Policy Formation in Democratic Society." In J. L. Bernd, *Mathematical Applications in the Social Sciences.* Dallas: Southern Methodist University Press, 1966.

Davis, O. A., M. J. Hinich, and P. C. Ordeshook. "An Expository Development of a Mathematical Model of the Electoral Process." *American Political Science Review* 64 (1970): 426–48.

de Tocqueville, A. *Democracy in America,* ed. J. P. Mayer, trans. G. Lawrence. Garden City, New York: Anchor Books, 1969.

Downs, A. *An Economy Theory of Democracy.* New York: Harper and Row, 1957.

Drew, E. *Portrait of an Election.* New York: Simon and Schuster, 1981.

Dubin, J. A., and R. D. Rivers. *Statistical Software Tools,* version 2.0. Pasadena: Dubin-Rivers Research, 1989.

Dubin, J. A., and R. D. Rivers. "Selection Bias in Linear Regression, Logit and Probit Models." *Sociological Methods and Research* 18 (1990): 360–90.

Enelow, J. M., and M. J. Hinich. *The Spatial Theory of Voting.* New York: Cambridge University Press, 1984.

Erikson, R. S., and D. W. Romero. "Candidate Equilibrium and the Behavioral Model of the Vote." *American Political Science Review* 84 (1990): 1103–26.

Faulkenberry, G. D., and R. Mason. "Characteristics of Non-Opinion and No Opinion Response Groups." *Public Opinion Quarterly* 42 (1978): 533–43.

Feick, L. F. "Latent Class Analysis of Survey Questions That Include Don't Know Responses." *Public Opinion Quarterly* 53 (1989): 525–47.

Fiorina, M. P. *Retrospective Voting in American National Elections.* New Haven: Yale University Press, 1981.

Finkel, S. E. "Reexamining the 'Minimal Effects' Model in Recent Presidential Campaigns." *Journal of Politics* 55 (1993): 1–21.

Fiske, S. T., R. R. Lau, and R. A. Smith. "On the Varieties and Utilities of Political Expertise." *Social Cognition* 8 (1990): 31–48.

Fiske, S. T., and M. A. Pavelchak. "Category-Based versus Piecemeal-Based Affective Responses: Developments in Schema–Triggered Affect." In R. M. Sorrentino and E. T. Higgins, *The Handbook of Motivation and Cognition.* New York: Guilford Press, 1986.

Flanigan, W. H., W. M. Rahn, and N. H. Zingale. "Political Parties as Objects of Identification and Orientation." Paper presented at the Annual Meeting of the Western Political Science Association, Salt Lake City, Utah, 1989.

Francis, J. D., and L. Busch. "What We Now Know About 'I Don't Know.' " *Public Opinion Quarterly* 39 (1975): 207–18.

Franklin, C. H. "Eschewing Obfuscation? Campaigns and the Perceptions of U.S. Senate Incumbents." *American Political Science Review* 85 (1991): 1193–1214.

Franklin, C. H., and J. E. Jackson. "The Dynamics of Party Identification." *American Political Science Review* 77 (1983): 957–73.

Frant, H. "Specifying a Model of State Policy Innovation." *American Political Science Review* 85 (1991): 571–73.

Germond, J. W., and J. Witcover. *Whose Broad Stripes and Bright Stars? The Trivial Pursuit of the Presidency, 1988.* New York: Warner, 1989.

Germond, J. W., and J. Witcover. *Mad as Hell: Revolt at the Ballot Box, 1992.* New York: Warner Books, 1993.

Glass, D. P. "Evaluating Presidential Candidates: Who Focuses on Their Personal Attributes?" *Public Opinion Quarterly* 49 (1985): 517–34.

Graber, D. A. *Mass Media and American Politics.* Washington, D.C.: Congressional Quarterly Press, 1980.

Graber, D. A. "Hoopla and Horse-Race in 1980 Campaign Coverage: A Closer Look." In W. Schulz and K. Schoenbach, *Mass Media and Elections: International Research Perspectives.* Munich, Germany: Oelschlaeger, 1983.

Graber, D. A. *Processing the News.* White Plains, New York: Longman, Inc., 1988.

Groves, R. M., and R. L. Kahn. *Surveys by Telephone.* New York: Academic Press, 1979.

Hamilton, A., J. Madison, and J. Jay. *The Federalist Papers.* New York: New American Library, 1961.

Hamill, R., and M. Lodge. "Cognitive Consequences of Political Sophistication." In R. R. Lau and D. O. Sears, *Political Cognition.* Hillsdale, New Jersey: 1986.

Hamill, R., M. Lodge, and F. Blake. "The Breadth, Depth, and Utility of Class, Partisan, and Ideological Schemata." *American Journal of Political Science* 29 (1985): 850–70.

Hanushek, E. A., and J. E. Jackson. *Statistical Methods for Social Scientists.* New York: Academic Press, 1977.

Harwood, R. *The Pursuit of the Presidency.* New York: Berkeley Books, 1980.

Hausman, J. A., and D. A. Wise. "A Conditional Probit Model for Qualitative Choice: Discrete Decisions Recognizing Interdependence and Heterogeneous Preferences." *Econometrica* 46 (1978): 403–26.

Heard, A. *Made in America*. New York: HarperCollins Publishers Inc., 1991.

Heckman, J. J. "Dummy Endogenous Variables in a Simultaneous Equation System." *Econometrica* 46 (1978): 931–60.

Hildebrand, D. K., J. D. Laing, and H. Rosenthal. "Prediction Analysis in Political Research." *American Political Science Review* 70 (1976): 509–35.

Holsti, O. R. "Public Opinion and Foreign Policy: Challenges to the Almond–Lippman Consensus." Paper presented at the Annual Meeting of the International Studies Association, Atlanta, Georgia, 1992.

Hurwitz, J., and M. Peffley. "How Are Foreign Policy Attitudes Structured? A Hierarchical Model." *American Political Science Review* 81 (1987): 1099–1120.

Husted, T. A., L. W. Kenny, and R. B. Morton. "Constituent Errors in Assessing Their Senators." *Public Choice* 83 (1995): 251–71.

Iyengar, S., and D. R. Kinder. *News That Matters*. Chicago: The University of Chicago Press, 1987.

Judge, G. G., R. C. Hill, W. E. Griffiths, H. Lutkepohl, and T.-C. Lee. *Introduction to the Theory and Practice of Econometrics*, second edition. New York: John Wiley and Sons, 1988.

Keane, M. P. "A Note on Identification in the Multinomial Probit Model." *Journal of Business and Economic Statistics* 72 (1978): 469–91.

Keane, M. P. "A Computationally Practical Simulation Estimator for Panel Data." *Econometrica* 62 (1994): 95–116.

Keene, K. H., and V. A. Sackett. "An Editors' Report on the Yankelovich, Skelly and White 'Mushiness Index.' " *Public Opinion* 4 (1981): 50–51.

Keith, B. E., D. B. Magleby, C. J. Nelson, E. Orr, M. C. Westlye, and R. E. Wolfinger. "The Partisan Affinities of Independent Leaners." *British Journal of Political Science* 16 (1986): 155–85.

Kelley, S., and T. W. Mirer. "The Simple Act of Voting." *American Political Science Review* 68 (1974): 572–91.

Kernell, S. "Campaigning, Governing, and the Contemporary Presidency." In J. E. Chubb and P. E. Peterson, *The New Direction in American Politics*. Washington, D.C.: The Brookings Institution, 1985.

Kessel, J. H. "Comment: The Issues in Issue Voting." *American Political Science Review* 66 (1972): 459–65.

Kessel, J. H. *Presidential Campaign Politics*. Homewood, Illinois: The Dorsey Press, 1984.

Key, V. O., Jr. *The Responsible Electorate*. New York: Vintage Books, 1966.

Kiewiet, D. R., and D. Rivers. "The Economic Basis of Reagan's Appeal." In J. E. Chubb and P. E. Peterson, *The New Direction in American Politics*.

Washington, D.C.: The Brookings Institution, 1985.

Kinder, D. R. "Presidential Character Revisited." In R. R. Lau and D. O. Sears, *Political Cognition*. Hillside: Lawrence Erlbaum, 1986.

King, G. *Unifying Political Methodology*. Cambridge: Cambridge University Press, 1989.

Kreps, D. M. *A Course in Microeconomic Theory*. Princeton: Princeton University Press, 1990.

Krosnick, J. A. "Expertise and Political Psychology." *Social Cognition* 8 (1990): 1–8.

Lau, R. R. "Political Schemata, Candidate Evaluations, and Voting Behavior." In R. R. Lau and D. O. Sears, *Political Cognition*. Hillsdale: Lawrence Erlbaum, 1986.

Lazarsfeld, P., B. Berelson, and H. Gaudet. *The People's Choice*. New York: Columbia University Press, 1944.

Lee, L. F. "Simultaneous Equations Models with Discrete and Censored Variables." In C. F. Manski and D. McFadden, *Structural Analysis of Discrete Data with Econometric Applications*. Cambridge: MIT Press, 1981.

Leege, D. C., J. A. Lieske, and K. D. Wald. "Toward Cultural Theories of American Political Behavior: Religion, Ethnicity and Race, and Class Outlook." In W. Crotty, editor, *Political Science: Looking to the Future, Volume Three, Political Behavior*. Evanston, Illinois: Northwestern University Press, 1991.

Lodge, M. G., and R. Hamill. "A Partisan Schema for Political Information Processing." *American Political Science Review* 80 (1986): 737–61.

Lodge, M. G., K. M. McGraw, and P. Stroh. "An Impression-Driven Model of Candidate Evaluation." *American Political Science Review* 83 (1989): 399–420.

Luskin, R. C. "Measuring Political Sophistication." *American Journal of Political Science* 31 (1987): 856–99.

Macdonald, S. E., O. Listhaug, and G. Rabinowitz. "Issues and Party Support in Multiparty Systems." *American Political Science Review* 85 (1991): 1107–32.

Maddala, G. S. *Limited-Dependent and Qualitative Variables in Econometrics*. Cambridge: Cambridge University Press, 1983.

Manski, C. F., and S. R. Lerman. "The Estimation of Choice Probabilities from Choice-Based Samples." *Econometrica* 45 (1977): 1977–88.

Markus, G. B., and P. E. Converse. "A Dynamic Simultaneous Equation Model of Electoral Choice." *American Political Science Review* 73 (1979): 1055–70.

McCullagh, P., and J. A. Nelder. *Generalized Linear Models*, second edition. London: Chapman and Hall, 1983.

McKelvey, R., and W. Zavoina. "A Statistical Model for Ordinal Dependent Variables." *Journal of Mathematical Sociology* 4 (1975): 103–20.

McGraw, K. M., M. Lodge, and P. Stroh. "On-Line Processing in Candidate Evaluation: The Effects of Issue Order, Issue Importance, and Sophistication." *Political Behavior* 12 (1990): 41–58.

Miller, A. H., M. P. Wattenberg, and O. Malanchuk. "Schematic Assessments of Presidential Candidates." *American Political Science Review* 79 (1986): 521–40.

Morrison, D., editor. *The Winning of the White House 1988*. New York: Time Books, 1988.

Nagler, J. "The Effect of Registration Laws and Education on U.S. Voter Turnout." *American Political Science Review* 85 (1991): 1394–1405.

Nagler, J. "Scobit—An Alternative Estimator to Logit and Probit." *American Journal of Political Science* 38 (1994): 230–55.

Natchez, P. B. *Images of Voting, Visions of Democracy*. New York: Basic Books, 1985.

Nelson, F. D. and L. Olson. "Specification and Estimation of a Simultaneous Equation Model with Limited Dependent Variables." *International Economic Review* 19 (1978) 695-710.

Neuman, W. R. *The Paradox of Mass Politics: Knowledge and Opinion in the American Electorate*. Cambridge: Harvard University Press, 1986.

New York Times Index 1976: A Book of Record, volume 64. New York: The New York Times Company, 1977.

New York Times Index 1980: A Book of Record, volume 68. New York: The New York Times Company, 1981.

New York Times Index 1984: A Book of Record, volume 72. New York: The New York Times Company, 1985.

New York Times Index 1988: A Book of Record, volume 76. New York: The New York Times Company, 1989.

Nie, N. H., S. Verba, and J. R. Petrocik. *The Changing American Voter*. Cambridge: Harvard University Press, 1979.

Niemi, R. G., and L. M. Bartels. "New Measures of Issue Salience: An Evaluation." *Journal of Politics* 47 (1985): 1213–20.

Page, B. I. "The Theory of Political Ambiguity." *American Political Science Review* 70 (1976): 742–52.

Page, B. I. *Choices and Echoes in Presidential Elections*. Chicago: University of Chicago Press, 1978.

Page, B. I., and R. A. Brody. "Policy Voting and the Electoral Process: The Vietnam War Issue." *American Political Science Review* 66 (1972): 979–95.

Page. B. I., and R. Y. Shapiro. *The Rational Public.* Chicago: The University of Chicago Press, 1989.

Palfrey, T. R., and K. T. Poole. "The Relationship Between Information, Ideology, and Voting Behavior." *American Journal of Political Science* 31 (1987): 511–30.

Patterson, T. C. *The Mass Media Election.* New York: Praeger, 1980.

Patterson, T. C., and R. D. McClure. *The Unseeing Eye.* New York: G. P. Putnam, 1976.

Polsby, N. W., and A. Wildavsky. *Presidential Elections,* eighth edition. New York: Free Press, 1988.

Pomper, G. M. "From Confusion to Clarity: Issues and American Voters, 1956–1968." *American Political Science Review* 70 (1972): 779–805.

Popkin, S. L. *The Reasoning Voter.* Chicago: The University of Chicago Press, 1991.

Przeworski, A., and H. Teune. *The Logic of Comparative Social Inquiry.* Malabar, Florida: Robert E. Krieger Publishing Company, 1982.

Rabinowitz, G., and S. E. Macdonald. "A Directional Theory of Issue Voting." *American Political Science Review* 83 (1989): 93–121.

Rabinowitz, G., J. W. Prothro, and W. Jacoby. "Salience as a Factor in The Impact of Issues on Candidate Evaluation." *Journal of Politics* 44 (1982): 41–63.

Rahn, W. M. "Perception and Evaluation of Political Candidates: A Social-Cognitive Perspective." Ph.D. Dissertation, University of Minnesota, 1990.

Rahn, W. M., J. H. Aldrich, E. Borgida, and J. Sullivan. "A Social-Cognitive Model of Candidate Appraisal." In J. Ferejohn and J. Kuklinski, *Information and Democratic Processes.* Champaign-Urbana: University of Illinois Press, 1990.

Rapoport, R. B. "Sex Differences in Attitude Expression: A Generational Explanation." *Public Opinion Quarterly* 46 (1982): 86–96.

Rapoport, R. B. "Like Mother, Like Daughter: Intergenerational Transmission of DK Response Rates." *Public Opinion Quarterly* 49 (1985): 198–208.

Rasmussen, E. *Games and Information.* Cambridge: Basil Blackwell, 1989.

RePass, D. E. "Issue Salience and Party Choice." *American Political Science Review* 65 (1971): 389–400.

Rivers, D. "Heterogeneity in Models of Electoral Choice." *American Journal of Political Science* 32 (1988): 737–57.

Rivers, D., and Q. H. Vuong. "Limited Information Estimators and Exogeneity Tests for Simultaneous Probit Models." *Journal of Econometrics* 39 (1988): 347–66.

Sartori, G. "Concept Misinformation in Comparative Politics." *American Political Science Review* 64 (1970): 1033–53.

Schattschneider, E. E. *The Semisovereign People.* New York: Holt, Rinehart and Winston, 1960.

Schuman, H., and S. Presser. *Questions and Answers in Attitude Surveys.* New York: Academic Press, 1981.

Shepsle, K. A. "The Strategy of Ambiguity." *American Political Science Review* 66 (1972): 555–68.

Shively, W. P. "The Development of Party Identification Among Adults: Explorations of a Functional Model." *American Political Science Review* 73 (1979): 1039–58.

Smith, E. R. A. N. *The Unchanging American Voter.* Berkeley and Los Angeles: University of California Press, 1989.

Sorauf, F. J. *Money in American Elections.* Glenview, Illinois: Scott, Foresman and Co., 1988.

Stokes, D. "Spatial Models of Party Competition." *American Political Science Review* 57 (1963): 368–77.

Sullivan, J. L., J. E. Piereson, and G. E. Marcus. "Ideological Constraint in the Mass Public: A Methodological Critique and Some New Findings." *American Journal of Political Science* 22 (1978): 233–49.

Theil, H. *Principles of Econometrics.* New York: John Wiley and Sons, 1971.

Valentine, D. C. and J. R. Van Wingen. "Partisanship, Independence, and the Partisan Identification Question." *American Politics Quarterly* 8 (1980): 165–86.

Wattenberg, M. P. *The Rise of Candidate-Centered Politics.* Cambridge: Harvard University Press, 1991.

Witcover, J. *Marathon.* New York: Viking Press, 1977.

Wolfinger, R. E., and S. J. Rosenstone. *Who Votes?* New Haven: Yale University Press, 1980.

Zaller, J. "The Effects of Political Involvement on Public Attitudes and Voting Behavior." Paper presented at the Annual Meetings of the American Political Science Association, 1986.

Zaller, J. "Bringing Converse Back In: Modeling Information Flow in Political Campaigns." *Political Analysis* 1 (1989): 181–234.

Zaller, J. "Political Awareness, Elite Opinion Leadership, and the Mass Survey Response." *Social Cognition* 8 (1990): 125–53.

Zechman, M. J. "Dynamic Models of Voting Behavior and Spatial Models of Party Competition." Chapel Hill, North Carolina: Institute for Research in Social Science, University of North Carolina at Chapel Hill, Working Papers in Methodology, Number 10.

Index

253